Our hymn-writers and their hymns

Let those refuse to sing
that never knew our God;
but children of the heavenly King
may speak their joys abroad.

Then let our songs abound,
and every tear be dry;
we're marching through Immanuel's ground
to fairer worlds on high.

Isaac Watts

Our hymn-writers
and their hymns

Faith Cook

EVANGELICAL PRESS

EVANGELICAL PRESS
Faverdale North Industrial Estate, Darlington, DL3 0PH, England

Evangelical Press USA
P. O. Box 825, Webster, New York 14580, USA

e-mail: sales@evangelicalpress.org

web: www.evangelicalpress.org

First published 2005

British Library Cataloguing in Publication Data available

ISBN 0 85234 585 2

Printed and bound in Great Britain by Creative Print and Design Wales, Ebbw Vale, South Wales.

Contents

Preface
and acknowledgements

During the last two years it has been my privilege to spend time working on the lives and contribution of some of our most gifted hymn-writers down through the generations. Hymns based on the great themes of the Christian message have their own unique ministry to the mind and heart; they can renew faith and hope in God especially in days of spiritual decline and apathy. Such timeless truths set into verse stimulate and enhance our worship, and confirm our love to God and our gratitude to the Saviour. If reading or rereading some of these moving hymns that I have quoted has this effect on others as well as on me, then the time expended in this work will be amply rewarded.

A number of books that detail the stories or circumstances behind the writing of some of our popular hymns have been published over the years. This has not been my aim in the present work. Instead, I have tried to trace the development of the English hymn from the early period of the Christian Church up until our present century by means of biographical sketches of a number of our best-known writers. I have also endeavoured to demonstrate the way in which their individual personalities and circumstances have often been reflected in the hymns they have composed.

Some analysis of the style and technique employed by each poet has been attempted and for this it has clearly been important to quote original texts as far as possible, rather than any edited or improved version of a hymn. This does not mean, however, that a hymn text should not be subject to sensitive editing. The poet Fred Pratt Green, who also wrote a number of hymns, has pointed out that although poetry, as distinct from hymnology, must stand as originally written, 'the hymn is the servant of the church',[1] and therefore must be primarily suited for use in Christian worship. Language is a living, changing thing, and over the years many hymns have been improved by editors of the ilk of John Wesley, Augustus Toplady, James Montgomery and Henry Baker, although, equally, some have suffered badly at the hands of less able editors.

Any work of this nature must necessarily rely at least to some extent on the research and comment of those who have tackled this subject before. Among today's writers, I have found the work of Professor J. R. Watson, Emeritus Professor of English at the University of Durham, particularly helpful and would recommend his books, listed in my bibliography, to any who wish a more detailed critique of the development of English hymnology.

I have appreciated the support of the staff of the Evangelical Library for the illustrations and the many books they sent me on long-term loan to facilitate this project. Also, in this respect, I would like to thank Dr Jack Milner for the photographs he has taken of Olney and of Benjamin Keach's chapel in Winslow. With his extensive knowledge of hymns, David Preston has checked over my work and saved me from a number of pitfalls, and for this I am very grateful. I am also indebted to our friend Ralph Ireland for looking through the manuscript with his eagle eye for grammatical and other mistakes. And, as always, I am specially grateful for the help and encouragement of my husband Paul. His lifelong love of hymns and his own work as an editor of *Christian Hymns* has made this book a shared endeavour.

Faith Cook
April 2005

Notes
1. For a fuller discussion on this, see *Lift Every Heart*, Timothy Dudley-Smith, Hope Publishing Company, 1984, pp.20-21.

Distant voices:

Ambrose to Watts

My song is love unknown,
  my Saviour's love to me,
love to the loveless shown,
  that they might lovely be.
    O who am I,
      that for my sake
      my Lord should take
  frail flesh and die?

Samuel Crossman

Distant voices:

Ambrose to Watts

Without doubt the people of God have always had cause to sing — for song is the natural medium of expression of a heart moved by deep feelings — and who has more reason to sing than the man or woman who knows the living God, the joy of forgiven sin, and the certainty of a life to come when sorrow, pain and failure will be things of the past? Old Testament believers marked God's mighty acts of deliverance from their enemies in song: Moses and the children of Israel sang on the banks of the Red Sea in recognition of their miraculous escape from Egypt; Hannah praised God in song for answer to her earnest prayer; the Psalms are packed with hymns of praise to God written by David, Asaph and others commemorating God's dealings with his people. And in the New Testament believers had yet more cause to sing: Mary poured out her thanksgiving to God as she contemplated his mercies to his people through the child she would bear. The early church sang hymns, and snatches of some of the words can be found in the letters written to the churches by the apostle Paul.[1] And one day the whole redeemed church of Jesus Christ will join in one great anthem of praise — the song of Moses and of the Lamb.

The story of the development of the English hymn is a long one, and in 1892 a hymnologist, Dr John Julian, took more than 1600 pages of close print with double columns to cover it satisfactorily.[2] And that was before what some have called 'the hymn explosion' of the last half of the twentieth century, when countless new writers added their voices to the songs of the church. However, in order to appreciate the work of those hymn-writers whose lives we have chosen to follow in these pages, it will help to know something of the story of the development of the English hymn — that foundation on which their endeavours were built.[3] Confining ourselves to those whose work was either written in English or appears in translation in our hymn books, a quick glance will reveal a number whose lives predated our first subject, Isaac Watts, some by many centuries.

Ambrose of Milan

Possibly the earliest of our hymn-writers of the Christian era

Ambrose of Milan

whose hymns are still sung today is Ambrose of Milan who lived in the fourth century (339-397). Initially Ambrose practised law in Milan, but in 374, at the young age of thirty-four, was made Bishop of Milan — and this by popular acclaim, even though he was only a 'catechumen' undergoing instruction prior to being baptized. It was a recognition by the people both of his sincere faith and godly life, and the knowledge that he was probably the only one who could stem the tide of Arianism that was sweeping the churches. As bishop, Ambrose had a significant and important ministry; under his preaching Augustine, whose wayward youth had brought his mother Monica near to despair, was converted. Far-sighted and with a deep concern for those who gathered to hear his preaching, Ambrose also made a noteworthy contribution to the development of hymns. Called 'the father of the church song' he encouraged congregational singing of both psalms and hymns. Almost one hundred hymns were originally ascribed to him but it is likely that only twelve were actually his work. Despite the revolution in English usage that has been part of the cultural change of recent years, two of Ambrose's own hymns can still be found in modern hymnals, one of them translated by Charles Wesley. Better known is 'O Jesus, Lord of heavenly grace', a morning hymn translated variously more than twenty times from the same Latin original. One version includes the following words:

> O Jesus, Lord of heavenly grace,
> thou brightness of thy Father's face,
> thou fountain of eternal light,
> whose beams disperse the shades of night;
>
> Come, holy Sun of heavenly love,
> shower down thy radiance from above,
> and to our inmost hearts convey
> the Holy Spirit's cloudless ray.[4]

The effect of Ambrose's attempt to introduce hymns into services of worship was short-lived, however, and even Augustine frowned on the practice.

Bernard of Cluny

Many other hymns were written over the following eight centuries but few have survived. Venantius Fortunatus was a sixth-century poet, but his work is little known today. Not until we reach the twelfth century do we find ourselves back on familiar ground with extracts from Bernard of Cluny's three-thousand-line Latin poem on the glories of the heavenly country. Distressed by the evils he witnessed in the world around him, Bernard, who lived in Brittany, retreated to a monastery, but was soon to discover that even there the wickedness of the human heart found plenty of opportunity for expression. His mind turned with longing to the world to come where sin is banished for ever. John Neale[5] translated selected verses from his poem which have been made into two or three separate hymns, the best known being 'Jerusalem the Golden'. The first verse of Neale's translation picks up Bernard's frame of mind:

> The world is very evil,
>   the times are waxing late;
> be sober and keep vigil,
>   the Judge is at the gate…

We catch the poet's longing for that 'sweet and blessed country' as he writes:

> I know not, O I know not
>   what joys await us there,
> what radiancy of glory,
>   what bliss beyond compare…
>
> Jesus in mercy bring us
>   to that dear land of rest,
> who art, with God the Father
>   and Spirit, ever blest!

Bernard of Clairvaux

Contemporary with Bernard of
Cluny was another Bernard,
Bernard of Clairvaux[6] — a
name familiar to many
because of the hymns
attributed to him. He too was
a French monk, and a man of
outstanding ability. He set up
a monastery in a desolate and
forsaken valley known as the
'Valley of Wormwood' and by
years of toil and self-sacrifice
transformed the area until it
became known as the 'Valley
of Light' (or 'Clairvaux' in
French). Bernard was a man
of contrasts; some of his
writings and actions were far
from attractive, particularly
his participation in the second
Crusade, but he was primarily
a preacher whose main
theme in both his writing and
preaching was the love and
beauties of Christ — a contrast
to the religion of fear so widely

Bernard of Clairvaux

propagated by the church of the day. Preaching, he insisted, is
'not so much to explain the words as to reach people's hearts'.
Martin Luther was a strong admirer of Bernard of Clairvaux
because 'he preaches Christ so excellently'. Bernard is thought
to be the author of a forty-eight-stanza Latin poem *Jesu dulcis
memoria* — a poem extolling the glories of Christ, and called
the 'sweetest and most evangelical hymn of the Middle Ages'.

One part of this poem, translated by Edward Caswall (1814-78), is the well-known hymn:

> Jesus, the very thought of thee
> with sweetness fills my breast;
> but sweeter far thy face to see,
> and in thy presence rest.

Two other portions have also been translated and have found warm acceptance in today's hymn books: 'Jesus, thou joy of loving hearts'[7] is often sung at Communion services:

> We taste thee, O thou living Bread,
> and long to feast upon thee still;
> we drink of thee, the fountain-head,
> and thirst our souls from thee to fill.

The last hymn in this trilogy, again translated by Caswall, is once more on the person of Christ, the source and sustainer of true inward religion:

> O Jesus, King most wonderful,
> thou Conqueror renowned,
> thou sweetness most ineffable,
> in whom all joys are found.

Although Bernard held tenaciously to many of the teachings of the Roman Catholic Church, propagating the notion that the virgin Mary could bestow favours because of her special access to her Son, his reliance on the foundation truths of the Christian gospel is demonstrated in a prayer he uttered as he lay dying: 'I have lived wickedly, [but] thou, loving Lord Jesus, hast purchased heaven with thy suffering and death. Thou hast unlocked heaven and presented it to me ... in this I have joy and comfort.'

Martin Luther

When Martin Luther came on the scene (1483-1546), and with him the great changes brought in by the Reformation, a new day was introduced in the development of hymn-singing. Luther, called the 'Ambrose of German hymnody', recognized both the importance of the participation of the people in services of worship and the power of the hymn to inspire, instruct and sustain the Christian. 'The hymns of Luther', said one who was deeply opposed to the truths the Reformer was

Martin Luther

preaching, 'have killed more souls than his sermons.' A hymn book brought out in 1524 contained twenty-three of Luther's hymns, six of which were metrical psalms. This same year saw the martyrdom of two of Luther's young followers, and we may well imagine the effect this would have had on a man of such intense feeling as Martin Luther. It is thought that his moving rendering of Psalm 130, 'From deep distress I cry to thee', was written with such circumstances in mind:

> Though great our sins and sore our woes,
>   his grace much more aboundeth;
> his helping love no limit knows,
>   our utmost need it soundeth;
> our kind and faithful Shepherd he,
> who shall at last set Israel free
>   from all their sin and sorrow.

Conflicting accounts exist as to when Luther composed the greatest of all his hymns, 'A safe stronghold our God is still' — based on Psalm 46. In *Here I Stand,* his important work on the life of Luther, Roland Bainton asserts that it was 1527, a year when another friend was martyred and when the tempestuous preacher experienced periods of depression. At such moments he could be tempted to doubt even the fundamental truths of the faith for which he was contending. Undoubtedly this hymn of confidence in God came straight from the conflict, both personal and on the wider front, as Luther faced fierce papal opposition. But it is more likely that it was composed in 1529 when the German princes entered their great 'Protest'[8] as they finally separated from the Church of Rome, insisting that 'they must *protest* and testify publicly before God that they should do nothing contrary to his Word'. And so Luther wrote:

> God's Word, for all their craft and force,
>   one moment will not linger,
> but, spite of hell, shall have its course;
>   'tis written by his finger.
>   And though they take our life,
>   goods, honour, children, wife,
>   yet is their profit small:
>   these things shall vanish all;
>   the city of God remaineth.

The hymns which Luther composed for his children each Christmas time demonstrate the tenderness of this rugged Reformer. 'From heaven above to earth I come' was composed for five-year-old Hans, and includes these words:

> Ah, dearest Jesus, holy child,
> make thee a bed, soft, undefiled,
> within my heart that it may be
> a quiet chamber fit for thee.[9]

John Calvin

While Luther wrote some thirty-seven hymns altogether and set a firm tradition of congregational singing in the Lutheran churches, John Calvin took a different position. Like Luther he also favoured the use of metrical psalms for congregational singing, and in 1539 had published a collection for such a purpose. Unlike Luther, however, he was unhappy about the use of words other than those of Scripture in the worship of God, although he was not as rigid on the issue as some of his followers. One beautiful hymn has even been attributed to him:

> I greet thee who my sure Redeemer art,
> my only trust and Saviour of my heart,
> who pain didst undergo for my poor sake:
> I pray thee from our hearts all cares to take.

Sternhold and Hopkins

Many of the exiles from Britain who fled from Queen Mary's cruel regime found a haven in Calvin's Geneva; and among them was the Scottish Reformer, John Knox. When these spiritual leaders, deeply influenced by Calvin's emphasis, returned home at the accession of Elizabeth I, they implemented the singing of only metrical psalms in their churches. This became the order of the day in Britain for at least one hundred and fifty years. Thomas Sternhold, a one-time groom in the court of Henry VIII, had been the first to work on a metrical version of the Psalms — a far cry from the bawdy songs usually sung at court. When the young Edward VI heard the courtier's 'holye songes' as he played them on his own organ, he was delighted, and it was to the boy-king that the former courtier dedicated his first collection of psalms, which he published in 1549.

Sternhold died soon afterwards and his friend John Hopkins, a Suffolk country parson, took up his work. He gathered together thirty-seven of Sternhold's renderings, added a further seven of his own and had them printed in 1551. A number of editions appeared over the next ten years, each adding new psalms and other modifications until in 1562 an expanded selection of these ballad-style arrangements was published, this time including a further twenty-four by William Kethe and a number by William Whittingham. It bore a long title, generally abbreviated to *The Whole Booke of Psalmes.*

Although John Wesley referred to the *Old Version* (the name that would be given to this collection) as 'wretched, scandalous doggerel', there was merit in the work. Through the metrical psalms of Sternhold and Hopkins, English church worshippers became familiar with congregational singing in their own language and learnt to appreciate the value of metre and rhyme in religious verse. They also became accustomed to untangling the inverted lines which Sternhold and Hopkins would use in order to produce a rhyming word (usually a verb at the end of the line) — a feature that has often characterized hymns ever since. The *Old Version* was frequently bound up with both the Geneva Bible and the 1611 Authorized Version; one psalm at least — a rendering of Psalm 100 by William Kethe — still finds a place in our hymn books:

> All people that on earth do dwell,
>   sing to the Lord with cheerful voice;
> him serve with fear[10] his praise forth tell,
>   come ye before him and rejoice.

While English and Scottish churches remained firmly dedicated to singing only words found in Scripture itself, Martin Luther had undoubtedly begun a new tradition in Germany. His encouragement of hymn-singing soon gave rise to a school of writers whose work has enriched not only the congregations for which they were written, but also the wider Christian church as they were translated into English and other languages.

Paul Gerhardt

Paul Gerhardt, a member of the Lutheran Church and called

Paul Gerhardt

the 'Wesley of Germany', was born in 1607. While reflecting all the strengths of Luther's theological position, his hymns also introduced a personal note. Sixteen of them begin with 'I' in the original German — refreshing and new in his day, although initiating a subjectivism which has today become the norm rather than the exception. Many of Gerhardt's hymns express a note of sadness, yet also a triumph of faith as he found strength from God to rise above his trials:

> Why should cross and trial grieve me?
> > Christ is near
> > with his cheer;
> > never will he leave me.
> Who can rob me of my heaven
> > that God's Son
> > for my own
> > to my faith has given?

A glance at the circumstances of Gerhardt's life soon shows why this is so. His ministry was set in tumultuous times. First, in the wake of the Reformation, came the outbreak of the Thirty Years War in 1618 when he saw his country torn apart by religious strife. Gerhardt also experienced many personal sorrows and trials, not least the early death of his wife and all but one of his five children. Unwilling to compromise his stand for the truth, the bold preacher eventually found himself stripped of his office and therefore also of the means of supporting his sick wife and remaining child. We may well imagine that a hymn such as 'Commit thou all thy griefs/and ways into his hand', arose from such circumstances:

> No profit canst thou gain
> from self-consuming care:
> to him commend thy cause; his ear
> attends thy softest prayer.
>
> When he makes bare his arm,
> who shall his work withstand?
> When he his people's cause defends,
> who, who shall stay his hand?

Other verses from the same poem, now forming a separate hymn, again suggest such circumstances:

> Give to the wind thy fears;
> hope and be undismayed:
> God hears thy sighs, and counts thy tears;
> God shall lift up thy head.

This hymn, together with a number of others from Paul Gerhardt's pen, was translated from the German by John Wesley. Still searching for spiritual certainty, Wesley had sailed to Georgia in October 1735. Aboard the same ship were a number of Moravians whose lives impressed him deeply, particularly when they showed no fear during a storm that threatened to sink the ship. He listened to them singing their hymns and, moved by their sincerity and confidence, wished to join with them. During the five-month voyage Wesley set himself to master German, and the Moravian hymn book became one of

John Wesley

his main textbooks. Five German hymns found a place in the first collection of hymns that Wesley published in 1737 and over the next forty years he included at least twenty-eight more from a number of German writers in his various publications. Those written by Gerhardt are still valued and sung today. Among the best known of Wesley's translations we find the following magnificent lines:

> Jesus, thy boundless love to me
>   no thought can reach, no tongue declare;
> O knit my thankful heart to thee,
>   and reign without a rival there!
> Thine wholly, thine alone I am,
> be thou alone my constant flame.

> O grant that nothing in my soul
>   may dwell, but thy pure love alone;
> O may thy love possess me whole,
>   my joy, my treasure, and my crown!
> Strange flames far from my heart remove;
> my every act, word, thought, be love.

Gerhardt's emphasis on the love of God in the soul of the believer, the fountain from which all other Christian graces spring, was one that the Wesley brothers themselves stressed repeatedly and finds a constant refrain in Charles Wesley's own hymns.

Little is known of Paul Gerhardt's later years, apart from the fact that during the last seven he ministered in Lübben. This preacher and hymn-writer, who had known so much bereavement, died in 1676 reciting words from one of his own hymns:

> Death can never kill us even,
>   but relief
>   from all grief
> to us then is given.

> It doth close life's mournful story,
>   make a way
>   that we may
> pass to heaven's glory.[11]

A portrait of Gerhardt marks his burial place in Lübben. Underneath the portrait is a caption which reads, 'A theologian experienced in the sieve of Satan'.

Catherine Winkworth

The greatest of all the translators of German hymns was undoubtedly Catherine Winkworth, and to her the English-speaking church owes an unquestionable debt for the enrichment it has received from her work. Born in 1827, Catherine belonged to a well-placed Manchester family which had many connections with the literary figures of the day, including Charlotte Brontë and Elizabeth Gaskell. She perfected her schoolgirl German by spending a year in Dresden when she was sixteen. Here she also learnt some of the great German hymns and, with marked poetic gifts herself, was in

Catherine Winkworth

an excellent position to translate them into English. When Catherine was only twenty-seven years of age she published *Lyra Germanica,* a handsomely bound and illustrated volume containing about one hundred of the best German hymns. Writing of Gerhardt in the introduction, Catherine maintains, 'He is without doubt the greatest of the German hymn-writers, possessing loftier poetical genius, and a richer variety of thought and feeling than any other.'[12]

Winkworth's translation of Gerhardt's work includes the Christmas hymn 'All my heart this night rejoices':

> Hark! a voice from yonder manger,
>   soft and sweet, doth entreat:
> 'Flee from woe and danger;
> Brethren, come: from all that grieves you
>   you are freed; all you need
> I will surely give you.'

A further hymn of Gerhardt's on the incarnation that has not
found its way into the hymn books has moving words:

> Since first the world began to be,
> how many a heart has longed for thee;
> long years our fathers hoped of old
> their eyes might yet thy light behold.
>
> Now thou art here, we know thee now,
> in lowly manger liest thou;
> a child — yet making all things great,
> poor — yet is earth thy robe of state.

John Milton

In 1608, the year after Paul Gerhardt's birth near Wittenberg, a
child was born in London who has been described as 'England's
mighty bard' and acclaimed second only to Shakespeare for his
contribution to English literature — John Milton. As a fifteen-
year-old schoolboy at St Paul's School in London, he tried his
hand at versifying two of the psalms. His attempt at Psalm 114
had no great merit as a hymn, but his work on Psalm 136,
beginning 'Let us with a gladsome mind' has found a place in
hymn books ever since. Originally it ran to twenty-four verses,
six of which appear in most hymn books, each ending with the
refrain:

> For his mercies shall endure,
> ever faithful ever sure.

The young Milton may well have set out to prove that it is
possible to write a psalm in metric form without sacrificing poetic
excellence, as Sternhold and Hopkins had done. In balancing
couplets, he traced the history of God's mighty acts from

creation up to the entry of the Israelites into the Promised Land
of Canaan. Milton's choice of words clearly shows a poet in the
making:

> He with all-commanding light
> filled the new-made world with light…
>
> He his chosen race did bless
> in the wasteful wilderness…

A tempestuous life lay ahead of John Milton, both personal
and political. His troubled marriage, political involvement
through all the uncertainties of the Civil War, bereavements,
coupled with his blindness before he had reached middle age,
all took their toll upon him. There is a gentler, sadder note in
his rendering of Psalm 84, 'How lovely are thy dwellings fair',
written shortly before the end of the war and the execution of
Charles I in 1649:

> My soul doth long and almost die
>   thy courts, O Lord, to see;
> my heart and flesh aloud do cry,
>   O living God, for thee.

Richard Baxter

Richard Baxter (1615-91), whose lines, like Milton's, are still sung
today, was another who was embroiled in all the pain, confusion
and suffering of the Civil War period. His valuable work *The
Saints' Everlasting Rest*, also published in 1649, encourages the
believer to look away from his present circumstances both of
trials and joys and to meditate on 'the rest that remains for the
people of God'[13] in the life to come. From 1641 onwards, apart
from a period during the Civil War, Baxter had ministered in

Richard Baxter

Kidderminster and seen an astonishing spiritual transformation in the town. But in 1662, despite the fact that he had supported the restoration of Charles II to his throne in 1660, Baxter, like two thousand other preachers, was cast out of his living for his refusal to compromise his conscience by signing the Act of Uniformity. From that time onwards he and his wife Margaret were harried, persecuted and driven to and fro by circumstance. Little wonder then that two of his hymns, published in his *Poetical Fragments* in 1681, take up the theme of the joys and security of heaven and encourage believers to look beyond death to a land where love and concord reign.

In 1681 Margaret died at only forty-five years of age. 'Under the power of a melting grief', Baxter wrote a short account of her life, in which he told of a covenant she had made with God at a time when she had been seriously ill, not long before they married. He had found a copy of this covenant among Margaret's papers after her death and had turned the words into verse. His lines form the basis of a familiar hymn:

> Lord, it belongs not to my care
> whether I die or live;
> to love and serve thee is my share,
> and this thy grace must give.

If life be long, I will be glad
    that I may long obey;
if short, then why should I be sad
    to soar to endless day?

Come, Lord, when grace has made me meet
    thy blessed face to see;
for if thy work on earth be sweet,
    what will thy glory be?

In another of his hymns beginning 'Ye holy angels bright', Baxter calls on the angels, the church militant and the church triumphant to join in the praises of God. Entitled 'A Psalm of Praise', it was set to the metre known as the 148th (i.e. 6.6.6.6.4.4.4.4.), a metre then used for Psalm 148 and still popular with hymn-writers today. Baxter's last verse, not included in present-day versions of the hymn, links up with the theme to which he so often delighted to return — the glories of the heavenly world:

With thy triumphant flock
    then I shall numbered be,
built on the eternal Rock,
    his glory we shall see.
      The heavens so high,
        with praise shall ring,
        and all shall sing
      in harmony.

Samuel Crossman

Samuel Crossman (1624-83), like Richard Baxter, was ejected from his living in 1662 for his unwillingness to sign up to the Act of Uniformity, although he would later conform. He too wrote verse and in 1664, just two years after he had been stripped of his home and means of livelihood, he published a small book of meditations and poems. Perhaps such circumstances turned his thoughts to the suffering of the Saviour and this became the subject of some lines he wrote, never imagining that one day they would become a well-loved hymn:

> My song is love unknown,
>   my Saviour's love to me,
> love to the loveless shown,
>   that they might lovely be.
>   O who am I,
>   that for my sake
>   my Lord should take
>   frail flesh, and die?

These words, like Baxter's, are also set to the 148th metre and contain an evocative play on the word 'love', using it five times in different forms in the opening lines. The direct question, 'O who am I?' immediately involves the reader personally in the unfolding narrative of the brutality of man and the sufferings of Christ, culminating in the crucifixion. Perhaps his own situation was in his mind as he wrote his fifth verse:

> In life, no house, no home
>   my Lord on earth might have;
> in death, no friendly tomb
>   but what a stranger gave.
>   What may I say?
>   Heaven was his home:
>   but mine the tomb
>   wherein he lay.

By the time Crossman reaches his final stanza, we are ready to join with full hearts in his conclusion:

> Here might I stay and sing,
>   no story so divine;
> never was love, dear King,
>   never was grief like thine!
>   This is my friend
>   in whose sweet praise
>   I all my days
>   could gladly spend.

Because the day of hymn-singing had not yet dawned for Britain, this poignant piece lay neglected for some two hundred years, until it was 'discovered' and appeared in *The Anglican Hymnbook* of 1868 — retaining its deserved popularity ever since.

Thomas Ken

Surprising as it may seem, the first hymns for young people did not come from the Victorian era, nor even from Isaac Watts, but from the redoubtable seventeenth-century figure of Bishop Thomas Ken (1637-1710). Ken had been educated at Winchester College and later

Bishop Ken

returned as chaplain,[14] and in *A Manual of Prayers for the Use of the Scholars of Winchester College,* he included his well-known morning and evening hymns. Addressing them to an imaginary boy called Philotheus, or Phil for short, he exhorted the pupils to sing the hymns before they left the dormitory in the morning and before they crept back into bed at night. Each morning they should sing:

> Awake, my soul, and with the sun
> thy daily stage of duty run;
> shake off dull sloth, and joyful rise
> to pay thy morning sacrifice.

Or alternatively they might sing:

> Direct, control, suggest this day
> all I design, or do, or say;
> that all my powers, with all their might,
> in thy sole glory may unite.

And at night they should pray for forgiveness of sins they had committed during the day:

> Forgive me, Lord, for thy dear Son,
> the ill that I this day have done;
> that with the world, myself, and thee,
> I, ere I sleep, at peace may be.

Each hymn ended with the words of the doxology, for ever associated with this fearless and godly bishop's name:

> Praise God from whom all blessings flow;
> praise him all creatures here below;
> praise him above, ye heavenly host;
> praise Father, Son and Holy Ghost.

Tate and Brady

Throughout the seventeenth century there had been numerous attempts to publish a more satisfactory metrical psalter for use in the churches, but none had gained the popularity necessary to replace *The Whole Booke of Psalmes* of Sternhold and Hopkins and others. During the last part of the century, however, a significant change in English usage made a new version a timely venture and the work of two Irishmen, Nahum Tate and Nicholas Brady, published in 1696, stood a far higher chance of success, and soon became known as the *New Version* — an abbreviated form of the title. More skilful as versifiers than the men who produced

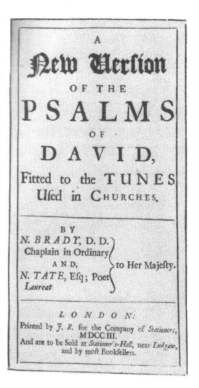

Title page
to *New Version* of 1696

the *Old Version,* Tate and Brady achieved a natural flow in their lines, making the psalms much easier to sing; some of their work has endured for more than three centuries. A version of Psalm 34 is a notable example:

> Through all the changing scenes of life,
>   in trouble and in joy,
> the praises of my God shall still
>   my heart and tongue employ.

Although attempts had been made from the time of the Reformation to introduce hymns to the English churches, none had succeeded. It might be thought that the Dissenters would have been more amenable to the practice of communal singing than the Established Church, but this was not the case. Persecution of Nonconformists after 1662 made it unsafe for worshippers to betray their presence by singing; but even if it had been safe, congregational singing of any form was deemed unacceptable. The General Baptist Assembly of 1689 prohibited all singing in a service of worship as it involved such 'carnal formalities' as the use of rhyme and metre and also allowed the unconverted to join in the praises of God. There were some brave spirits, however, who were prepared to follow their own convictions in this matter, and one was Benjamin Keach.

Benjamin Keach

Born in 1640, Benjamin Keach became the pastor of a General Baptist church in Winslow, Buckinghamshire, when he was just twenty years of age. The old chapel where he once preached, steeped in historical interest, is still opened once a year for worship. Pilloried in the town stocks for his brave stand against the religious trends of the day, Keach would not swerve but declared, 'My Lord Jesus was not ashamed to suffer on the cross for me and it is for his cause I am made a gazing-stock.' Not long after moving to London in 1668, Keach suffered the loss of his first wife. His second wife, whom he married two years later, was a Particular Baptist and it seems that she brought her husband around to her theological views, so that before long he became pastor of a Particular (or Calvinistic) Baptist church in Southwark — a church that would eventually call C. H. Spurgeon to its pulpit a hundred and fifty years later.

Keach's chapel at Winslow

The importance of Keach from the perspective of the development of hymnody is found in the lone stand he took in encouraging hymn-singing in his Southwark congregation at Horsley Down. At first it was only the singing of one hymn at the Lord's Supper, but this was soon extended to include a hymn each Sunday. Usually this would take place at the close of the service to allow those who were unhappy with the innovation to leave the building. In 1689 Keach challenged the Particular Baptist Assembly on the issue and two years later published his own hymn book entitled *Spiritual Melody,* containing some three hundred hymns. Such an innovation caused an outcry and even more so when the intrepid preacher published a controversial book entitled *The Breach Repaired in God's Worship; or Singing of Psalms, Hymns and Spiritual Songs proved to be a Holy Ordinance of Jesus Christ.* The issue was not whether it was right to sing only psalms, but whether it was right to sing at all. There were undeniably deep fears among some that the worship of the God of glory was being corrupted by such novelties. But attitudes were gradually changing and in 1690 the Bedford Independent (Congregational) Church permitted the public singing of psalms provided they were only sung by those 'with grace in their hearts'. Keach, however, persevered in his solitary stand and gradually the value of hymn-singing began to sway opinion. It is therefore true to say that Benjamin Keach, whose own hymns had little poetic excellence and have not survived, in a very real sense must take the credit for having introduced hymns to the English churches and prepared the way for Isaac Watts, born in 1674, whom we have described as the 'pioneer of English hymns'.

Notes

1. For example 1 Timothy 3:16 & 2 Timothy 2:11-13.
2. John Julian, *A Dictionary of Hymnology*, London: John Murray, 1892.
3. For an excellent and detailed study of the development of English hymnody, see J. R. Watson, *The English Hymn*, Oxford University Press, 1995.
4. Translated by John Chandler, 1806-76. A variant translation is found in the hymn 'O splendour of God's glory bright', translated by the compilers of *Hymns Ancient and Modern*, 1904.
5. 1818-66.
6. 1091-1153.
7. Translated by Ray Palmer, 1807-87.
8. This is the origin of the name Protestants.
9. Translated by Catherine Winkworth, 1827-78.
10. In the original Kethe uses the word 'mirth' to convey 'gladness' as in the AV.
11. Translated by John Kelly, d.1890.
12. *Lyra Germanica*, 1856, p.xi.
13. Hebrews 4:9.
14. For further details of Ken's life see *Companion to Christian Hymns*, compiled by Cliff Knight, 1992.

Isaac Watts
(1674-1748)

Pioneer of English hymns

Come, let us join our cheerful songs
  with angels round the throne;
ten thousand thousand are their tongues,
  but all their joys are one.

'Worthy the Lamb that died,' they cry,
  'to be exalted thus:'
'Worthy the Lamb,' our lips reply,
  'for he was slain for us.'

Isaac Watts

Isaac Watts
(1674-1748)

Pioneer of English hymns

The Watts family had gathered for their customary time of daily worship. Isaac, the oldest of the children, was then about six years of age. Together they all knelt to pray. Then, as the father of the family led in prayer, the unthinkable happened: Isaac began to titter. An offence of that nature in the Watts household would have serious consequences, and the child knew it. When his father demanded the reason for such merriment, he had his answer ready. He had spotted a mouse running up the bell-rope that hung in the fireplace, and a couplet of verse had flashed into his head:

> There was a mouse for want of stairs
> ran up a rope to say his prayers.

His father was unimpressed. When he reached for his stick to chastise his erring son, young Isaac fell on his knees and implored:

> O father, father, pity take,
> and I will no more verses make.

Whether the child's ingenuity won the day, we are not told.

The privilege of prayer in his family and in public worship was one that had cost Isaac's father dear. In 1662, twelve years before Isaac was born, the Act of Uniformity had been imposed by Charles II and his government in order to crush any dissent from the set prayers and canons of the Church of England. Two thousand had been ejected from their livings for refusing to comply with the terms of the act. Nathaniel Robinson, rector of All Saints, Southampton, and pastor of the church that Isaac Watts' father attended, was among them. Twelve years later, after a brief respite from persecution, the elder Isaac Watts himself (for father and son shared the same name) was thrown into the dank unhealthy jail in Southampton — called 'God's House Tower' — for his refusal to use the set prayers and liturgy of the church. Sarah Watts, his young wife, had recently given birth to their first child Isaac; now she would bring her baby, a frail, underweight child, and nurse him outside the prison — a silent protest at the inhuman treatment meted out to her husband and many other men of conscience and conviction.

The early sufferings of his family would leave a lasting mark on young Isaac who, despite an inauspicious beginning to life, was destined in God's purposes to make an indelible imprint on the unfolding history of the Christian Church both in Britain and far beyond. Words written in later years reflect the convictions etched on the mind of a boy growing up in the home of a Dissenting family:

> I'm not ashamed to own my Lord,
>   or to defend his cause;
> maintain the honour of his word,
>   the glory of his cross.
>
> Jesus, my God! I know his name,
>   his name is all my trust;
> nor will he put my soul to shame,
>   nor let my hope be lost.

Even though young Isaac, born in July 1674, had earnestly undertaken that he would 'no more verses make', his parents actively encouraged their precocious son to progress in every branch of learning, including the composition of poetry. When his father opened a small school in Southampton, Isaac's mother offered a reward of one farthing to any of her husband's pupils who could compose some good lines of poetry. Determined that his work should be better than anything others could produce, the seven-year-old wrote:

> I write not this for a farthing, but to try
> how I your farthing-writers can outvie.

At four years of age Isaac began to study Latin under his father's tuition, attending the local Free School when he was six. By the age of eight or nine he was learning Greek, with French at ten years of age and Hebrew when he was thirteen.

A further period of persecution saw Isaac Watts senior once more behind bars and then forced to live in hiding in London, away from his family for a period of six months. In 1688, when the young Isaac Watts was fourteen, William of Orange landed on British soil and James II fled the country. With the vicious persecution against Dissenters eased, the congregation of the church to which the Watts family belonged was able to meet openly once more. By this time the faith that had strengthened his parents to endure through years of intimidation and duress was becoming a personal one for their son Isaac, too.

During his Southampton schooldays he kept a private *Memorandum*. Only a brief entry describes the spiritual transaction that took place during this period when the boy was fourteen to fifteen years of age.

> Fell under considerable convictions of sin.   1688
> And was taught to trust in Christ, I hope.   1689

Even though none of his later hymns were intentionally autobiographical in character, we may discern references to his conversion experience in a number of his lines:

> How heavy is the night
> that hangs upon our eyes,
> till Christ with his reviving light
> over our souls arise!
>
> Our guilty spirits dread
> to meet the wrath of heaven;
> but, in his righteousness arrayed,
> we see our sins forgiven.

Sometimes he recollected the relief that the repentant sinner knows when he first realizes that his debt of sin has been cancelled:

> My soul looks back to see
> the burden thou didst bear,
> when hanging on the accursed tree,
> and knows her guilt was there.
>
> Believing, we rejoice
> to see the curse remove;
> we bless the Lamb with cheerful voice,
> and sing his wondrous love.

When only seventeen years of age, Isaac Watts' young faith was put to a severe test. Recognizing his exceptional abilities, a Southampton doctor offered to cover all the costs of a university education for the youth. But Oxford and Cambridge, the only two English universities at the time, would not allow any student who did not conform to the Church of England to become graduates. To take advantage of this offer of financial help, Isaac Watts would need to turn his back on the Dissenting principles of his home and upbringing — convictions that had also become his own. This he was not prepared to do: he declined the generous proposal.

Instead it was decided that the young man should attend a Dissenting academy at Stoke Newington, north of London, then a village surrounded by fields. Such academies, run by preachers in conjunction with their work in their own churches, were the answer that the Dissenters gave to the ban on gaining a university degree, and often provided a more rounded and useful education than the universities themselves. The Stoke Newington academy, run by a Thomas Rowe to whom Isaac became warmly attached, was no exception. In a tribute to his tutor, he later wrote:

> I love thy gentle influence, Rowe,
> thy gentle influence like the sun
> only dissolves the frozen snow,
> then bids our thoughts like rivers flow,
> and choose the channels where they run.

Not many weeks had passed before Watts had drawn around him a group of like-minded students who would remain his lasting friends. The group vied with each other in their studies and enjoyed communicating in verse. The curriculum included philosophy, astronomy, mathematics, detailed studies of the great English poets, Greek and Latin authors and, of course, theology. Isaac Watts gave himself unstintingly to his work, not only during stated hours of study, but often far into the night. Never strong, such excessive concentration undermined his health and seriously disturbed his sleep pattern, leading to an ever-worsening problem of insomnia.

A significant suggestion

In 1694, after four years at Thomas Rowe's academy, Watts, now twenty years of age, returned to his Southampton home. He had long felt called by God to enter the ministry but, though now qualified, delayed taking any appointment for the time being. Several suggestions have been made for this: perhaps he lacked assurance to undertake so responsible a task at his age; perhaps he wished more time to study. Whatever the reason, we see an overarching providence of God in this decision.

As he attended worship Sunday by Sunday at the Above Bar Independent Church, the young poet became increasingly dismayed at the doggerel verse he was obliged to sing. The congregation was using the metrical version of the Psalms arranged by Thomas Sternhold and John Hopkins and others, published in 1556 and known as *The Whole Booke of Psalmes*, which, as we have seen, was the standard singing material in English churches. Even though there had been numerous attempts to improve the *Old Version*, as it was called, and Nahum Tate and Nicholas Brady were currently working on an improved rendering of the Psalms, it was still Sternhold and Hopkins' Psalter that was in general use.[1] Described by the poet James Montgomery as bearing as much resemblance as the dead to the living, these ungainly paraphrases were stifling the life of Christian worship. Congregations would have found greater benefit from reading Psalm 102 than from singing such clumsy lines as:

> By reason of my groaning voice
>   my bones cleave to my skin,
> as pelican in wilderness
>   such case now am I in;
> and as an owl in desert is,
>   lo! I am such a one;

> I watch, and as a sparrow on
> the housetop am alone.

Returning from the morning service one Sunday, young Isaac Watts felt he had had enough. 'Such words', he exclaimed heatedly, 'are entirely wanting in the dignity and beauty that should characterize every part of a Christian service.' His father had a ready answer for his son, both reasonable and obvious: 'Try, then, whether you can do something better' — a seed thought only, but one that would bring incalculable blessings to the church of Christ. Taking up the challenge, Isaac began to write hymns, the first reflecting his new commission:

> Behold the glories of the Lamb
> amidst his Father's throne:
> prepare new honours for his name,
> and songs before unknown...

Above Bar Independent Church was willing to try out his verses, but with a largely illiterate congregation and no ready means of circulating a few copies, they had to be 'lined' — a process that involved the stanza being read out line by line, with each line sung in turn. This naturally made the whole sound disjointed, but Watts was undeterred. Every Sunday the congregation tried out a further composition, and during the two years he spent at home he wrote most of the hymns for which his name was to be known and loved. Fresh, vibrant and vigorous, they reflect the strong earnest faith of a young Christian eager to sing the glories of his God and the wonders of salvation. These early hymns cover the wide spectrum of Christian worship and experience. First came hymns to lift the worship of the Lord's people above the dreary effusions of Sternhold and Hopkins:

> Come let us join our cheerful songs
>   with angels round the throne;
> ten thousand thousand are their tongues,
>   but all their joys are one.

The faithful character of God, underpinning all his promises in salvation, was a theme that Watts loved to extol:

> His every word of grace is strong
>   as that which built the skies;
> the voice that rolls the stars along
>   speaks all the promises.

Watts showed a deep concern for his eight younger brothers and sisters and would often speak to each of them, using the 'wonderful works of God' in nature to lead them on to a personal knowledge of the Creator. Ever a keen observer of the natural world in all its varied expressions, Watts finds in the beauty he saw around him a starting point for his thought. The following words are typical:

> Nature with open volume stands
>   to spread her Maker's praise abroad,
> and every labour of his hands
>   shows something worthy of a God.

> But in the grace that rescued man
>   his brightest form of glory shines;
> here on the cross 'tis fairest drawn
>   in precious blood and crimson lines.

> O the sweet wonders of that cross,
>   where God the Saviour loved and died!
> Her noblest life my spirit draws
>   from his dear wounds and bleeding side.

And it is when he is dealing directly with the cross itself that Watts is at once most moving and powerful. Lines that have brought many to salvation, including Fanny Crosby, the blind hymn-writer of New York, and have led countless worshippers to new depths of understanding and gratitude to God, are found in these verses:

> Alas! and did my Saviour bleed
>   and did my Sovereign die?
> Would he devote that sacred head
>   for such a worm as I?
>
> Was it for crimes that I had done,
>   he groaned upon the tree?
> Amazing pity! Grace unknown!
>   And love beyond degree!
>
> But drops of grief can ne'er repay
>   the debt of love I owe:
> here, Lord, I give myself away;
>   'tis all that I can do.

Without question, the greatest treatment of this theme is found in the well-known words:

> When I survey the wondrous cross,
>   on which the Prince of glory died,
> my richest gain I count but loss,
>   and pour contempt on all my pride.
>
> See from his head, his hands, his feet,
>   sorrow and love flow mingled down;
> did e'er such love and sorrow meet
>   or thorns compose so rich a crown?

The inadequacy of any righteous deeds on our part to earn the favour of God is a subject that Watts pursues in a number of his hymns:

> No more, my God, I boast no more
>   of all the duties I have done;
> I quit the hopes I held before,
>   to trust the merits of thy Son.
>
> The best obedience of my hands
>   dares not appear before thy throne;
> but faith can answer thy demands
>   by pleading what my Lord has done.

He understood how a Christian feels when beset with temptations on every side; but more than this, he knew the remedy:

> Amidst temptations sharp and long,
>   my soul to this dear refuge flies:
> hope is my anchor, firm and strong,
>   while tempests blow and billows rise.
>
> The gospel bears my spirit up;
>   a faithful and unchanging God...

A further keynote of Isaac Watts' verse is one of joy. Perhaps he noticed that Christian congregations often seemed dour and sad. It was his strong contention that:

> Religion never was designed
>   to make our pleasures less.

And so he could urge believers to cast away their gloom:

> Come, we that love the Lord,
>   and let our joys be known;
> join in a song with sweet accord,
>   and thus surround the throne.
>
> Let those refuse to sing
>   that never knew our God;
> but children of the heavenly King
>   may speak their joys abroad.

Not only does a believer anticipate joy in the world to come, but even here may know foretastes of all that is in store. So he could sing in a verse usually omitted:

> Yes, and before we rise
>   to that immortal state,
> the thoughts of such amazing bliss
>   should constant joys create.

And on a similar theme could exclaim:

> My God, the spring of all my joys,
>   the life of my delights,
> the glory of my brightest days
>   and comfort of my nights.

That last line carries a poignancy of its own for the poet. Insomnia, begun in his academy days as he studied far into the night, became a lifelong problem for Isaac Watts. Only an opiate such as laudanum could bring him any relief. His achievements, in spite of this affliction, might well astound us.

For a young man of twenty-one years of age to be writing funeral hymns may seem strange from the hedonistic perspective of society in our day. But families living in the seventeenth and eighteenth centuries were no strangers to death. Hardly a household had not experienced the sorrow of burying young children. Isaac himself had been seriously ill with smallpox as a young teenager. One day as he stood on the east bank of Southampton Water looking across to the west bank and to the bright flowery fields merging into the majestic greens of the New Forest, he thought of the beautiful land of the heavenly Canaan beyond the narrow stream of death. And in words that remind us of John Bunyan's 'Beulah Land' where the flowers never fade, he wrote:

> There is a land of pure delight,
>   where saints immortal reign;
> infinite day excludes the night,
>   and pleasures banish pain.
>
> There everlasting spring abides,
>   and never-withering flowers;
> death like a narrow sea divides
>   this heavenly land from ours.
>
> Sweet fields beyond the swelling flood
>   stand dressed in living green:
> so to the Jews old Canaan stood,
>   while Jordan rolled between.

Many Christians have felt their spirits lift, despite the open grave before them, as they have sung such words as:

> Give me the wings of faith to rise
>   within the veil and see
> the saints above, how great their joys,
>   how bright their glories be.

> I ask them whence their victory came;
>   they, with united breath,
> ascribe their conquest to the Lamb,
>   their triumph to his death.

By the time Watts was twenty-one years of age he had already completed the majority of his hymns, although not his paraphrases of the Psalms and other Scriptures. The hymns were passed from hand to hand in manuscript form, but he did not attempt to publish them until a further ten years had elapsed.

Entering the ministry

Meanwhile, in 1696 a wealthy Dissenter, Sir John Hartopp, invited Isaac Watts to become tutor to his family, consisting of a son and seven daughters. Having his home in Stoke Newington where Watts had previously studied, Sir John would have known of the young man's exceptional abilities. The arrangement was one that Watts happily accepted, for it enabled him to continue his studies and his writings. A natural educationalist, Watts found a sense of fulfilment in his work and a warm spiritual affinity with Sir John Hartopp and his wife Elizabeth. Like Isaac's own father, Sir John had paid a heavy price for his Nonconformity, and his love of spiritual things was intense and real. The Hartopps worshipped at Mark Lane Independent Church — a well-known London church with a noble pedigree in terms of its previous ministers. These included Joseph Caryl, David Clarkson[2] and none other than the renowned Dr John Owen himself, whose widow was still in the congregation. But the church had recently been in decline, largely owing to the uninspiring ministry of the learned Isaac

Chauncey. To this church Sir John introduced his young tutor.

Before long the well-heeled congregation at Mark Lane became aware of Isaac Watts' abilities and on his twenty-fourth birthday, 17 July 1698, he preached his first sermon there. It must have been with some trepidation that he mounted that pulpit, but the appreciation was widespread, and within a few months he was pressed to accept an invitation to become an assistant to Dr Chauncey. With Watts preaching each Sunday morning, the condition of the church rapidly improved. Three years later, on the resignation of Dr Chauncey, the church approached the twenty-seven-year-old Watts, urging him to accept the pastorate. Ill at the time, he demurred, but in January 1702 agreed to take the position — one that he would hold for the rest of his life, although his ministry was necessarily intermittent because of his indifferent health.

A book of poems

Throughout these years Watts continued to write hymns and had begun to try his hand at an enhanced rendering of the Psalms. One of his friends from his student days wrote approvingly in 1697: 'I give you my hearty thanks for your ingenious paraphrase in which you have so generously rescued the noble Psalmist out of the butcherly hands of Sternhold and Hopkins.' Despite this, Watts was not yet ready to allow any of his verse to be put into print. His preaching and work as tutor to the Hartopp family engrossed his time, as did a major treatise on which he was engaged, later to be published under the title *Logic*. However, in March 1700 he received a long and highly significant letter from one of his younger brothers, Enoch. Knowing well the quality of Isaac's hymns, Enoch was now urging his brother to publish them. Nor was this the first time he had done so: 'I have frequently importuned you to it before now,' he tells him, but Isaac had always managed to find an excuse. Piling argument on argument, Enoch earnestly begged his brother to take this significant step. Referring to the pressing need for a new version of the Psalms, he maintained, 'I have been persuaded a great while since that were David to speak English, he would have chosen to make use of your style.'

Still Watts hesitated, but at last in 1706 he took an important initial step: he published a book of his own poems, entitled *Horae Lyricae*. 'I make no pretences to the name of poet,' said Watts modestly of his own work. Others thought differently. The unlikely Dr Samuel Johnson, the great lexicographer of the eighteenth century, and poet in his own right, considered that Watts' poems certainly merited recognition. They earned for the Mark Lane preacher a lasting place among the English poets. Many of the items in *Horae Lyricae* were in all probability the work of his student days when he corresponded with his friends in verse. Some pieces were hymns, while others were composed to commemorate national events such as the death of William III. Narrative poems, moral exhortations and poetical renderings of Scripture narratives were all included.

Although most of the verses found in *Horae Lyricae* were not intended as hymns, the closer his lines approached to the subject nearest his heart — the majesty and glory of God in creation and redemption — the more memorable they became:

> Thy hand unseen sustains the poles
> on which this huge creation rolls:
> the starry arch proclaims thy power,
> thy pencil glows in every flower;
> in thousand shapes and colours rise
> thy painted wonders to our eyes...

> Across the waves, around the sky,
> there's not a spot or deep or high,
> where the Creator has not trod
> and left the footstep of a God.

In such words we discover a cosmic grandeur, an immensity of thought that lifts the reader beyond the narrow confines of his daily circumstances. Watts scours the English vocabulary to convey the wonders of creation:

> Thy hand, how wide it spreads the sky!
>   How glorious to behold!
> Tinged with the blue of heavenly dye,
>   and starred with sparkling gold…

But as he speaks of the resurrection and ascension of the Saviour his tone is at once more tender, more triumphant:

> Here's love and grief beyond degree;
>   the Lord of glory dies for men!
> But lo! what sudden joys we see;
>   Jesus, the dead, revives again!
>
> The rising God forsakes the tomb;
>   up to his Father's court he flies;
> cherubic legions guard him home,
>   and shout his welcome to the skies.

In *Horae Lyricae* Watts allows the reader a rare glimpse into his own personal experiences of Christ's presence:

> Once I beheld his face, where beams divine
> broke from his eyelids, and unusual light
> wrapt me at once in glory and surprise.

> My joyful heart, high leaping in my breast,
> with transport cry'd, 'This is the Christ of God!'
> And threw my arms around in sweet embrace,
> and clasp'd, and bow'd adoring low, till I was lost in him.

One young woman who read *Horae Lyricae* was so impressed with the poet's command of language, his depth of thought and, above all, his spirituality of mind, that she longed to meet him. Described as 'a haunting beauty', Elizabeth Singer also came from a family that had suffered persecution under Charles II, and was a poet in her own right. With auburn hair, lovely complexion and animated eyes, Elizabeth not only possessed stunning looks, but appears to have known it, decorating her hair with flowers, and writing under the pseudonym of Philomela.[3] Enamoured with the thought of a man who could compose such words as she read in *Horae Lyricae*, she wrote to Watts in verse in July 1706:

> Seraphic heights I seem to gain;
>   and sacred transports feel,
> while WATTS, to thy celestial strain,
>   surprised I listen still.

Not unexpectedly, Isaac Watts found himself drawn to such an attractive admirer. He responded to her in verse:

> Let all my powers with awe profound,
> while Philomela sings,
> attend the rapture of the sound,
> and my devotion rise on her seraphic wings.

Elizabeth imagined that the poet's personal appearance would match the magnificence of his verse. She had a shock coming. When at last they met she saw before her a man scarcely

five feet in height, with prominent nose and a sallow, heavy
complexion scarred from smallpox, and showing the marks
of sleeplessness. She found herself having to re-evaluate her
impressions. A friendship grew up between them nevertheless,
but on her part it was based on affinity of thought rather than
physical attraction. When at last the thirty-two-year-old Watts
plucked up courage to broach the question of marriage, Miss
Singer gave a well-intentioned but tactless reply: 'Mr Watts, I
only wish I could say that I admire the casket as much as I
admire the jewel.'[4] Watts would remain single for the rest of his
life. Perhaps lines such as these reflect his disappointment:

> How vain are all things here below!
> How false, and yet how fair!
> Each pleasure has its poison too,
> and every sweet, a snare…
>
> The fondness of a creature's love,
> how strong it strikes the sense!
> Thither the warm affections move,
> nor can we call them thence.

Hymns and Spiritual Songs

In 1707, following the favourable reception given to *Horae
Lyricae,* Isaac Watts decided at last to offer his hymns to a
publisher — who bought the copyright for a mere £10. Called
Hymns and Spiritual Songs, the whole, comprising 365 items,
was divided into three books or sections, the first containing
one hundred and fifty hymns based on passages of Scripture,
the last of these being a twelve-verse hymn, 'Join all the glorious
names' — much loved since the day it was first published:

HYMNS

AND

Spiritual Songs.

In Three BOOKS.

I. Collected from the Scriptures.
II. Compos'd on Divine Subjects.
III. Prepared for the Lord's Supper.

With an ESSAY

Towards the Improvement of Chri-
ftian Pfalmody, by the Ufe of E-
vangelical Hymns in Worfhip, as
well as the Pfalms of *David.*

By *I. WATTS.*

*And they fung a new Song, faying, Thou art
worthy, &c. for thou waft flain and haft redeemed us, &c.* Rev. 5. 9.
Soliti effent (*i. e. Chriftiani*) convenire, car-
menque Chrifto quafi Deo dicere. *Plinius
in Epift.*

LONDON,

Printed by *J. Humfreys,* for *John Lawrence,*
at the Angel in the *Poultrey.* 1707.

Title page to 1707 edition of *Hymns and Spiritual Songs*

> Jesus, my great High Priest
>   offered his blood and died;
>   my guilty conscience seeks
>   no sacrifice beside:
>   his powerful blood did once atone
>   and now it pleads before the throne.

The second book contained a further one hundred and seventy free compositions on biblical themes and Christian experience, with the third adding another forty-five pieces, mainly relating to the Lord's Supper, and some doxologies. The work had a mixed reception: instantly popular with some, from others it met with stiff resistance. With a long tradition of singing only psalms in the churches, it is not surprising that many were suspicious and fearful. But very gradually *Hymns and Spiritual Songs* won its way and a second edition was called for in 1709. James Montgomery, himself a poet and hymn-writer, born thirty years after the death of Watts, wrote:

> Dr Watts may almost be called the inventor of hymns in our language, for he so far departed from precedent that few of his compositions resemble those of his forerunners, while he so far established a precedent to all his successors that none have departed from it otherwise than according to the [individual] turn of mind of the writer.[5]

The title 'Pioneer of English hymns' is one that Watts well deserves. As we have seen, seventeenth-century poets such as Thomas Ken, Samuel Crossman, John Milton and Richard Baxter all wrote before Watts, but theirs were more verses of personal devotion and not initially intended to enrich congregational worship. Like them, however, Watts was predominantly a poet of the seventeenth century, and wrote within the restrictions that language usage and circumstances of the day imposed upon him. His hymns were mainly in simple four-line verses and written in common metre, short metre or long metre. Despite his exceptional poetic ability, he deliberately chose a path of self-denial for the greater good of the worshipper. Although conversant with the Latin poets and classical literature, he rarely allowed himself the luxury of using erudite Latin-based vocabulary. Instead he expressed his thoughts in the plain Anglo-Saxon diction of the common man.

By the time that Charles Wesley wrote his early hymns, more than forty years later, language, as in our own generation, had undergone a fundamental change. The essayists Joseph Addison, Richard Steele, Charles Lamb and others had forged a new style of written English, liberating eighteenth-century writers from the restrictions of the past. Some of the vocabulary Watts had used regularly was now out of vogue — even regarded as distasteful to the cultured eighteenth-century ear. However, his hymns live on, and appear to date less than the work of many of his successors.

Despite his predominant use of basic metres and language, the hymns of Isaac Watts so far transcend the ordinary that the singer is at once engaged, moved and uplifted by his words. His use of the unexpected in adjective, adverb and rhyme never allows the singer any degree of mental boredom. Words such as these, describing the joys of believers in heaven, illustrate all that is best in Watts' thought:

> Then I shall see thy lovely face
>   with strong immortal eyes,
> and feast upon thy unknown grace
>   with pleasure and surprise.

We come across expressions like 'hellish darts', 'fruits immortal', 'guardian grace', 'my wandering soul', 'leaning on all-sufficient grace', 'unmingled joys', 'our helpless miseries', Christ's 'dear

majestic head', 'his dying crimson like a robe' (a reference to
the purple robes of emperors); and many, many more. Then we
discover couplets that we have sung and cannot forget, though
we may hardly know in which hymn they are found:

> This world is ours, and worlds to come;
> earth is our lodge and heaven our home.

> Where reason fails with all her powers,
> there faith prevails, and love adores.

> Joy to the world! The Lord is come!
>   Let earth receive her King.

Another poetic device that Watts used to great effect was
the repetition of words in reverse order for cumulative impact.
A notable example of this is found in perhaps his best-loved
hymn of all, 'When I survey the wondrous cross', a meditative
hymn primarily intended for use at the Lord's Supper. In the
third verse Watts writes:

> See from his head, his hand, his feet,
>   *sorrow* and *love* flow mingled down;
> did e'er such *love* and *sorrow* meet,
>   or thorns compose so rich a crown?

Again in the fourth verse we have a further example of this
reversal of word order:

> Then am I *dead* to all the *globe*,
>   and all the *globe* is *dead* to me.

Each verse of this moving hymn describes the sufferings of
Christ in the first two lines and in the last two anticipates the
response due from the worshipper.

Bound up with Watts' 1707 edition of *Hymns and Spiritual Songs* was a highly significant piece entitled, *A Short Essay towards the Improvement of Psalmody*. In the word 'psalmody' Watts included not only the metrical psalms, but all verse forms for use in public worship. He presented strong arguments intended to counter the barrage of criticism he knew he would receive from those who felt that any human composition was an improper medium in which to sing the praises of God. Making the point that Christians should be able to bring their own thanksgiving to God in song as did Zacharias and Mary, he concluded that new favours received from God demanded new songs of love and gratitude. He backed up his comments by quoting such exhortations as 'Sing unto the Lord a new song' and the apostle Paul's words to the Ephesians on making melody to the Lord with 'psalms and hymns and spiritual songs'.[6] These remarks were an important pointer to the future and an unmistakable foreshadowing of what was soon to come from the hymn-writer's pen. He had already been at work on an improved version of the Psalms commonly sung in the churches, but planned to go much further than this. He determined to express himself 'as I suppose David would have done, had he lived in the days of Christianity'. 'Why', he enquired:

should I address God my Saviour in a song with burnt sacrifices and the fat of rams? Why should I bind my sacrifice with cords to the horns of the altar?... Why must I join David in his legal or prophetic language to curse my enemies when my Saviour has taught me to love and bless them? ... What need is there that I should wrap up the shining honours of my Redeemer in dark and shadowy language?

Why, in fact, should children of the New Covenant be obliged to sing exclusively the songs of the Old Covenant when that covenant has passed away?

A further eleven years would elapse, however, before the promised volume of Psalms materialized. His duties in the Hartopp household still demanded his time, as did his pulpit ministry. The Mark Lane premises had become dilapidated and after a period in temporary accommodation the congregation at last settled in its new home in Bury Street in 1709. Most of all, however, it was illness that disrupted the poet's endeavours. An assistant was appointed to fill the pulpit on the many Sundays that Watts was unable to preach. When this happened he would try to write a pastoral letter to his people instead.

In 1712, as Watts was halfway through his projected work on the Psalms, his health broke entirely. With little medical aid available he was prostrated for many months and grieved that although 'David's harp was ready strung for Messiah's name', the harpist was 'confined to sit in silence'. Watts spent much of his time convalescing at his family home in Southampton. Perhaps words he had written, such as these, came to his mind:

> With joy we meditate the grace
>   of our High Priest above;
> his heart is made of tenderness,
>   and overflows with love.
>
> Touched with a sympathy within
>   he knows our feeble frame,
> he knows what sore temptations mean
>   for he has felt the same.

When he began to regain strength in the spring of 1714, a friend, Sir Thomas Abney, thought that a week's break at his country mansion, Theobalds, in Cheshunt, Hertfordshire, would give the poet-preacher a much-needed change. Probably among the longest 'visits' ever recorded, the one week turned into thirty-eight years — in fact to the end of Watts' life. His welcome was beyond doubt. After thirty years Lady Abney was to declare quaintly that in her view it had been 'the shortest visit my family ever received'. This was a remarkable provision for the ailing poet, and there in the quiet beauty of the majestic trees and walks and the surrounding parkland of the Abney home, Watts' health improved. With his own suite of rooms he was able to write and think without interruption. In return he assisted with the education of the three Abney girls.

Songs for children

A year after he moved to Theobalds, Watts published a delightful collection of hymns for children. In a slim volume of thirty-six hymns entitled *Divine Songs Attempted in easy Language for the Use of Children*, a volume that has gone through hundreds of editions, he wrote with stark clarity and simplicity.

> There is beyond the sky
> a heaven of joy and love;
> and holy children when they die,
> go to that world above.

The work was dedicated to the Abney girls and written while he was their tutor. Clearly eighteenth-century children were much the same as children today, and so Watts could admonish against lying, stealing, laziness, but most notably, quarrelling:

> Let dogs delight to bark and bite,
> for God hath made them so;
> let bears and lions growl and fight,
> for 'tis their nature too.

> But, children, you should never let
> such angry passions rise;
> your little hands were never made
> to tear each other's eyes.

The only hymn in regular use to have survived from this collection is the one beginning 'I sing the almighty power of God'. Built around the creation narrative of Genesis 1, it ends with memorable words:

> God's hand is my perpetual guard,
> he keeps me with his eye;
> why should I then forget the Lord
> who is for ever nigh?

The Psalms of David Imitated

The year 1714 was one that Dissenters would not easily forget. Queen Anne, the last of the Stuart monarchs, had come to the throne in 1702. Her sympathy with the Church of Rome, and equally her antipathy towards the Dissenters, were well known. On 1 August 1714 an act known as the Schism Act, aimed at the dissolution of Nonconformist schools, was to come into force. This repressive act was likely to lead to renewed persecution; but the death of the queen on that very day spelt deliverance from such a plight, and was seen as a remarkable intervention of God on their behalf. 'Queen Anne's dead' would remain a term of relieved greeting among the Dissenters for many years to come, but Watts commemorated the occasion in a worthier fashion by his poetic rendering of Psalm 90 — words that would become something of a national anthem:

> Our God, our help in ages past,
>> our hope for years to come;
> our shelter from the stormy blast
>> and our eternal home.
>
> Beneath the shadow of thy throne
>> thy saints have dwelt secure;
> sufficient is thine arm alone,
>> and our defence is sure.

This hymn, with its terse iambic lines stressing the uncertainty of all human life, took its place under the title 'Man frail, and God eternal' in the completed work on the Psalms, ready at last in 1719. The publication carried a typically long title, so favoured by eighteenth-century writers: *The Psalms of David Imitated in the Language of the New Testament, and Applied to the Christian State and Worship.* To this Watts attached a preface, some thirty pages in length, in which he discussed all the arguments raised against the singing of anything but the actual words of Scripture in worship. The touchstone of 'Christ in all the Scriptures' laid down by the Lord himself to his troubled disciples on the road to Emmaus was the guiding principle directing all his endeavour. He did not attempt to adapt every psalm into a hymn — some he maintained were not suitable. Others, such as Psalm 103, had as many as five pieces based on it. Perhaps best known of all is his rendering of Solomon's prayer in Psalm 72. To Watts it was a prefiguring of Christ's triumphant and ever-increasing kingdom:

> Jesus shall reign where'er the sun
> doth his successive journeys run;
> his kingdom stretch from shore to shore,
> till moons shall wax and wane no more.

In his version of Psalm 136 Watts announced his theme of the wonders of God in creation:

> He built the earth, he spread the sky,
> he fixed the starry lights on high:

But then his mind ran on to a yet greater wonder:

> He sent his Son with power to save
> from guilt and darkness and the grave:

David's prayer of penitence in Psalm 51 after his grievous fall is interpreted with sensitivity, providing words with which many have been able to express their own need. When Daniel Webster, American orator and statesman, was dying, these were the words he was repeating, not once, but many times over:

> Show pity, Lord, O Lord, forgive;
> let a repenting rebel live;
> are not thy mercies large and free?
> May not a sinner trust in thee?
>
> A broken heart, my God, my King,
> is all the sacrifice I bring;
> the God of grace will ne'er despise
> a broken heart for sacrifice.

A young minister once asked an older preacher what commentary he would recommend on the Psalms. The immediate reply was 'Watts' version of them'. Called the 'Evangeliser of the Psalter' by Josiah Conder, himself a hymn-writer of considerable note, Watts had attempted, as he had already indicated, to baptize the songs of the Old Covenant with the glories of the

New. Not all were of equal merit, and the great majority have not stood the test of time, but others have brought immeasurable enrichment to Christian worship for almost three hundred years, and proved the foundation on which other writers were later to build. Watts' version of Psalm 146 was on John Wesley's lips as he lay dying. Again and again through his last night on earth he struggled to repeat the magnificent words:

> I'll praise my Maker, while I've breath
> and when my voice is lost in death
>   praise shall employ my nobler powers.
> My days of praise shall ne'er be past
> while life, and thought, and being last,
>   or immortality endures.

As he had anticipated, the publication of *The Psalms of David Imitated* brought an outcry against the poet. This came both from those who objected to singing any psalms or hymns at all and from those whose loyalty to the *Old Version* of Sternhold and Hopkins, bound up for generations with their Bibles, made them fearful that the faith itself was being destroyed. A typical eighteenth-century 'pamphlet war' broke out with outspoken publications appearing on each side of the divide, though it does not appear that Watts wrote in his own defence.

'The greatest name among hymn-writers'

By 1720 Isaac Watts' work as a hymn-writer was almost done, even though he had nearly thirty years of life ahead of him. James Montgomery is generous in his praise of this man whom he described as 'the greatest name among hymn-writers', declaring that his hymns have brought:

a more abundant and universal blessing than the verses of any uninspired penman that ever lived... His *Psalms and Hymns* throw light upon every secret movement of the human heart and describe every kind of trial, temptation, conflict, doubt, fear and grief; as well as the hope, faith, love, joy, peace, labour of the Christian in all stages of his course upon earth.[7]

In addition to his poetry Watts wrote educational books[8] and also a treatise on the theory of education. In compiling his *Dictionary*, Dr Samuel Johnson took hundreds of examples and illustrations from Watts' book on *Logic,* a work he had undertaken while he lived with the Hartopp family. Numerous printed sermons and several catechisms, one particularly for children, were among the many productions of his pen. But it is as a hymn-writer that we remember him above everything else. And there is a further unusual element about his work: unlike Wesley, Watts wrote in a day of spiritual decline — a fact that adds immeasurably to the stature of this unremarkable-looking little man.

Watts remained with the Abney family in Cheshunt for twenty-one years and then accompanied them when they moved to Stoke Newington in 1735. From there he continued to write and preach, but often under a cloud of illness and suffering — frequently the effects of insomnia. As a leader among the Dissenters and as an educationalist, his name was revered, but never had Watts lived merely for earthly reputation; always he had kept the eternal perspective fully in view. The title of one of his later works, *The World to Come,* published in 1745 just three years before his death, reveals the trend of his thoughts. Many years earlier he had written:

> There is a house not made with hands,
> eternal and on high;

> and here my waiting spirit stands,
> till God shall bid it fly.

And it was in that same frame of mind that George Whitefield found him when he visited him just half an hour before his death. When he asked the dying man how he was, Whitefield received the reply, 'I am one of Christ's waiting servants.' The wait was nearly over. And on 25 November 1748 Isaac Watts was at last ushered into the land of 'pure delight' of which he had sung, and experienced the fulfilment of that hope expressed long years before:

> Then shall I see and hear and know
> all I desired or wished below;
> and every power find sweet employ
> in that eternal world of joy.

Notes

1. An earlier improvement on Sternhold and Hopkins was to be found in the 'purer version' of William Barton, 1644. Some have suggested that this may have been the version in use at Above Bar Independent Church.
2. The three volumes of Clarkson's *Works* have recently been republished by the Banner of Truth Trust.
3. A poetic name for the nightingale.
4. Elizabeth Singer eventually married a Thomas Rowe, nephew of Isaac Watts' tutor. Her complete works were published in four volumes in 1739.
5. James Montgomery, *The Christian Psalmist*, 1846, p.20.
6. Psalms 96:1; 98:1; 149:1; Isaiah 42:9-10; Ephesians 5:19.
7. James Montgomery, *The Christian Psalmist*, p.19.
8. *The Art of Reading and Writing English* (1721), *First Principles of Astronomy and Geography* (1726), *Principles of Philosophy* (1733), *The Improvement of the Mind* (1741 & 1751).

Philip Doddridge
(1702-1751)

'To serve the cause
of such a Friend'

Hark, the glad sound! the Saviour comes,
　the Saviour promised long;
let every heart prepare a throne,
　and every voice a song.

Our glad hosannas, Prince of Peace,
　thy welcome shall proclaim,
and heaven's eternal arches ring
　with thy beloved name.

Philip Doddridge

Philip Doddridge
(1702-1751)

'To serve the cause of such a Friend'

When Monica Doddridge gave birth to her twentieth child, the infant was gently laid on one side, presumed to be stillborn as most of Monica's previous nineteen babies had been. Only a shallow sigh alerted the midwife to the fact that the child was alive — an inauspicious beginning for one who would become greatly used in the hands of God, not only for his own generation, but down the years, even to the present day.

Only surviving son of Daniel Doddridge, a London tradesman, and his wife Monica, Philip Doddridge was born in London in June 1702. The first two decades of the eighteenth century were marked by the birth of a remarkable number of men and women of outstanding significance in the purposes of God. Among them were such influential characters as John and Charles Wesley, Jonathan Edwards, William Grimshaw, Selina, Countess of Huntingdon, George Whitefield, Howell Harris, William Williams, Daniel Rowland, to name a few. Each would play a strategic role in God's unfolding plan of blessing for his church.

Both Philip Doddridge's father and his mother sprang from families who had suffered for their faith. His grandfather on his father's side was ejected from his living in 1662 for his refusal to compromise his conscience by submitting to the terms of the

Act of Uniformity; while his maternal grandfather, disguised as a peasant, had fled a persecution of Lutheran pastors in Prague and had eventually come to Britain. Even after the Toleration Act of 1689 strictures against Dissenters were still in operation, stiffening after Queen Anne's accession to the throne in the year of Philip's birth. However, it was a secure and godly home and Philip would later record the influence of his mother's early teaching on his life.

But these days were not to last. In 1711, when Philip was not yet nine years of age, his mother died; four years later his father also died. The orphaned thirteen-year-old had early found a spiritual foundation for his life through faith in Christ and now expressed his faith in a diary he had started to keep: 'God is an immortal Father, my soul rejoiceth in him. He hath hitherto helped me and provided for me.' Perhaps he was recalling these experiences in later years when he wrote:

> How gentle God's commands,
> how kind his precepts are!
> Come cast your burden on the Lord
> and trust his constant care.
>
> While providence supports,
> let saints securely dwell;
> that hand which bears all nature up
> shall guide his children well.
>
> His goodness stands approved
> down to the present day;
> I'll cast my burden at his feet
> and bear a song away.

But the provision of God for young Philip Doddridge did not come through his appointed guardian. At this point the youth came under the influence of a Presbyterian minister in

St Albans, Samuel Clark, who took him into his own home for several years and undertook to oversee the rest of his education, caring for him like a parent.

As in the case of many children privileged with Christian parents, it would not be easy to determine when young Philip Doddridge actually became a Christian. If he himself knew, he left no record of it. Perhaps, however, an answer can be found in the words of one of his best-known hymns — words that many since have been able to take to themselves to express that moment of self-dedication to the Saviour:

> O happy day that fixed my choice
>   on thee, my Saviour and my God!
> Well may this glowing heart rejoice
>   and tell its raptures all abroad.

This hymn was chosen by Queen Victoria at the confirmation service for one of her children.

But there was a day, a long-remembered day, when young Doddridge, still only fifteen years old, was received into the membership of Samuel Clark's church. In his diary for 1 January 1718, he wrote:

> I this day, in the strength of Christ, renewed my covenant with God, and renounced my covenant with sin. I vowed against every sin, and resolved carefully to perform every duty.

Other words from the hymn quoted above may well refer to that occasion:

> High heaven, that heard the solemn vow,
>   that vow renewed shall daily hear,
> till in life's latest hour I bow,
>   and bless in death a bond so dear.

As Philip Doddridge began to consider his future course, one desire above all others dominated his thinking: a desire to serve his God and to enter the Christian ministry. But his circumstances were not favourable for such a course. How could he receive training without financial backing? As he was pondering his problems he received an amazing offer from none other than the Duchess of Bedford. Philip's uncle worked for the Duke and Duchess and had told his employer about his promising nephew and his aspirations to be a preacher. As a result the Duchess offered not only to finance Philip's course at one of the universities, but also to settle him in a charge after he had completed his studies. But there was a condition attached. He must abandon his Dissenting principles and become a member of the Established Church, because unless he did so he could not complete a course at Oxford or Cambridge. Like Isaac Watts before him, Doddridge faced a hard choice, and like Watts he remained steadfast to his principles. He turned down the generous offer.

Soon after this, Philip approached Dr Edmund Calamy, considered the 'bishop' of the Dissenters at the time, and told him of his sense of call to the Christian ministry. Looking at the youth before him who had little financial support and uncertain health (for Philip had never been robust), Dr Calamy advised him to turn his back on such thoughts and enter some other profession instead. 'It was with great concern that I received such advice,' recorded Philip, 'but I desire to follow providence and not to force it. The Lord give me grace to glorify him in whatever station he sets me.'

Doddridge reluctantly began to consider alternatives. The legal profession seemed best suited to his turn of mind and abilities, and when he received a proposal from an eminent lawyer offering him a position, Philip felt that this was God's indication of his purposes for his life. He wrote a letter of acceptance. But just before posting it he decided to set aside a morning to wait on God and seek assurances of his will. As he prayed he heard the approach of the postman. Quickly opening a letter addressed to him, Philip could scarcely believe its contents. His kind friend Samuel Clark, who had cared for him in his early teens, was offering to secure him a place at one of the Dissenting academies to train for the ministry.

> This I looked upon almost as an answer from heaven, and while I live shall adore so seasonable an interposition of divine providence ... I beg God to make me an instrument of doing much good in the world.

The Dissenters, barred from graduating from the universities, were seriously concerned that their young candidates for the ministry should receive the best training possible. To facilitate this, a number of academies had been opened in different areas. As we have seen, Isaac Watts was trained under Thomas Rowe in Stoke Newington, and it was to John Jennings' academy in Kibworth Harcourt, Leicestershire, that Philip Doddridge travelled in October 1719, not long after his seventeenth birthday.

The young Londoner found country life a delightful contrast to the bustle and business of all he had known, and he settled well. He quickly mastered not only his studies in theology but also in the classics, philosophy and other branches of learning. After two years in Kibworth Harcourt, his tutor and pastor John Jennings accepted a call to an Independent church in nearby Hinckley, and the academy, consisting of some seven students, moved with him. By now Doddridge had completed his course and was ordained in July 1722, preaching his first sermon in Hinckley. His aspiration to serve God had long been his 'great desire' and when he heard that two had professed faith as a result of that first sermon, it must have been a seal of God's approval on his chosen course. One of his best-loved hymns expresses his resolve — one that became his lifelong purpose:

My gracious Lord, I own thy right
to every service I can pay;
and call it my supreme delight
to hear thy dictates and obey.

The unexpected death of John Jennings from smallpox in 1723 was a serious loss to Philip Doddridge who had only recently received a call from Jennings' previous congregation in Kibworth to become their pastor. For the next five years Doddridge served as a country pastor in several small Leicestershire towns including Market Harborough, refusing a number of pressing calls to larger and more influential churches. But young Doddridge was lonely. With no family apart from one married sister, he felt his isolation intensely, even though he still appreciated country life: 'I am like Adam in paradise; and it is my only misfortune that I want an Eve, and have none but the birds of the air and beasts of the field for my companions.' After a number of brief friendships, Doddridge, now twenty-seven, met Mercy Maris, a young woman of twenty-two, early orphaned like himself, and in her he found a life partner of supreme worth.

Following the death of John Jennings the students had disbanded, but as the years passed an increasing need for the academy to be reopened became apparent. And who better than Philip Doddridge to take charge of such an institution? He had studied closely his former tutor's methods and was unquestionably well prepared for such a task. But feeling his youthfulness and inexperience, Doddridge hesitated, until a man of the status of Isaac Watts, among the Dissenters, pressed him to consider it seriously, regarding him as the best suited man for such a dual ministry. At last he agreed. With the wife of his former tutor installed as housekeeper, Doddridge soon gathered around him a group of young men eager to receive training. Scarcely had he established his new academy at Kibworth when he received an urgent call from Castle Hill Independent Church in Northampton to leave Kibworth and become their pastor. Objections crowded into Doddridge's mind. The timing seemed quite wrong. Repeated invitations from the church coupled with its promises to provide not just for their new pastor, but also for the fledgling academy, at last inclined him to consider the invitation. Friends whose advice he valued added their encouragement until Doddridge was eventually persuaded; together with his students he moved from Kibworth Harcourt to Northampton in December 1729. Still only twenty-seven years of age, he was to remain there for the rest of his life, fulfilling the double role of pastor to his people and tutor to the most famous of all the Dissenting academies. Well might he sing:

> Thus far his hand has led me on,
> thus far I make his mercy known;
> and while I tread this desert land,
> new mercies shall new songs demand.

In their marriage Mercy and Philip Doddridge were admirably suited. Tender and devoted letters found their way back to Northampton whenever Philip had to be away from home. 'Dearest of women, dearest of creatures, my very soul is with you by night and day. You are my thought, my wish, my prayer,' he would write. Mercy, tall, dark-haired and dark-eyed, responded with equal warmth. A number of children were born into the Northampton manse. 'Tetsy' or Elizabeth, their first child, was sunny and warm-hearted in disposition. Once asked by her father why it was that everyone loved her, she replied, 'Indeed, Papa, I cannot think, unless it is that I love everyone.' In an attempt to catechize the family dog, the little girl cried out in despair to the unresponsive animal, 'You, Dr Doddridge's dog, and not know who made you!'

When five-year-old Tetsy succumbed to tuberculosis and died, it was a bitter grief for Philip and Mercy. Resting his paper on the small coffin, Doddridge wrote a moving message on the words 'It is well with the child'. As he buried his daughter he said, 'This day my heart hath been almost torn to pieces by sorrow, yet sorrow so softened and sweetened that I number it among the best days of my life.' Such an experience, hard indeed to bear, gave to Philip Doddridge a deepened understanding of the griefs and needs of his people — an understanding that would find expression in some of his hymns. For the sorrows of others he could say:

> When the most helpless sons of grief
>   in low distress are laid,
> soft be our hearts their pains to feel,
>   and swift our hands to aid.

And for himself:

> If thou, my Jesus, still be nigh,
>   cheerful I live and joyful die;
> secure when mortal comforts flee
>   to find ten thousand worlds in thee.

Eight other children were born to Philip and Mercy Doddridge, although, as was so common at the time, only four attained adult years.

Student numbers at Doddridge's academy in Northampton varied, with sometimes as many as forty-six training in the course of a single year. Not all were preparing for the ministry, for as none of the sons of the Dissenters were able to attend the universities, this opportunity to receive a wider education prepared young men for many different callings, benefiting society as a whole.

Quite apart from his prolific correspondence, Philip Doddridge's literary output was extraordinary for a man seeking to fulfil the calling of both pastor and principal — not to mention his family commitments. During his lifetime he prepared fifty-three different works for the press, some of which were short treatises, but others ran to several volumes apiece. All his work was eventually published in ten volumes early in the next century. Among the best known was *The Rise and Progress of Religion in the Soul* — a book presented to the dying Frederick, Prince of Wales, at the request of Selina, Countess of Huntingdon. 'His Royal Highness is fast verging towards Methodism,' was the cynical comment of Lord Bolingbroke. Better known is the fact that this was the book used by God to awaken William Wilberforce, politician and campaigner against the slave trade, to his spiritual need, subsequently leading to his conversion.

Yet for Christians today the name of Doddridge is familiar not for any learned treatise but because they have seen it at the bottom of the hymns they sing. However, Doddridge did not set out to be a hymn-writer: his first aim was to impress the truths he had just preached on the memories and hearts of his hearers. Taking the text of the sermon, he would elaborate its main points in verse, knowing well that words that are sung impress the truth on the mind in a unique way. In 1755, four years after Doddridge had died, one of his former pupils and his first biographer, Job Orton, published three hundred and fifty-three hymns from the pen of his warm-hearted principal.

Arranged in scriptural order, the hymns in this first edition demonstrate the width of Doddridge's choice of biblical passages during his ministry. Twenty-seven are based on Old Testament books from Genesis to Job, a further fifty-two from the Psalms and the book of Proverbs, with ninety-one from the prophetic books of the Old Testament. The remaining one hundred and eighty-three come from the New Testament books. Perhaps only a handful are of permanent value, but these few still speak directly to the heart of the believer.

James Montgomery, himself a hymn-writer and poet, valued Doddridge's work highly, and spoke particularly of 'the tenderness of Doddridge', expressed in his hymns. In the opinion of Dr Erik Routley, writing more than a century later, Doddridge holds the fourth place in the line of excellence, only superseded by Isaac Watts and Charles Wesley as joint first, with James Montgomery third. Comparing his work with that of John Newton and William Cowper in *Olney Hymns*, Routley says, 'In technique, consistency, sound doctrine, and the sense of what is fit for congregational use, he gives place to neither of our friends from Olney. He is less of a poet than Cowper, more of a scholar than Newton, and we here claim, a better hymn-writer than either.' We may wish to differ from Routley and place Newton as equal fourth, although the eminent gift of the Welsh hymn-writer, William Williams, should not be forgotten.

Among the best known of all Doddridge's hymns is the one dated in his manuscript 18 December 1735, 'Hark, the glad sound! the Saviour comes'. 'A more sweet, vigorous and perfect composition is not to be found in the whole body of ancient hymns,' wrote one commentator in reference to this hymn.[1] Entitling the piece 'Christ's message', Doddridge puts into verse the words of Christ spoken in the synagogue at Nazareth (Luke 4:18), quoted from Isaiah 61: 'He has anointed me to preach the gospel to the poor … to heal the broken-hearted, to preach deliverance to the captives and recovery of sight to the blind.'

> He comes the prisoner to release,
>   in Satan's bondage held;
> the gates of brass before him burst,
>   the iron fetters yield.

> He comes the broken heart to bind,
>   the bleeding soul to cure,
> and with the treasures of his grace
>   to enrich the humble poor.

Doddridge skilfully writes so that the first two lines of each verse form a unit, and the second two another unit, usually echoing the thought in the first two. In a verse sometimes omitted today because the construction of the lines leads to misunderstanding, Doddridge borrows freely from the poet Alexander Pope. Doddridge wrote:

> He comes, from thickest films of vice
>   to clear the mental ray;
> and on the eyeballs of the blind
>   to pour celestial day.

And Pope in a work published in 1712 had written:

> The Saviour comes! By ancient bards foretold:
> hear him, ye deaf, and all ye blind behold!
> he from thick films shall purge the visual ray,
> and on the sightless eyeball pour the day.[2]

Clearly, like Wesley and many other poets both before and after him, some words that Doddridge had read were so lodged in his mind that he repeats them here: a practice not regarded as plagiarism in the eighteenth century but as a compliment to the original writer.

Not unexpectedly Doddridge's work is often compared with that of his friend and mentor, the senior Dissenter of his day, Isaac Watts, and certainly the comparison is valid for it is natural that he should follow in the tradition forged by Watts. But there are differences. Watts had based his first hundred and fifty hymns on various texts of Scripture and his lines usually enlarged on the chosen passage itself, whereas Doddridge was more concerned to bring out the message of the text on which he had been preaching. His, therefore, are sermons in verse:

> And will the Judge descend?
> And must the dead arise?
> and not a single soul escape
> his all-discerning eyes?
>
> How will my heart endure
> the terrors of that day,
> when earth and heaven before his face
> astonished shrink away?
>
> Ye sinners, seek his grace,
> whose wrath you cannot bear;
> fly to the shelter of his cross,
> and find salvation there!

The use of the rhetorical question, as in the first verse of this hymn, is one often employed by the preacher and used by Doddridge to considerable effect in a number of his hymns. He will sometimes question himself: 'What is my being but for thee?' or he will question his God:

> Thou glorious sovereign of the skies,
> and wilt thou bow thy gracious ear?
> While feeble mortals raise their cries,
> wilt thou, the great Jehovah, hear?

The last thirteen years of Doddridge's life coincided with the early years of the great evangelical revival, under the preaching of the Wesleys and Whitefield. But Philip Doddridge might well be called the forerunner of that powerful work of God, for the spirit of earnest zeal for the salvation of the lost had characterized him well before the beginning of the revival. This concern is seen in another Doddridge hymn, once a firm favourite:

> Arise, my tenderest thoughts, arise,
> to torrents melt my streaming eyes!
> and you, my heart, with anguish feel
> those evils which you can not heal.

He then describes the pitiable state of men and women who live without any knowledge of God or of the way of forgiveness, and concludes:

> But feeble my compassion proves,
> and can but weep where most it loves:
> thine own all-saving arm employ,
> and turn these drops of grief to joy.

In 1735, three years before Wesley had any assurance of forgiveness of sins, and the same year that Whitefield was converted, Doddridge was already preaching deeply moving sermons such as one entitled 'Christ's Invitation to Thirsty Souls':

Behold then the tears of a Redeemer over perishing souls, and judge by them the compassion of his heart... and if our Lord could not give up the impenitent sinners of Jerusalem without weeping over them, surely he will not despise the humble and penitent soul who is perhaps with tears seeking his favour, and flying to his grace as his only refuge.

With such a spirit, we cannot be surprised that it was Philip Doddridge, almost alone among the Dissenters, who in 1739 was prepared to extend a welcome to George Whitefield and even allow him to preach in his pulpit — a gesture for which he paid a heavy price of ignominy among his fellow Dissenters. Like each of the great men of the revival, Doddridge shared an earnest desire to see the church of Jesus Christ renewed and glorious once more. In words based on Psalm 48, he wrote:

> Triumphant Zion, lift thy head
> from dust and darkness and the dead;
> though humbled long, awake at length,
> and gird thee with thy Saviour's strength.
>
> God from on high has heard thy prayer;
> his hand thy ruins shall repair;
> reared and adorned by love divine,
> thy towers and battlements shall shine.

As Isaac Watts before him and John Newton after him, and for the same reasons, Doddridge adopted short metre, common metre and long metre for the great majority of his hymns. Simplicity was all important if the words were to be lined out, and certainly in Doddridge's case there would have been no time to print a hymn that was intended for use directly after a sermon. These early hymn-writers were also dependent on these three metres because they were used for the tunes commonly set to the metrical psalms. There were exceptions, however, and his bright triumphant resurrection hymn clearly demanded something different. Here he chose the metre known as the 148th, from the *Old Version* of Sternhold and Hopkins:

> Yes, the Redeemer rose,
> the Saviour left the dead,

and o'er our hellish foes
high raised his conquering head;
in wild dismay
the guards around
fell to the ground
and sunk away.

The rhyming schemes adopted by Doddridge were also chosen with simplicity and ease of recall, bearing in mind that the congregation was without the aid of printed words. Frequently he used rhyming couplets, as, for example, hymns designed for singing at the close of a year:

I midst ten thousand dangers stand,
supported by his guardian hand,
and see, when I review my ways,
ten thousand monuments of praise.

or in another:

With grateful hearts the past we own;
the future, all to us unknown,
we to your guardian care commit,
and peaceful leave before your feet.

It has been said that Doddridge's hymns resemble Jacob's ladder: they begin on earth and end in heaven. With this in mind it is possible to trace such a development in almost all his compositions. We may cite as an example his hymn on prayer which begins:

Our heavenly Father calls,
and Christ invites us near...

but prayer must one day turn to praise:

> Here fix my roving heart!
> Here wait my warmest love!
> till the communion be complete
> in nobler scenes above.

Irenic by nature and broad-minded in considering the views of others, Doddridge was nevertheless consistent in his own theological stand, seeing in God the first cause in all events and most particularly in the salvation of his people. Even in a hymn that some have thought could suggest that salvation springs from the decision of man, as in:

> O happy day, that fixed my choice
> on thee, my Saviour and my God,

we have only to read on into the third verse where he confesses:

> He drew me and I followed on,
> charmed to confess the voice divine.

Or if we still had any doubt, it would be dispelled by verses from 'God of salvation, we adore/thy saving love, thy saving power…'

> We love the stroke that breaks our chain,
> the sword by which our sins are slain;
> and while abased in dust we bow,
> we sing the grace that lays us low.
>
> Perish each thought of human pride,
> let God alone by magnified…

Although John Wesley had a good argument when he insisted that his brother's poetry could not be improved, this is not the case with the majority of our hymn-writers, even the best. Certainly it is not true of Doddridge, and some of his best-loved hymns bear the fingerprints of others upon them. Changes made to 'O God of Bethel', a hymn universally loved and chosen at many national occasions, illustrate this. Sung at the funerals of both W. E. Gladstone and David Livingstone, the first verse as Doddridge originally wrote it only varies in the second line from the version sung today:

> O God of Bethel, by whose hand
>> thine Israel still is fed,
> who through this weary pilgrimage
>> hast all our fathers led.

Job Orton changed the opening words to 'O God of Jacob...'. However, in the version published in *Scottish Translations and Paraphrases* in 1781, a version now commonly found in our hymn books, Doddridge's original opening was restored, with the word 'people' in place of 'Israel' in the second line. In addition, John Logan takes up each of Doddridge's lines and improves it, adding a last verse of his own, to produce the excellent version in general use.

However, one aspect of Doddridge's original thought has been lost in the changes: the aspect of covenanting with God, illustrated by Jacob at Bethel in Genesis 28. In this biblical practice, much favoured in Puritan times and particularly in Scotland, the believer promises to serve his God with all his energies and seeks that in response God will undertake for him in all the circumstances of life and sustain him in the hour of death. In his best-known work, *The Rise and Progress of Religion in the Soul,* Doddridge provided a sample covenant which he recommended believers to undertake with prayer and fasting and renew at least four times each year. In a typical sentence of this covenant the believer declares: 'In thy service I desire and purpose to spend all my time, desiring thee to teach me to spend every moment of it to thy glory.' And in response he prays that God will supply him with 'all needful influences of thy cheering and comforting Spirit, and lift up that light of thy countenance upon me which will put the sublimest joy and gladness into my heart'. This concept of a covenant with God is veiled by Logan's changes to Doddridge's original words which read:

> If thou thro' each perplexing path
>   wilt be our constant guide;
> if thou wilt daily bread supply
>   and raiment will provide;
>
> If thou wilt spread thy shield around
>   till these our wand'rings cease,
> and at our Father's loved abode
>   our souls arrive in peace:
>
> To thee as to our covenant God
>   we'll our whole selves resign;
> and count that not one tenth alone,
>   but all we have is thine.

Another of Doddridge's well-known hymns, 'Grace, 'tis a charming sound', contains three verses that were added by that prime hymn-improver, Augustus Toplady. Based on Ephesians 2:5, 'By grace you have been saved', Doddridge traces his debt to God's grace not just at the start of the Christian life but through each day:

> Grace taught my wandering feet
> to tread the heavenly road,
> and new supplies each hour I meet
> while pressing on to God.

And in typical Doddridge style he assures himself and all who sing his words that such grace will not only carry him through life but keep him to the very end:

> Grace all the works shall crown
> through everlasting days;
> it lays in heaven the topmost stone,
> and well deserves the praise.

Doddridge was not afraid to include unexpected words in his hymns — a feature, used in moderation, that marks out poetry from mere verse. Describing the sufferings of the Son of God on the cross, he writes:

> …God stood afar, nor would afford
> one *pitying* look, one *cheering* word.

We find similar surprising adjectives scattered throughout the Northampton preacher's hymns: referring to the future punishment of the devil, he writes:

> See the old dragon from his throne
> sink with *enormous* ruin down!

Other expressions include such phrases as '*peerless* glories', *capacious* powers', '*glowing* seraphs', '*briny* tears', '*untainted* Eden', God's '*all-animating* voice' and many more.

An early biographer has suggested that Philip Doddridge seemed to live many lives at once: tutor, pastor, church leader, writer and family man. But by the late 1740s his strength was almost gone. 'Use me, O Lord, I beseech thee, as the instrument of thy glory ... that I may bring praise to thy name and benefit to the world in which I live', he had prayed in his covenant with God — a prayer that had been remarkably answered. The death of Isaac Watts in 1748 had brought added responsibilities to Doddridge, but it was the passing of his lifelong friend, Samuel Clark, in December 1750, one who had come to his aid when Philip was a youth, that seemed to spark off a steady decline in his health. Symptoms of tuberculosis, the illness that had taken his young daughter Tetsy away, soon became evident.

Thoughts of death were not new to Philip Doddridge. He had frequently meditated on the subject, preparing himself spiritually for it. Five of his own children had died, and some of his closest friends as well. As he had written:

> Death may my soul divide
> from this abode of clay;
> but love shall keep me near his side
> through all the gloomy way.
>
> Since Christ and we are one,
> what should remain to fear?
> If he in heaven has fixed his throne,
> he'll fix his members there.

In the summer of 1751 Mercy and Philip Doddridge travelled to Bristol to see if the Hot Wells, with their supposed medicinal value, could bring relief to his persistent symptoms. But they did not help. The only expedient left appeared to be a voyage to a warmer climate. Selina, Countess of Huntingdon, with her typical generosity, canvassed around among her friends and soon raised enough money to send the sick man and his wife to Lisbon. But Doddridge seemed to sense that his days were fast slipping to a close; and God too was preparing him by unusual disclosures of his love:

> My profuse night sweats are very weakening to my mortal frame; but the most distressing nights to this frail body have been the beginning of heaven to my soul. God hath as it were let heaven down upon me in those nights of weakness and waking.

Just before his journey to Falmouth to embark for Lisbon, Philip Doddridge, together with Mercy, spent a day or two with the Countess in Bath. She too was recovering from severe illness, and had prayed that even if God were to take her, he would spare Doddridge for many years to come for the good of his church. Coming into his room on the morning he was due to leave she found her friend in tears. Open before him was his Bible. The words that had moved him so deeply were from the book of Daniel, 'O Daniel, a man greatly beloved.'

Selina, Countess of Huntingdon

'You are in tears, Sir,' said Selina.

'I am weeping,' replied Philip, 'but they are tears of comfort and joy. I can give up my country, my relations and friends into the hands of God; and as to myself, I can as well go to heaven from Lisbon as from my study in Northampton.'

As he had written in one of his hymns many years before:

> I'll speak the honours of thy name
> with my last labouring breath;
> then speechless clasp thee in my arms,
> the antidote to death.

A temporary recovery on the voyage to Lisbon soon gave way to renewed illness, but throughout these last weeks Philip Doddridge was favoured with the brightness of the presence of God, so much so that Mercy afterwards was to say that the radiant expression on his face reminded her of a verse of one of his hymns:

> When death o'er nature shall prevail,
> and all the powers of language fail,
> joy through my swimming eyes shall break,
> and mean the thanks I cannot speak.

Trying to reassure Mercy as the end approached, Philip spoke words she would never forget: 'So sure am I that God will be with you and comfort you that I think my death will be a greater blessing to you than ever my life has been.'

''Tis to my Saviour I would live,' Philip Doddridge had once written and he had indeed lived his forty-nine years to the full in 'the cause of such a Friend'. On 26 October 1751, he at last saw that Friend face to face. The parting was painful indeed, but Mercy knew the consolations of God's grace in exceptional measure and could write to her children from Lisbon: 'Such comforts has he granted to the meanest of his creatures that my mind at times is held in perfect astonishment and is ready to burst into songs of praise under its most exquisite distress... I mourn the best of husbands and of friends, removed from this world of sin and sorrow to the regions of immortal bliss and light. What a glory!' And Mercy knew well that Philip joined her in singing those 'songs of praise' about which he too had once written, and now sang perfectly in a better world:

> But O when that last conflict's o'er,
> and I am chained to earth no more,
> with what glad accents shall I rise
> to join the music of the skies.
>
> Soon shall I learn the exalted strains
> which echo through the heavenly plains;
> and emulate, with joy unknown,
> the glowing seraphs round the throne.

Notes

1. John Julian, *Dictionary of Hymnology*, 1909, p.489.
2. Cited by J. R. Watson, *An Annotated Anthology of Hymns*, p.155.

Charles Wesley
(1707-1788)

Singing a new song

O for a thousand tongues to sing
  my great Redeemer's praise,
the glories of my God and King,
  the triumphs of his grace!

My gracious master and my God,
  assist me to proclaim,
to spread through all the earth abroad
  the honours of thy name.

Charles Wesley as a young man,
painted by Henry Hudson

Charles Wesley
(1707-1788)

Singing a new song

Would Susanna Wesley's eighteenth baby survive? Eight of her infants had already died and this frail, premature child seemed likely to follow his brothers and sisters to an early grave. Wrapped in soft wool, scarcely reacting and with eyes shut, little Charles Wesley's grasp on life seemed fragile at best. But God had unusual purposes of grace for this child and contrary to all expectations he gradually gained strength. Born on 18 December 1707, his life would leave an indelible mark on the history of the Christian Church.

Samuel Wesley, for thirty-eight years rector of Epworth in Lincolnshire, was unpopular with his parishioners. Accounts of his trials, his place-seeking, his inability to manage his finances, his temporary abandonment of his wife and his unforgiving attitude towards his daughter Hetty have all been well chronicled, but despite these things he was held in honour by his sons. He did all in his power to give Samuel, his eldest, and the two younger boys, John and Charles, the best education available. Poetry became part of the life of the young Wesley children from earliest days. Their father spent long hours locked in his study transcribing the whole of the book of Job into verse — a task scarcely completed before his death. Both his younger boys inherited his poetic gift, as did Hetty also, to a marked degree. All Susanna's children were educated first in her own 'home school', with the boys later going to public school, John to Charterhouse and Charles, at nine years of age, to Westminster School. Favoured by the nobility of the day, the school was at that time housed in the former dormitories of the monks who had once served Westminster Abbey. From there Charles would matriculate to Oxford at the age of nineteen.

Already Charles had begun to express himself in verse. This is well illustrated by John Wesley's description of his dismay when his younger brother entered his room during his Oxford days. In a 'fine frenzy' Charles, short-sighted and a little clumsy, would come in, his head crammed full of the lines of a poem he was composing. Knocking into his brother's desk, he would disarrange all the meticulously organized papers, repeat some poetry, ask some questions and without waiting for answers depart, leaving the orderly John Wesley to put everything back to rights once more.

The classical education that Charles received at home, school and university was to provide him with the basic foundation and equipment that was vital for his future contribution to the Christian Church. The study of rhetoric, Greek, Latin, mythology and the works of poets of past generations all played a part in God's preparation of this young man for the task of composing hymns that would enable Christians to express their devotion, zeal and praise to God in language of unsurpassed excellence.

During his first year at Oxford, Charles admitted spending much time in 'diversions', relaxing and enjoying his new environment far from watchful parental eyes. When his older brother John, by this time preparing for ordination, accosted him on the subject of religion, he would reply testily, 'What, would you have me to be a saint all at once?' During his second year, however, Charles attempted to reform his ways. Reading William Law's classic, *A Serious Call to a Devout and Holy*

Life, and writers such as Thomas à Kempis, the young man decided to give up the light-hearted company he had been enjoying and devote himself to the pursuit of a life pleasing to God. With two friends he met regularly to study the Greek New Testament and other religious works, mainly written by men of High Church persuasion. This was the beginning of the 'Holy Club', so dubbed by scornful fellow students. When John returned to Oxford in 1729 he took over the leadership of this group of seriously-minded students, but Charles is recognized as being the originator of the Holy Club.

Seven years of restless striving to please God by his own high standards of noble endeavour and religious observances would follow. Charles joined his older brother John as a missionary to Georgia where their ship docked in February 1736. But neither of the Wesleys knew any degree of freedom from the bondage of seeking a gateway to salvation through their own righteous deeds. His stay in America was a disaster for Charles; he decided to return home and reached England in December of that same year, weary, ill and depressed. Another seventeen months of earnest searching after peace of conscience would pass before Charles was finally brought into spiritual liberty. Sunday 21 May 1738 was a day Charles Wesley never forgot; he spoke of it in his journal as 'the Day of Pentecost', both literally in the church's year and figuratively in his own experience:

> I now found myself at peace with God, and rejoiced in hope of loving Christ ... I saw that by faith I stood; by the continual support of faith kept from falling, though by myself I am ever sinking into sin.

Three days later his brother John entered into a similar experience of assurance of faith. The date of John's actual conversion, however, may well have been some time before that notable date of 24 May 1738 when he felt his heart 'strangely warmed' by the certainty that Christ 'had taken away my sins, even mine, and saved me from the law of sin and death'.

Released from the bondage of trying to earn his salvation, Charles Wesley began to express his joy in verse — the medium that came most naturally to him. On Tuesday 23 May he wrote in his journal, 'At nine I began a hymn on my conversion':

> Where shall my wondering soul begin?
> How shall I to heaven aspire?
> A slave redeemed from death and sin,
> a brand plucked from eternal fire...

But then he stopped — surely this was pride to use his poetic gift in this way — God would not be pleased with such expressions... Charles wrestled with this anxiety, an evident stratagem of Satan to restrain him from using his God-given gift. When a friend encouraged him to resist such a thought, Charles recognized the source of his fears and continued in his journal: 'I clearly discerned that it was a device of the enemy to keep back glory from God.' And so he resumed his hymn:

> And shall I slight my Father's love
> or basely fear his gifts to own?

The following night, the very night when John Wesley knew at last the joy of assurance that his sins were forgiven, Charles records, 'Towards ten, my brother was brought in triumph by a troop of friends, and declared, "I believe!" *We sang the hymn*[1] [the one so recently written] with great joy, and parted with prayer.' Charles Wesley, the hymn-writer, had begun his life's work. From this date onwards we find him writing lines that have become the treasured heritage of the Christian Church ever since.

Released from his scruples and rejoicing in the wonder of God's grace to a sinner, Charles was soon to write in lines of heartfelt eloquence the words of one of his best-known hymns, published the following year in a collection called *Hymns and Sacred Poems*:

> And can it be that I should gain
> an interest in the Saviour's blood?
> Died he for me, who caused his pain,
> for me, who him to death pursued?
> Amazing love! how can it be
> that thou, my God, shouldst die for me?

The threefold use of 'for me' expresses his amazement that at last he too should know for certain that 'Jesus, and all in him, is mine'. He had longed to *feel* his acceptance with God and, in a verse usually omitted from the hymn, rejoices in that new-found assurance:

> Still the small inward voice I hear,
> that whispers all my sins forgiven;
> still the atoning blood is near,
> that quenched the wrath of hostile heaven:
> I *feel*[2] the life his wounds impart;
> I *feel* my Saviour in my heart.

Unable to contain his joy, Charles Wesley could scarcely be restrained. To all he met and at every opportunity, he spoke of the need to acknowledge and confess sin and seek forgiveness through the merits of Christ's sacrifice. Many were affronted at such language:

In the coach to London I preached faith in Christ; a lady was extremely offended; avowed her own merits in plain terms; asked if I was not a Methodist and threatened to beat me. I declared I deserved nothing but hell; so did she; and must confess it before she could have a title to heaven. This was most intolerable to her.[3]

This interview may be considered a prototype of the next ten years of Wesley's life. Abuse, both physical and verbal, was the order of the day as he preached boldly wherever and whenever he could. Excluded from the pulpits of the churches, like George Whitefield and his brother John, Charles began to preach in field, barn, wasteland and prison yard. Persecution inevitably followed. Stones were hurled by furious mobs, houses where he was preaching were torched or dismantled and he himself forcefully ejected from his makeshift pulpits. Walsall and Wednesbury witnessed violent attacks on the valiant preachers. John Wesley was dragged by his hair down the main street of Walsall and Charles too was menaced and assaulted. Soused with stagnant ditch water, threatened with gunfire and struck by stones or other missiles, Charles held on his course, travelling and preaching undeterred. If ever he were tempted to give up, he looked to Christ for new grace to persevere:

> To leave my Captain I disdain,
>   behind I will not stay;
> though shame and loss and bonds and pain
>   or death obstruct the way.
>
> Then shall I bear thy utmost will,
>   when first the strength is given:
> come, foolish world, my body kill,
>   my soul shall rise to heaven.

In 1744 Charles and John Wesley jointly published a small collection of hymns entitled, *Hymns for Times of Trouble and Persecution.* Containing thirteen hymns for 'times of trouble', sixteen for persecution and four to be sung 'in a tumult', it reflects the turbulent scenes the brothers witnessed in the early days of the revival. We may well sing these hymns today with a cheerful spirit, not realizing that they arose out of such scenes of distress. A verse often omitted from 'Ye servants of God, your Master proclaim', reads:

> Men, devils engage, the billows arise,
> and horribly rage, and threaten the skies:
> their fury shall never our steadfastness shock,
> the weakest believer is built on a Rock.

'And are we yet alive,/and see each other's face?' was a hymn with which the Methodists would open their annual conference. It was a serious question. Already one of their number, William Seward, converted under Charles' ministry, had died after being stoned by a mob at Hay-on-Wye. Well could Wesley record:

> What troubles have we seen,
> what conflicts have we passed!
> Fightings without and fears within,
> since we assembled last.

The final verse was a rallying cry to those who might be finding the cost too great:

> Let us take up the cross,
> till we the crown obtain,
> and gladly reckon all things loss,
> so we may Jesus gain.

Throughout the next thirty years Charles Wesley wrote continuously. His hymns, sometimes scribbled on scraps of card, were often composed as he travelled from place to place. Many of his rhythms suggest that the words came to his mind as he jogged along on horseback. Perhaps as he set off before dawn for some distant town, watched the stars pale and the sun slowly lightening up the eastern sky, there came into his mind such thoughts as:

> Christ, whose glory fills the skies,
> Christ, the true, the only light,
> Sun of righteousness, arise,
> triumph o'er the shades of night:
> Day-spring from on high, be near,
> Day-star, in my heart appear!

Metaphor and reality, Old Testament and New mingle throughout this hymn. Christ is the Sun of Righteousness of Malachi 4:2, the Dayspring of Luke 1:78 and the Day-star of 2 Peter 1:19. As light floods the morning sky, so Christ 'the true, the only light' pours his 'radiancy divine' into the heart, scattering unbelief:

> Visit then this soul of mine,
> pierce the gloom of sin and grief;
> fill me, Radiancy divine!
> scatter all my unbelief:
> more and more thyself display,
> shining to the perfect day.

Sights and sounds that greeted the travelling preacher on his journeys sometimes provided the seed-thought for a hymn. Seeing quarrymen at work gave rise to the lines:

> Come, O thou all-victorious Lord,
> thy power to us make known;
> strike with the hammer of thy word
> and break these hearts of stone.

The glow of furnaces at night was the inspiration behind:

> See how great a flame aspires,
>   kindled by a spark of grace!
> Jesu's love the nations fires,
>   sets the kingdoms on a blaze.

A London friend recalled the times when Charles would arrive at his home clearly in another 'fine frenzy', tethered his pony in the garden and entered the house crying out, 'Pen and ink, pen and ink.' With these supplied, he would write down the lines that had been burning in his mind during his journey. Then he would smile, greet his hosts, ask after their health and announce a hymn for them all to sing together.

Many penny pamphlets and larger collections of hymns and psalms appeared during the 1740s and 1750s: *Funeral Hymns, Children's Hymns, Hymns for Earthquakes and Tumults.* The books were published jointly by John and Charles Wesley and no distinction made to indicate which of the two had written each piece. At last in 1780 the many smaller publications were gathered together and John Wesley issued *A Collection of Hymns for the Use of the People Called Methodists* — a book that was in use until 1904. Originally containing 525 hymns, this work served not merely as a hymnal but as a devotional classic with a number of indices to aid the worshipper to find a hymn and also to direct attention to every aspect of the Christian life. No authorship is ascribed to the items, but John himself makes it plain in the preface that 'but a small part of these hymns is of my own composing'. So he did not consider it out of place to add, 'I do not think it inconsistent with modesty to declare that I am persuaded no such hymn-book as this has yet been published in the English language.' Commending his brother's verse, John continued:

In these hymns there is no doggerel, no botches, nothing put in to patch up the rhyme, no feeble expletives. Here is nothing turgid or bombast, on the one hand, or low and creeping, on the other. Here is no *cant* expressions, no words without meaning… Here are, allow me to say, both the purity, the strength and the elegance of the English language.

And with a warning to lesser versifiers, he adds that although others may imitate great verse 'unless he be *born* a poet, he will never attain the genuine spirit of poetry'. Nor was John Wesley happy with any who attempted to tinker with (as he himself had sometimes done with the work of Isaac Watts), or improve his brother's lines:

Many gentlemen have done my brother and me the honour to reprint many of our hymns. Now they are perfectly welcome so to do, provided they print them just as they are. But I desire they would not attempt to mend them; for they really are not able. None of them is able to mend either the sense or the verse. Therefore I must beg of them … to let them stand just as they are … that we may no longer be accountable either for the nonsense or for the doggerel of other men.

Surprisingly, there was an outstanding hymn of his brother's which John Wesley omitted from his 1780 collection: 'Jesu, lover of my soul'. The reason usually given for this is that he regarded such terms of affection for the Saviour as inappropriate. Yet among all Wesley's hymns this is one that has frequently moved believers most deeply. Tempest-tossed and helpless, the Christian finds a haven from 'the nearer waters' of his troubles. Facing the battles of life, he seeks protection under 'the shadow of thy wing'. J. R. Watson, commenting on this hymn, points

out that 'every stage of the hymn leads on to the next, and
relates back to the central truth of Jesus as the lover of the
human soul, however undeserving it may be'.[4] An example
of chiasmus is found in the structure of the second part of the
third verse. The first and fourth lines describe the character of
Christ and sandwiched in between, in the second and third lines,
we have a description of the sinner, coupled with the double
use of the words 'I am' but in reversed position in each line:

> Just and holy is thy name
>   *I am* all unrighteousness,
> False and full of sin *I am*
>   Thou art full of truth and grace.

A number of books have appeared that examine in detail
Charles Wesley's unique craft as a poet and hymn-writer. Frank
Baker, in his work *Charles Wesley's Verse,* has computed that
some 8,990 items of poetry from Wesley's hand have survived.
Not all are hymns, in fact only about 3,500 could be classified as
such and amongst these the quality varies considerably. Some
he revised carefully and these number among his better pieces;
others came white-hot from the fire of his creative genius and
were either never finalized or were allowed to go forward for
publication with little editorial work. Others again were found
in manuscript form after Wesley's death — some only snatches
of verse — that were probably never intended for publication
or were still only in an embryonic state.

One manuscript containing many items of verse from the
pen of Charles Wesley was almost lost. During the 1750s the
poet had transcribed parts of the book of Psalms into verse.
Carefully writing out each composition in his neat hand, he
presented the collection to Selina, Countess of Huntingdon,
with whom Charles and his wife Sally enjoyed a close friendship
during this time. After the death of the Countess in 1791,

and the removal of her college from Trevecca to Cheshunt, a number of her books and papers were sold or dispersed. Eventually Wesley's manuscript was accidentally discovered by someone who recognized the handwriting when it was up for sale in a London market. By his quick thinking, Henry Fish rescued the manuscript and published it in 1854 under the title, *A poetical version of nearly the whole of the Psalms of David.* One hundred and twenty of the psalms are covered in Wesley's manuscript, although some only represented by a single verse. Treasures such as Wesley's rendering of Psalm 45, 'My heart is full of Christ and longs/its glorious matter to declare' were preserved to the Christian Church in this way.

His *Psalms,* however, do not rank among his best work. The stricture of working within the preset guidelines of the Scripture text tended to act as a curb on Wesley's poetic genius. Some of his lines followed the words in the Psalter closely; but whenever he detected references to the Messiah, he gave a New Covenant rendering to his verse as Isaac Watts had done before him. So part of his version of Psalm 23 reads:

> Jesus the good Shepherd is,
>   Jesus died the sheep to save;
> he is mine and I am his,
>   all I want in him I have…
>
> Jesus loves and guards his own;
>   me in verdant pastures feeds;
> makes me quietly lie down,
>   by the streams of comfort leads:

Wesley, however, allowed himself more much latitude with the text than Watts did, as may be seen in comparing the above with a rendering of the same psalm by Watts:

> My Shepherd will supply my need,
>> Jehovah is his name;
> in pastures fresh he makes me feed
>> beside the living stream.

The hymns of Charles Wesley, like the book of Psalms itself, reflect the wide spectrum of Christian experience. There is scarcely a mood or aspiration common among believers — from conversion until the approach of death and the glories of heaven — that does not find its counterpart in words from Wesley's pen. Virtually every hymn to which we turn discovers an echo in the heart of the believer. When grieving for sin or backsliding, we may find consolation in such words as:

> Though my sins as mountains rise,
>> and swell and reach to heaven,
> mercy is above the skies,
>> I may be still forgiven.

Or:

> The ruins of my soul repair
> and make my heart a house of prayer.

When prayer seems hard, Wesley supplies us with words to express our desires:

> To help our soul's infirmity,
>> to heal thy sin-sick people's care,
> to urge our God-commanding plea,
>> and make our hearts a house of prayer,
> the promised Intercessor give,
> and let us now thyself receive.

If we find a longing for closer communion with Christ, we discover that the hymn-writer has been there before us:

> O Love divine, how sweet thou art!
> When shall I find my willing heart
>   all taken up by thee?
> I thirst, I faint, I die to prove
> the greatness of redeeming love,
>   the love of Christ to me.

If the joy of forgiveness of sin and the sense of the presence of Christ is predominant in the believer's experience, he is given words with which to express it:

> My God, I am thine;
>   what a comfort divine,
> what a blessing to know that my Jesus is mine!
>   In the heavenly Lamb
>   thrice happy I am,
> and my heart it doth dance at the sound of his name.

Surprisingly, there are few hymns by Wesley that fall into the category entitled 'Worship' in most hymn books. One piece in the section 'The Lord's Day' is the nearest to it in a book such as *Christian Hymns*.

Unlike many modern writers, in each of his hymns Wesley follows a theme throughout, bringing it to a triumphant conclusion in the final verse. A hymn such as 'Love divine, all loves excelling' begins by describing that love, pleading that it may 'enter every trembling heart'; he then prays that Christ will take from us the love of sinning and in the third verse anticipates a day when his people will serve him as the heavenly hosts. He finishes on a sustained crescendo of adoration and desire for the day when we will love him perfectly:

> Changed from glory into glory,
>> till in heaven we take our place,
> till we cast our crowns before thee,
>> lost in wonder, love and praise.

Charles Wesley's use of Scripture is one of the outstanding qualities in his hymns. A son of a Church of England rector, the young Wesley was taught the Scriptures from his earliest days: his first reading book was the Gospel of John. The *Book of Common Prayer*, with its litanies, confessions and collects, also draws heavily on biblical language, and by constant repetition of these words, the boy would have his mind saturated with scriptural concepts. Some have attempted to put a reference to every line of such hymns as 'Hark! the herald angels sing' and found twenty-eight biblical references. One writer affirms that it is possible to discover fifty references to biblical themes, narratives or verses in the hymn that begins, 'With glorious clouds encompassed round'; while J. E. Rattenbury has ventured to suggest that 'A skilful man, if the Bible were lost, might extract much of it from Wesley's hymns.'[5]

In addition to scriptural references, Wesley used a wide range of metaphorical allusions, particularly from the Old Testament, to develop his theme — allusions that might leave many of his singers baffled unless they had unusual biblical knowledge. An example of this is found in his hymn for the New Year that begins 'Sing to the great Jehovah's praise':

> Our residue of days or hours
>> thine, wholly thine, shall be,
> and all our consecrated powers
>> a sacrifice to thee;
>
> till Jesus in the clouds appear
>> to saints on earth forgiven,

> and bring the grand *sabbatic* year,
> the *jubilee* of heaven.[6]

In the words of Frank Baker, who made an extensive study of Charles Wesley's verse, 'His verse is an enormous sponge filled to saturation with Bible words, Bible similes, Bible metaphors, Bible stories, Bible themes.'[7]

The best and most highly acclaimed example of Wesley's use of biblical narrative occurs in the piece known as 'Wrestling Jacob', based on Genesis 32 — verses that Isaac Watts is said to have rated above all the poetry that he himself had written. This spiritually powerful poem, for it is scarcely a hymn, is more suited to personal devotion. Wesley printed twelve verses in his 1780 collection, although only six are included in most hymn books. The hymn opens with Jacob's challenge to the 'Man who wrestled with him until the breaking of day':

> Come, O thou Traveller unknown,
> whom still I hold but cannot see!
> My company before is gone
> and I am left alone with thee.

And then he sets the theme for the entire poem in two unforgettable lines:

> With thee all night I mean to stay,
> and wrestle till the break of day.

As Wesley traces Jacob's long conflict with the one whom the patriarch recognizes to be none other than the divine person himself in the form of an angel, the believer readily identifies with the struggle that must sometimes accompany intercessory prayer. Wesley depicts Jacob's urgent fight to know the name of his antagonist, for in Old Testament terms the name stood for a person's innermost nature and character. At last there is a breakthrough as Jacob triumphantly declares:

> 'Tis Love! 'Tis Love! Thou diedst for me;
>   I hear thy whisper in my heart.
> The morning breaks, the shadows flee,
>   Pure universal Love thou art:
> To me, to all, thy mercies move —
> Thy nature and thy name is LOVE.

Each stanza after that ends with those words of conquest and joy: 'Thy nature and thy name is LOVE'. In the exultant final stanza Wesley portrays Jacob, weak yet elated, affirming:

> Lame as I am, I take the prey,
>   hell, earth and sin with ease o'ercome;
> I leap for joy, pursue my way,
>   and as a bounding hart fly home,
> through all eternity to prove
> thy nature and thy name is LOVE.

Not only did Wesley glean ideas for his hymns from Scripture but it is sometimes possible to trace the source material from which his lines have been garnered. Hardly any poets or writers would profess total originality and like Isaac Watts before him Wesley made no such claim, but at least he improved on lines he used. One example must suffice. His brother Samuel had written a 'Hymn to Easter Day' that contains these lines:

> In vain the stone, the watch, the seal,
>   forbid an early rise,
> to him who breaks the gates of hell
>   and opens paradise.

In his younger brother's hymn the words appear in a far more poetic form:

> Vain the stone, the watch, the seal,
> Christ has burst the gates of hell;
> Death in vain forbids his rise;
> Christ has opened paradise.

Only in recent years has there been a movement in literary circles to recognize Charles Wesley, not just as a highly gifted hymn-writer, but as one of the country's major poets. In a comparison between Watts and Wesley, Bernard Lord Manning makes this assessment:

> If I were asked to compare Watts with Wesley in a word, I should say, I think, though with great diffidence, that Watts seems to me to have the greater mind, the wider outlook, the more philosophic approach to human life and to the Christian revelation… But Wesley is the greater artist. He flies more surely. He crashes far less often. He reaches the heights far more often, though perhaps he does not go quite as high… But in essentials they are one.[8]

Because Wesley's lines were intended primarily for singing and not merely for reading, they have often been dismissed by literary critics. But his achievement, despite having to restrict his verse to regular metres and stanzas of consistent lengths, is a measure of his greatness. It is thought that Charles usually composed his words with a tune in mind. The musical gifts which both he and his wife Sally shared, and which were inherited by their sons to an extraordinary degree, placed a far wider selection of tunes and metres at the poet's command than those to which writers like Watts and Doddridge were limited. Although he often wrote in four-line verses, Wesley clearly preferred the longer stanza as it gave him more scope to develop his theme. One of his favourites would seem to be a six-line iambic verse; it has been computed that he wrote more than 1,100 of these. A fine example is:

> Thou hidden source of calm repose,
> > thou all-sufficient love divine,
> my help and refuge from my foes,
> > secure I am, if thou art mine.
> And lo! from sin, and grief, and shame,
> I hide me, Jesus, in thy name.

The verse just quoted illustrates another of Charles Wesley's favourite techniques. Once it has been observed, it is possible to discover it in numerous verses from the pen of this genius. He sets out his proposition in the first four lines of the stanza and in the last two draws out the practical implications of those truths for the lives of believers. Another illustration comes from his great hymn, 'And can it be that I should gain…':

> No condemnation now I dread,
> > Jesus, and all in him, is mine!
> Alive in him, my living Head,
> > and clothed with righteousness divine,
> bold I approach the eternal throne,
> and claim the crown, through Christ my own.

The poetic skill that lies behind Wesley's work as a hymn-writer is a wide subject. We may only mention a few of the most important characteristics of his ability. The art of repetition — an art that few hymn-writers have used without stumbling — is one that Wesley masters with consummate skill. In 'Come, thou long-expected Jesus' he introduces the word 'born' in the first verse, *'Born* to set thy people free', and then takes up the theme in the third verse:

Born thy people to deliver,
born a child and yet a king,
born to reign in us for ever,
now thy gracious kingdom bring.

Again he sings:

Wash me, and make me thus thine own,
wash me, and mine thou art,
wash me, but not my feet alone,
my hands, my head, my heart.

An elaboration of this ability to use repetition effectively is illustrated in Wesley's use of the last phrase of one line to introduce the next, leading the worshipper on naturally from one concept to another:

Died he for me, who caused his pain,
for me, who him to death pursued?

Or alternatively from one verse to the next:

This all my hope, and all my plea,
for me the Saviour died!

My dying Saviour, and my God,
fountain for guilt and sin...

Each line or phrase bears a connection with the preceding one, holding the singer's attention and building the theme to its climax.

The use of oxymoron, apparently contradictory terms placed side by side in order to increase their impact, is a marked characteristic in Wesley's work. Startling expressions such as 'The *immortal* God hath *died* for me' compel the singer to pause in amazement. Alternatively Wesley can marry contrary concepts in a line such as 'And let thy *glorious toil* succeed'. Yet more frequent is his use of paradox to gain the intended effect on the minds of the worshippers. Examples can be found throughout his hymns, but we may notice these:

> *Impoverish*, Lord, and then relieve,
> and then *enrich* the poor;
> the knowledge of our *sickness* give,
> the knowledge of our *cure*.

Or again:

> Assert thy claim, maintain thy right,
> come quickly from above;
> and *sink me* to perfection's *height*,
> the depth of humble love.

Piling one contrasting allusion on another, he writes:

> Jesus, my all in all thou art,
> my *rest* in *toil*, my *ease* in *pain*,
> the *medicine* of my *broken heart*,
> in *war* my *peace*, in *loss* my *gain*;
> my *smile* beneath the tyrant's *frown*,
> in *shame* my *glory* and my *crown*.

Such a literary technique in Wesley's hand reaches a climax in the well-known hymn, 'O for a thousand tongues to sing/my great Redeemer's praise':

> *Hear* him, ye *deaf*; his praise, ye *dumb*,
> your *loosened tongues* employ;
> ye *blind*, *behold* your Saviour come,
> and *leap*, ye *lame*, for joy.

This hymn, which originally ran to eighteen verses, was first published in 1740 in the collection the brothers had entitled *Hymns and Sacred Poems*. It was written, probably in May 1739, to commemorate the first anniversary of his conversion. We can still feel Wesley's contagious joy at the wonder of God's grace to him:

> On this glad day the glorious Sun
> of righteousness arose;
> on my benighted soul he shone
> and filled it with repose.

Unlike Isaac Watts, who aimed to stoop to the level of the worshippers, many of them illiterate, Wesley always sought to raise the standards of those who sang his verses; and although some of the early Methodists complained about it, he often introduced words with which they might well be unfamiliar:

> Unmarked by human eye,
> the *latent* Godhead lay.

Other examples might include such words as 'our gloomy *hemisphere*'. His ability to use polysyllabic words with impunity is one that few other poets can match:

> Our God contracted to a span
> *incomprehensibly* made man.

Or:

> There let it for thy glory burn
> with *inextinguishable* blaze.

Unusual hyphenated words are a further feature of Wesley's verse, so we find such expressions as 'our God-commanding plea', 'never-ceasing prayer' and 'all-redeeming God'. In all Wesley's verse there is a tight economy of words — nothing extraneous is added to make up the required syllables; rarely are lines inverted unnecessarily to facilitate rhyme. A further technique employed by this remarkable poet is the use of the rhetorical question. He could express wonder, even incredulity at the grace of God: 'Died he for me who caused his shame?' and penitent surprise: 'Can my God his wrath forbear,/me, the chief of sinners, spare?'

Above all, Wesley's lines have given Christians strength and hope to live by and confidence to die by. When John Badock, young Cornish fisherman and brave pioneer missionary to Tierra del Fuego, south of Patagonia, was dying of starvation in a hapless missionary enterprise, he suddenly sat upright and called to those who stood around, 'Shall we sing a hymn?' He then began to sing in a clear voice words he remembered from childhood days:

> Arise, my soul, arise,
> > shake off thy guilty fears:
> the bleeding sacrifice
> > in my behalf appears.
> Before the throne my Surety stands;
> my name is written on his hands.

And then he died.

Even children drew consolation from Wesley's words; when twelve-year-old Jane Grimshaw, only daughter of William Grimshaw of Haworth, lay dying in Bristol, far from her Yorkshire home, she repeated in a clear voice:

> He has loved me, I cried,
> he has suffered and died,
> to redeem such a rebel as me.

As we might expect, Wesley's temperament led him to intense and often impulsive reactions to varying situations. His feelings are portrayed in his hymns. In a bright frame of mind he might write:

> How happy are they
> who the Saviour obey,
> and have laid up their treasure above!
> Tongue cannot express
> the sweet comfort and peace
> of a soul in its earliest love.

And in another hymn, perhaps composed soon after the former when oppressed by a sense of sin and failure, he could write:

> Depth of mercy! can there be
> mercy still reserved for me?
> Can my God his wrath forbear,
> me, the chief of sinners spare?
>
> I have long withstood his grace,
> long provoked him to his face,
> would not hearken to his calls,
> grieved him by a thousand falls.

Not surprisingly Charles Wesley showed little patience with the doggerel compositions of others. William Darney was a case in point. The rugged Scotsman wrote screeds of appalling verse for his unlettered hearers to sing after he had addressed them. They loved them, and the message they had just heard was imprinted on their hearts by this means. But Charles Wesley found Darney a serious trial and insisted that he should be prevented from 'railing, begging and printing nonsense'.

In his marriage to Sally Gwynne, Charles Wesley found much joy, and the musical Welsh girl, twenty years his junior, entered into the poet's feelings in a remarkable manner. He continued to write poetry throughout his life: long epitaphs of his friends called away from earth; grievous laments as his infants were taken from him in death; joyful birthday poems for his beloved Sally. And it was to Sally that he dictated his last verse of poetry not many days before his death:

> In age and feebleness extreme,
> who shall a sinful worm redeem?
> JESUS, my only hope thou art,
> strength of my failing flesh and heart;
> O could I catch a smile from thee
> and drop into eternity.

'Do you want anything?' asked Sally earnestly as she saw Charles slowing slipping away. 'Nothing but Christ,' whispered the dying man. It was even as he had written many years before:

> Happy if with my latest breath
>   I may but gasp his name

and on 29 March 1788 Charles Wesley knew in its fulness that experience long anticipated:

> I view the Lamb in his own light,
>   whom angels dimly see,
> and gaze, transported with the sight,
>   through all eternity.

Notes

1. Italics mine.
2. Italics mine.
3. Quotes from *The Journal of Charles Wesley*, vol. 1, republished Baker Book House, Michigan, US, 1980.
4. *An Annotated Anthology of Hymns* (OUP, 1992), p.175.
5. J. E. Rattenbury, *The Evangelical Doctrines of Charles Wesley's Hymns* (London: Epworth Press, 1941), p.48.
6. *See* Leviticus 25.
7. Frank Baker, *Charles Wesley's Verse*, Epworth Press, 1988, p.34.
8. Bernard Lord Manning, *The Hymns of Wesley and Watts*, Epworth Press, 1942, pp.104-5.

William Williams
(1717 -1791)

Poet of the revival

When I tread the verge of Jordan
bid my anxious fears subside;
death of death and hell's destruction,
land me safe on Canaan's side;
songs of praises
I will ever give to thee.

William Williams

William Williams
(1717-1791)

Poet of the revival

'I have been roving and ranging over the rough mountains and wild precipices of Wales in search of poor illiterate souls chained in the dens of darkness and infidelity,' wrote William Williams with a touch of the poet's rhetoric. These words, found in a letter to his friend Selina, Countess of Huntingdon, in 1769, form a succinct summary of the life of William Williams, the Welsh preacher, poet and hymn-writer of the eighteenth-century evangelical revival. At seventy-three years of age he could look back on the last forty-three years of his life and tell another friend that he had travelled between forty and fifty miles each week during that long period, an astounding total of some 100,000 miles or more. Much of this had been undertaken on horseback, but where the terrain became too rough for even the most sure-footed animal, Williams would pick his way doggedly along on foot, seeking always to reach men and women with the gospel of Jesus Christ.

Born in 1717 in Cefn-coed, three miles from Llandovery, Carmarthenshire, William Williams, better known to his friends as Billy Williams[1], was a farmer's son. His parents, John and Dorothy Williams, were members of an Independent church. His father, however, died when William was quite young, leaving the child to be brought up by his mother. An inheritance from a well-placed uncle lifted the family above the anxiety that such a loss would normally have entailed. Included in this inheritance was a farmstead near Llandovery known as Pantycelyn. Here Dorothy and the children moved after her husband's death, and this would eventually become William's permanent home. Good-looking, spirited and intelligent, the boy showed considerable interest in the study of medicine, and in his late teens began to attend the Nonconformist Academy near Hay-on-Wye, finding accommodation in nearby Talgarth.

These were the days immediately prior to the beginnings of the evangelical revival in England. The year 1738, crucial in the annals of God's purposes for his church, had seen both the Wesley brothers, John and Charles, brought into a full assurance of their salvation, while George Whitefield was already preaching with astonishing effect both in England and in the New World. But for Wales, and William Williams personally, a yet more significant event had taken place three years earlier in 1735, with the conversion of a young Talgarth school teacher, Howell Harris. Enlightened by the truth, Harris was now taking every opportunity he could to gain a hearing for the gospel and with his passionate preaching was stirring up the people to seek forgiveness of sins through the sacrifice of Christ.

Although he had been taught Christian truth from his early years, Williams himself was still unconverted when he began his medical studies, but before long he too became troubled about his spiritual state. Fearful of the final judgement, he was later to describe himself as 'a wounded soul' at this time. Perhaps that is why he drifted into the Talgarth churchyard one Sunday morning in 1738 as the congregation was spilling out of the old church. A look of anticipation was written on many faces and soon Williams understood the reason. A young man, whom he recognized as Howell Harris himself, mounted a gravestone and a stillness descended. Then the medical student heard preaching such as he had never listened to before. As Harris pleaded with his hearers and warned of coming judgement on the impenitent, anticipation turned to terror on many faces. The effect on William Williams was swift and dramatic as the Spirit of God applied the words to his conscience. The debt he owed to Howell Harris was one he never forgot.

Not long after his conversion, Williams, now twenty-three years of age, also felt the urgency of the spiritual needs of his countrymen. In 1740 he gave up any thought of a medical career and applied for ordination, first as deacon in the Church of England, later hoping to gain full ordination as priest. Appointed as curate to a cluster of small churches in the vicinity of his home in Cefn-coed, he toiled for three years, preaching to unreceptive congregations, and facing the hostility of an unsympathetic and critical bishop.

Despite the antipathy of the clerics of his day, Williams could not be restrained by the strictures of his church and could regularly be found travelling beyond the bounds of his own parishes, preaching wherever he could gather hearers. Danger and malice were the constant accompaniments to his outspoken preaching, and it cannot have been a surprise for Williams when in 1743 he discovered that his bishop refused to ordain him. Nineteen charges were brought against the young preacher, amongst them his refusal to make the sign of the cross when baptizing infants and, of course, his 'irregularity' in transgressing parish boundaries. This effectively signalled the end of his ministry in the Established Church.

Rejected by the church he might be, but God accepted and owned his servant, and even so powerful a preacher as Howell Harris could declare, 'Hell trembles when he comes and souls are daily taken by Brother Williams in the gospel net.' From late 1742 onwards William Williams increasingly found his future ministry as an itinerant preacher, working together with Howell

Harris and Daniel Rowland of Llangeitho, in the newly-formed Welsh Calvinistic Methodist movement.

Daniel Rowland, acclaimed by some to be second only to Whitefield in the power of his preaching, and by others to be supreme, had been converted a few months before Harris. Soon Llangeitho, where he served as curate, became the scene of deep-felt sorrow for sin and an outpouring of God's Spirit in converting power as the people responded to the new message from their pulpit. A warm bond quickly grew up between Rowland and William Williams and by October 1742 Rowland could write to Harris: 'Brother Williams was here last Sunday, and a sweet day it was. I love him more and more because of his simple, honest, plain way of dealing with people.'

A historic milestone in the development of this new movement was passed when the first Association Meeting combining both English and Welsh Calvinistic Methodists was held at Watford, Glamorganshire, in January 1743. An important decision for Williams came at the conclusion of this meeting. Daniel Rowland needed help and most particularly at the monthly communion services when the people flocked across the mountains for the privilege of hearing the preaching and joining in the season of fellowship and worship. William Williams was asked if he could give this needed assistance — a service which he fulfilled for the rest of his life, trekking at least once a month across the Cambrian Mountains from his farmstead home, Pantycelyn.

But a yet more significant Association Meeting in terms of William Williams' own spiritual contribution was held later that same year in Carmarthenshire. Howell Harris, Daniel Rowland and Williams were present, together with two or three lay preachers. Harris raised the question of the need of a poet to set the truths of the gospel into song in the same way as Charles Wesley was doing for the English Methodist movement. Each man was invited to write a hymn and to submit it to the others for assessment to see whether God had given to any the gift of creating verse. The work submitted by William Williams so far outshone that of any other that he was quickly commissioned to compose hymns that would set the Welsh people singing the liberating truths that he and the other preachers were declaring.

By the following year, 1744, Williams had composed and published his first book of hymns, written in Welsh and entitled *Hallelujah*. In his preface he describes the subjects which his verses address: assurance of faith, spiritual joys, longings for heaven and triumph over enemies of the gospel. The people received his work with delight and the small volume soon ran through three editions. Many of his fellow-countrymen were illiterate, few had ready access to copies of the Scriptures, and through the hymns that Williams wrote the people learned their theology as they sang the great truths of the faith. 'The hymns of William Williams', wrote Martyn Lloyd-Jones in a lecture delivered in 1968, 'are packed with theology and experience… You get greatness, and bigness, and largeness in Isaac Watts; you get the experimental side wonderfully in Charles Wesley. But in William Williams you get both at the same time, and that is why I put him in a category entirely on his own. He taught the people theology in his hymns…'[2] The ascription 'poet of the revival' is therefore well merited. A ready example of this combination of theology and experience may be found in such words as these:

> Awake, my soul, and rise
> amazed and yonder see
> how hangs the mighty Saviour God
> upon a cursèd tree!
>
> How gloriously fulfilled
> is that most ancient plan
> contrived in the Eternal Mind
> before the world began.

> Now hell in all her strength,
> her rage and boasted sway,
> can never snatch a wandering sheep
> from Jesus' arms away.

The devotional fervour and depth of spiritual experience expressed in such hymns could never be the result of mere study and skill with words. Williams wrote with a degree of inspiration that has always characterized the work of the most gifted poets. Many verses 'came' to him in the dead of night, and so he always went to bed prepared with pen, ink and a board on which to rest his paper. As he lay musing on the profound truths of the Christian life, the thoughts would begin to burn themselves into his mind. Sometimes in the early hours of the morning he would suddenly cry out, 'O bring light, my vessel is running over!' Then he would write down the words racing through his brain. Words such as these, originally in his own native Welsh, could well have been born at such times:

> Jesus, Jesus, all-sufficient,
> beyond telling is thy worth;
> in thy name lie greater treasures
> than the richest found on earth.
> Such abundance
> is my portion with my God.
>
> In thy gracious face there's beauty
> far surpassing every thing
> found in all the earth's great wonders
> mortal eye hath ever seen.
> Rose of Sharon,
> thou thyself art heaven's delight.[3]

Another hymn literally translated from the Welsh reads:

Invisible One, I love you,
wonderful is the power of your grace,
pulling my soul so sweetly
away from its choicest pleasures;
you did more in one brief minute
than the whole world ever did,
winning for yourself a quiet seat
in this heart of stone.

These words have been freely rendered in the following way:

Unseen, yet loved, my God, my friend,
 I sing the wonders of your grace,
that in this stubborn heart of stone
 has won a quiet resting-place.

Sweetly from earth's beguiling charms
 you drew my restless soul away;
in one bright moment heaped on me
 ten thousand blessings more than they.

Although it is true that all the best hymns must spring from a degree of immediate and inspired thought, this does not mean that Williams did not expend much time and effort in order to create such lines. In our own day when there has been an explosion of song-writing for use in Christian worship, with results ranging from the deeply moving to the inconsequential — or worse — it is of interest to note the guidelines which William Williams laid down for would-be hymn-writers:

1. To seek for real grace themselves, and a saving knowledge of God in his Son; for without such qualifications, it is a most daring presumption to touch the ark.

2. To read … every work of suitable poetry they may obtain to enlarge their understanding, to know poetry well, to perceive where its excellence exists…

3. To read over and over again the works of the Prophets, the Psalms, Solomon's Song, the Lamentations, the Book of Job and the Revelation which are not only full of poetical flights, figurative speech, rich variety, easy language and lively comparisons, but also a spirit that enkindles fire, zeal and life in the reader…

4. Never to attempt to compose a hymn till they feel their souls near to heaven, under the influence of the Holy Spirit, and then the Spirit will be ready to bless his work.

Often called the 'Sweet Singer of Wales', William Williams was to write more than 850 hymns, some in English, but mostly in Welsh. With skilful hand he was able to touch a chord in the hearts of his fellow-countrymen. He understood the mystical and poetic elements in the Welsh temperament, and his hymns, lyrical and intense, gave expression to the deepest desires of the Christian heart. Much of his imagery he drew from the natural world around him. As he travelled among the rugged mountains, across barren tracts of land and beside the rivers that flowed through the valleys, he would see comparisons that gave him substance for his verses. The theme of pilgrimage is one to which Williams often returned, reflecting his journeys as he carried out his preaching ministry. In 1745, at twenty-eight years of age, he composed the Welsh version of his best-known hymn:

> Guide me, O thou great Jehovah,
>   pilgrim through this barren land.
> I am weak, but thou art mighty,
>   hold me with thy powerful hand.

Another hymn pursues the same theme:

> A pilgrim in a desert land,
>   I wander far and wide,
> expecting I may some time come
>   close to my Father's side.

Perhaps he sometimes missed his way as he journeyed:

> So prone am I when on my own
>   to stray from side to side,
> I need each step to paradise
>   my God to be my guide.[4]

Sometimes night overtook him and he would be left to find his way in the dark:

> The fearful desert night,
>   perils in every place,
> and fear of death, all take their flight
>   when God reveals his face.

Dangers were ever present, as any climber in the Welsh mountains could well testify:

> In thy hand I cannot fall
> though the weakest of them all;
> in thy hand at length I come
> from my trials safely home.

As he watched the waterfalls cascading down the mountainside after heavy rain, they reminded him of the strength of God, to cleanse and conquer sin:

> O that now like mighty torrents
>   strength descended from above;
> not the strongest of my passions
>   could withstand his conquering love.

When William Williams courted and married Mary Francis in 1748, he found a life partner delightfully suited to him. Mary's musical gifts gave her a ministry of her own and William would take his young wife with him on his travels. Often when they were staying overnight at some wayside tavern, Mary would start to sing in her lilting Welsh voice the tune of some familiar song of the day but set to words composed by her husband. Attracted by the strains of a well-known tune, fellow travellers stopped their conversations and began to listen. This opened the way for William to preach to them. However, such opportunities must have been curtailed with the arrival of a numerous family at Pantycelyn — a name that was becoming synonymous with Williams himself. Two sons (both of whom would also become preachers) and six daughters were born to William and Mary Williams.

A man of a kindly and serene disposition, 'Billy' Williams was the one sent for when any dispute arising among his neighbours and friends seemed to threaten the peace of the community. Again and again he seemed able to put the unresolved issues in the light of eternal truths, in a way that made them appear trivial and even paltry in the eyes of the contending parties. Then the quarrelling neighbours would feel ashamed that they had disagreed over such petty matters.

But in 1750 a dispute arose that even William Williams with his irenic nature was unable to solve: a dispute between the two men whom he held in the highest esteem, Howell Harris and Daniel Rowland. Undoubtedly the burden of responsibility rested on Harris, who resented the increasing prestige and leadership that Rowland was exercising in Welsh

Calvinistic Methodism. Exhausted by the constant demands of travelling and preaching without sufficient rest, Harris confessed, 'My nature is worn out and spent, and my body so impaired that I have not sufficient strength.' Coupled with this, Harris had embraced a certain doctrinal aberration known as Patripassianism,[5] leading some to question his orthodoxy. He had also been behaving most unwisely in other respects as well. His expulsion from the Association brought about a split among the Calvinistic Methodists that would last for the next twelve years. Although grieving deeply over the sorry position of his friend and spiritual father, William Williams remained with Daniel Rowland. Perhaps words such as these express his source of consolation at this difficult time:

> Thy presence can, without delay,
> drive all my numerous cares away,
>   as chaff before the wind.
> Compose my thoughts to adore and love
> thee, as an object far above,
>   to thee alone inclined.

Throughout the sorrows and pain of the next ten or more years, Williams drew constantly on the grace of God; and the trials he faced, both in the work and from divided loyalties, took him back again and again to Christ who alone could give him strength. Many of his best hymns were penned during this period of distress in the Welsh Methodist societies.

In 1758 William Williams published another book of hymns with the title *Alleluia*, containing 242 further compositions. The following year, probably at the request of his English-speaking friends, came a book of hymns in English called *Hosanna to the Son of David*. Some of these were translations of his Welsh verse; others were new and composed in English. Among the best known in this collection is one that speaks eloquently of

the anguish and love of the Saviour as he bore the weight of
the sins of his people:

> The enormous load of human guilt
>   was on my Saviour laid;
> with woes as with a garment, he
>   for sinners was arrayed.
>
> And in the fearful pangs of death
>   he wept, he prayed for me;
> loved and embraced my guilty soul
>   when nailèd to the tree.
>
> O love amazing! love beyond
>   the reach of human tongue;
> love which shall be the subject of
>   an everlasting song.

The sacrifice of Calvary was the focal point on which most of the
poet's hymns centred. Unhampered by the rigorous demands
of contemporary poetic diction, they spoke directly to the mind
and heart of the worshipper rather than to a fastidious or élitist
taste.

The divisions in Welsh Methodism led to general decline in
the joy, expectancy and spiritual life that had characterized it
for almost fifteen years. The Society or 'Experience' meetings
continued but became less vibrant and more routine. In this
context William Williams demonstrated exceptional pastoral gifts:
encouraging, consoling, restraining and guiding the societies. A
small work entitled *The Experience Meeting* written by Williams
as a handbook to guide the local leaders of the societies reveals
this ability. 'His genius, his spiritual understanding, and what
would now be termed as psychological insight stand out
everywhere and are truly astonishing,' wrote Lloyd-Jones in a

preface to the translated version of this book.[6] Nor was this the only product of the Pantycelyn poet's pen; over the years he published more than ninety other books, sermons, essays and pamphlets to enrich the Welsh Methodist societies.

At last in 1761 the clouds that hung over Welsh Methodism began to disperse. A reconciliation between Harris and Rowland brought healing to a wound that had festered for more than ten years. Meanwhile a new visitation of God's power was becoming evident in many parts of England, so that John Wesley could write, 'God was pleased to pour out his Spirit this year on every part of England and Ireland, perhaps in a manner we have not seen before, certainly not for twenty years.' By 1762 this floodtide of blessing had spread to Wales and was first felt under the penetrating preaching of Daniel Rowland. Called 'The Great Revival', it coincided with the publication of yet another collection of Welsh hymns from the pen of the poet, under the translated title, *The songs of those who are on the Sea of Glass*. As they sang these moving truths of God's grace to sinners, hearts were set aflame and many traced their conversion to this 'time of refreshing'. The people clamoured to obtain copies of the hymns and the book rapidly went through five editions. Words such as these throb with hope and expectation of the ultimate triumph of the kingdom of Christ:

> Onward march, all-conquering Jesus,
>   gird thee on thy mighty sword;
> sinful earth can ne'er oppose thee;
>   hell itself quails at thy word...
>
> Even today I hear sweet music,
>   praises of a blood-freed throng;
> full deliverance, glorious freedom,
>   are their themes for endless song.

Whiter than the snow their raiment,
victor palms they wave on high,
as they pass with fullest glory,
into life's felicity.

'He would frequently mount on very strong wings which would lift him to the heights of splendour,' wrote Thomas Charles of Bala as he described Williams' poetry, and continued, 'some verses of his hymns are like coals of fire, warming every passion when sung.' And as they sang such words the people were often unable to contain the exuberance and gladness of heart that welled up within them. Then they would literally leap and jump for joy. Such physical manifestations brought a considerable measure of criticism on the new work of God, and undoubtedly it was open to counterfeit as Jonathan Edwards, the New England theologian whose works he had studied, had warned. Williams now found himself in a position where he had to defend the genuine expressions of spiritual delight from hostile censure. Equally eloquent in prose as poetry, he mounted a strong defence, personifying his argument by putting words into the mouth of a fictitious young woman, a convert of the revival, named Martha:

O blessed hour, when my soul was in the greatest extremity, the day dawned on me. In a moment I felt my sins forgiven... I often cannot stop my tongue crying out, 'God is good.' I bless and magnify God; I leap and shout for joy in so great salvation, that I never knew before.

This work, together with many other theological treatises, became a further important contribution to the work of God in Wales at this time.

For some years Williams had taken an interest in the enterprising work of Selina, Countess of Huntingdon, as she opened chapels in a number of English towns and engaged preachers to occupy the pulpits. But when she equipped and opened a college for training young preachers at Trevecca, near Talgarth, his attention was quickened. Aided and encouraged by Howell Harris, who also lived in Trevecca and had established a religious community there, the college was opened in August 1768. George Whitefield was the preacher and to mark the occasion another Welsh preacher, Peter Williams, had translated 'Guide me, O thou great Jehovah' into English. Known subsequently as the 'Trevecca hymn', these memorable lines, echoing

Pulpit at Trevecca from which William Williams preached

around those Welsh mountains as they were sung by the thousands gathered for the occasion, expressed the aspirations of students and supporters alike. The translation, finalized in its English form by William Williams himself, concluded with a triumphant verse not found in our hymn books:

All my hope is in your power,
    wonders you have ever done;
death, hell, Satan are your captives,
    victory is already won;
        glorious conquest!
    This on Calvary was gained.

Williams showed an active interest in the progress of the fledgling college, and was regularly among the preachers who took part in the crowded open-air services held each August to mark its anniversary. The wrought iron pulpit from which he and others such as Daniel Rowland, John Fletcher, Augustus Toplady, John Wesley and George Whitefield preached can still be seen at Howell Harris' Trevecca Institute. Eventually one of his sons, John, would become the main tutor at Trevecca.

Lady Huntingdon shared William Williams' vision for the worldwide triumph of the gospel, and when she sent six of her students out to Savannah in Georgia to begin evangelistic work among the Indian peoples she asked him to compose some hymns especially for that endeavour. Her friend complied with the request and in 1772, the year the students sailed, he published his further collection of English hymns, this time entitled *Gloria in Excelsis*. Some of the Welsh poet's most notable hymns originate from this collection. One found in many hymn books begins with the words 'O'er the gloomy hills of darkness'. Its exultant final verse conveys the hope in the hearts of these men and women of faith as they watched eagerly for the increase of the kingdom of God:

> Fly abroad, thou mighty gospel,
>   win and conquer, never cease;
> may thy lasting wide dominion
> multiply and still increase!
>   Sway thy sceptre,
> Saviour, all the world around.

The metre, 87.87.47, which Williams employed for this hymn and also for 'Guide me, O thou great Jehovah', was one scarcely, if ever, utilized before in hymn-writing. It would later be taken up and used by a number of others, notably Joseph Hart and Thomas Kelly.

Constant travel, preaching and writing took a heavy toll on Williams' health. Like many of a poetic and sensitive disposition, he suffered from nervous exhaustion at several different periods of life. Writing to one of his sons in 1777 he said, 'There is no complaint so distressing as the nervous one which came upon me by too great attention to reading, writing, over-exertions in travelling and preaching.' His caution to his son was advice he needed to heed himself: 'Take great care to go soon to bed, to rise early and to walk out often. Don't sit long at your books...' Williams had a reputation for working long into the night — maybe the only time when he could be sure of uninterrupted time for creative thought. Perhaps the words of one of his most moving hymns, found in the 1772 English collection, came out of such time of suffering:

> Speak, I pray thee, gentle Jesus!
>   O how passing sweet thy words,
> breathing o'er my troubled spirit
>   peace which never earth affords.

As the 1790s approached, William Williams' constitution finally gave way under the strain of his ceaseless endeavours. At seventy-three years of age, his increasing illness meant that he was soon confined to one room. Looking back on days when he used to travel 3,000 miles in a year, he commented sadly to a friend that he could now move no more than forty feet in a day: from the bed to the fireside and back again. When he became virtually bedridden his wife Mary sat by him much of the time, reading to him from the Psalms and the New Testament. 1790 and 1791 were years of great loss for the Christian Church. In October 1790 Daniel Rowland was called away from his long ministry of preaching that had shaped Welsh Calvinistic Methodism, spanning fifty years. Williams felt the loss keenly and, ill as he was, managed to write one last poem — a moving elegy in memory of his lifelong friend. When anyone came to see him he had only one exhortation: 'Cleave to the Lord with full purpose of heart.' But as the end drew near, the man who had penned so many stirring and consoling words to help his fellow-pilgrims on their journey fell silent himself, being unable to articulate even the briefest sentence. Yet the look of triumph and serenity that marked his features told of his confidence in the redeeming work of Jesus Christ to undertake for him at the last. It was even as he had prayed long years before:

> When I tread the verge of Jordan
>   bid my anxious fears subside;
> death of death and hell's destruction,
>   land me safe on Canaan's side;
>   songs of praises
>   I will ever give to thee.

And on 11 January 1791 William Williams ended his pilgrimage, joining those songs of praises above, safe at last in the heavenly Canaan. Writing shortly after the poet's death, Thomas Charles was to say, 'Mr Daniel Rowland's sermons and the hymns of Mr William Williams made the age in which they lived more remarkable than almost any age in the history of Wales.'

Notes

1. He signed himself as 'Billy Williams' in letters to close friends, as in the one cited above to the Countess of Huntingdon.
2. D. M. Lloyd-Jones, *The Manifold Grace of God,* Puritan and Reformed Studies Conference, 1968; also included in *The Puritans, Their Origins and Successors*, Banner of Truth Trust, Edinburgh, 1987.
3. Translated by Robert Maynard Jones (Bobi Jones).
4. Translated by Robert Maynard Jones (Bobi Jones).
5. The teaching that God the Father was also suffering and dying in the person of his Son.
6. *The Experience Meeting*, trans. Bethan Lloyd-Jones, Evangelical Press and Evangelical Movement of Wales, 1973.

Joseph Hart
(1712-1768)

The penitent poet

How good is the God we adore,
our faithful, unchangeable friend!
His love is as great as his power,
and knows neither measure nor end.

H Y M N S, &c.

COMPOSED ON
Various Subjects.

By J. HART.

O sing unto the Lord a new Song; for he hath done MARVELLOUS THINGS: *His right Hand, and his holy Arm hath gotten him the Victory.* Psalm xcviii. 1.

THE SEVENTH EDITION,
With the AUTHOR'S EXPERIENCE,
the SUPPLEMENT, and APPENDIX.

L O N D O N:

Printed by M. LEWIS, in Pater-noster-Row; And sold by F. NEWBERY, at the Crown, the corner of St. Paul's Church-Yard, Ludgate-Hill; and by the AUTHOR's WIDOW, (the Lamb) near Durham-Yard, in the Strand; and at the MEETINGS in Jewin-Street, and Bartholomew-Close.

Price bound Two-Shillings.

Title page of Hart's hymns,
1770 (7th edition)

Joseph Hart
(1712-1768)

The penitent poet

The road of death with rash career
  I ran, and gloried in my shame;
abused his grace, despised his fear,
  and others taught the same.
Far, far from home on husks I fed,
  puffed up with each fantastic whim;
with swine a beastly life I led,
  and served God's foe instead of him.

These words form part of a long poem in which Joseph Hart made a sorry confession of his way of life prior to his conversion at the age of forty-five. Never could he forget the unexpected mercy of God that rescued him in mid-life from his pride, waywardness and bold, blasphemous behaviour.

Born in London in 1712, two years before George Whitefield and five years after Charles Wesley, Joseph Hart was the son of God-fearing parents who attended an Independent Meeting. Like all Independents or Dissenters, his parents would have known days of religious discrimination if not outright persecution, particularly before the Toleration Act of 1688. Even at the time of Joseph's birth, Queen Anne's strong dislike of any who refused to conform to the Church of England was a cause of constant concern. Once again these men and women of strong spiritual convictions saw their few privileges threatened.

Joseph's quick intelligence and obvious abilities encouraged his parents to give him the best classical education available at the time for children of Nonconformists. More than this, the boy was taught the truths of Scripture from his infancy. Looking back in later years, Joseph Hart recognized that even in those early years of life he had experienced many 'touches of heart, checks of conscience by the secret strivings of God's Spirit with me'. But such serious thoughts were soon brushed aside as ambition to succeed and love of popularity mastered the boy's thinking. A good student, he became skilled at French, Latin, Greek and Hebrew, particularly enjoying the literature of ancient Greece and Rome. He developed a love of poetry, taking much delight in the work of the Latin poets, and was to spend many hours translating some of their works into English verse. With his own education complete, Joseph Hart then became a proficient teacher of classics.

Soon after his twenty-first birthday the young teacher began to have fresh concerns about his own spiritual condition. All that his parents had taught him crowded into his mind, and he determined to amend his life and live in a way that would be pleasing to God. He fasted, prayed and tried to subdue his natural desires by stringent ascetic practices. Nothing seemed to quieten his disturbed conscience. He started to express his deepest thought in verse — lines which he probably later destroyed. If he was conscious that he had transgressed against God's commandments, he would urgently seek forgiveness; and if he could manage to add a few tears to his prayers, he would confidently hope that God would reckon him sincere enough to merit forgiveness ... until he stumbled and sinned and the cycle began again. 'Sinning, repenting, working and dreading, I went on for about seven years,' wrote Hart. Many more years would pass before he discovered that:

> Only by faith in Jesus' wounds
> the sinner gets release;
> no other sacrifice for sin
> will God accept but this.

In 1740, when he was twenty-eight years of age, a circumstance arose in his life which he describes as 'a great domestic affliction'. He did not divulge the nature of this affliction, but commented that in it he was a 'moderate sufferer but a monstrous sinner'. It appears to have brought a new dimension into his spiritual quest. Now he knew he did not merit salvation: it no longer became a question of whether he wished to follow the way of Christ or not, but whether God would ever accept him. After some weeks in this condition, with despair ever tightening its grip upon him, he began to feel a marked degree of spiritual comfort. The Bible took on new meaning for him, and he imagined that he had at last found the peace with God for which he had been searching.

These were the early years of the eighteenth-century evangelical revival. Both John Wesley and George Whitefield were preaching to vast crowds of hearers on Kennington Common and at Moorfields. As a Londoner, Hart followed the activities of these preachers with much interest, and when a division between them emerged over the doctrines of free will and election, Hart, whose early teaching gave him a strong empathy with Whitefield, tracked the development of the dispute with apparent concern.

Confident that he had already solved his own spiritual problems, Hart took upon himself the role of a religious connoisseur. With his background of careful instruction, he had acquired considerable head-knowledge and, as he expressed it, 'rushing impetuously into notions beyond my experience, I hastened to make myself a Christian by mere doctrine, adopting other men's opinions before I had tried them'. Full of self-confidence, Hart was confusing head-knowledge with true heart experience. A day would come when he would warn others of this dangerous position:

> For a living soul really to trust in Christ alone, when he sees nothing in himself but evil and sin is an act as supernatural as for Peter to walk on the sea... Mere doctrine, though ever so sound, will not alter the heart; consequently to turn from one set of tenets to another is not Christian conversion.

In 1741 when John Wesley published the sermon which he called 'Free Grace', expressing himself in the strongest terms against Whitefield's doctrinal position on election and the final perseverance of believers, it was Joseph Hart who sprang to Whitefield's defence. For the first time, he ventured into print in a long article entitled 'The Unreasonableness of Religion'. With a tightly argued critique, he demonstrated that reason and religion (or nature and grace) must ever stand in opposition to one another. While there is little that is objectionable in the earlier part of the article, towards its close Hart took a dramatic leap into antinomian territory and declared that 'a sinner's sins do not destroy but increase his comfort even here'. This was the very heresy of which the apostle Paul warned when he asked scathingly, 'Shall we continue in sin that grace may abound?'[1]

Worse than this, Joseph Hart now carried these notions through into his daily living. Assured of his own security in grace, he took that security as an open cheque to indulge in all and any sin as he pleased. 'In a word,' he confessed, 'I ran to such dangerous lengths both of carnal and spiritual wickedness that I even outwent professed infidels, and shocked the irreligious and

profane with my horrid blasphemies and monstrous impieties.'
If the grace of Christ would be magnified by the extent of his
sinning, his perverted reason suggested, then the more sins he
could commit the more it would demonstrate God's mercy.
A tender conscience, he thought, revealed weakness, while
prayer and broken-hearted confession of sin was useful only
for religious novices and weak-minded bigots.

For the next nine or ten years Joseph Hart, ever a popular
figure in the dance halls, taverns and playhouses of the day,
continued as 'an audacious apostate, a bold-faced rebel'. Not
only did he indulge an impure lifestyle, he encouraged others
to follow his course of action. He translated and published a
number of works from Greek and Latin writers, including a
preface to each, and added footnotes in which he continued to
extol godless and corrupt conduct. Later he confessed:

> Bold blasphemies employed my tongue;
> I heeded not my heart unclean;
> lost all regard of right and wrong,
> in thought and word and act obscene.

Yet God in his infinite mercy and grace had not forgotten
Joseph Hart. Even during his worst years, he had felt occasional
'meltings of heart' and the inner longing that one day he might
reform his ways and be a better man. In 1751, at almost forty
years of age, Hart made some attempt at self-reformation and
about the same time courted and married a young woman
fourteen years his junior. Perhaps his desire to please his wife
Mary was part of the reason for the change. Even though he
now counted his new morality as evidence of his good standing
with God, he could sometimes be found on his knees seeking
the face of God in prayer and would spend many hours reading
the Scriptures. One doctrine above all, however, seemed a
stumbling block: he found within himself a total reluctance to

accept the value of the cross of Christ and his death on behalf of sinners. He could not bring himself to believe it was either necessary or important in the scheme of salvation, regarding it as an affront to intelligence to accept such a concept. Like the Greeks whose works he had studied, the cross appeared 'foolishness' to Joseph Hart.

The early years of married life were not easy for Joseph and Mary Hart. After little more than a year they experienced the sorrow, so common in those days, of burying their first child. And when a son was born in 1754 they soon discovered that he was an epileptic; his needs were a constant anxiety to them. Meanwhile Joseph Hart's parents, who must have been much distressed over their son's conduct, had become regular in their attendance at Whitefield's Tabernacle in Moorfields — a barn-like structure before a more permanent building took its place in 1753. When Whitefield himself returned from America in 1755, the numbers attending Moorfields multiplied if it became known that the great evangelist would be preaching. And in amongst the crowds that thronged to hear him was a middle-aged man with a burdened conscience — Joseph Hart.

He heard the fearsome warnings and the impassioned appeals; he saw the tears of repentance streaming down the faces of other listeners. At last Hart became thoroughly alarmed about his own condition. One thought only gripped his mind: the words of the Prodigal who said, 'I will arise and go to my Father.' But would the Father receive him? Hart did not know. He longed for some sign, some voice from heaven, to assure him of his acceptance with God. But no voice came. Days passed and the burden of his sins grew ever more pressing. He could scarcely eat; he avoided all company and often went on long solitary walks, all the time begging God to pardon his sins and receive him. Then one day he thought he heard words addressed directly to him: which would he choose, the voice demanded, the visions and revelations for which he had been praying or would he at last trust himself to 'the low despised mystery of a crucified Man'? This touched on the core of his problem, and in agony of spirit he chose the latter.

From that moment onwards, although dejection and gloom still oppressed his naturally buoyant spirit, he had an inner assurance that somehow, somewhere, he would find the peace and forgiveness which his wounded spirit craved. However, two more years would pass before he reached that point: years of distress of soul that in some measure tallied with the depths of degradation to which he had fallen. Fearing he had 'trampled underfoot the blood of Christ', it seemed that all the promises of the gospel only mocked him. His anguish of spirit had physical effects as well. The pains he experienced were so intense that he thought he must be dying. But when he took to his bed he was afraid to close his eyes lest he should wake up in hell. He discovered in those grievous days that mere head-knowledge of Christian doctrine, however orthodox, could not 'sustain a soul in the day of trial'.

Not long after Easter in 1757 Hart attended a service in the Moravian Chapel in Fetter Lane. He listened intently to the sermon but afterwards could recollect little of it. But what took place when he returned home is best told in his own words:

> I was hardly got home when I felt myself melting away into a strange softness of affection which made me fling myself on my knees before God. My horrors were immediately dispelled and such light and comfort flowed into my heart as no words can paint. The Lord by his Spirit of love came … with such divine power and energy into my soul, that I was lost in blissful amazement. I cried out, 'What, me Lord?' His Spirit answered to me, 'Yes, thee'. I objected, 'But I have been so unspeakably vile and wicked'. The answer was, 'I pardon thee fully and freely.'

Hart's reaction to such a declaration of mercy and acceptance was instant and intense. 'Tears ran in streams from my eyes,' he recalled, 'I threw my soul willingly into my Saviour's hands; lay weeping at his feet, wholly resigned to his will, only begging that I might … be of some service to his church and people.'

Overcome at the wonder of God's forgiving mercy he began to express his gratitude and surprise in verse:

> My God, when I reflect
>   how all my lifetime past
> I ran the roads of sin and death
>   with rash impetuous haste,
>
> My foolishness I hate,
>   my filthiness I loathe;
> and view, with sharp remorse and shame,
>   my filth and folly both.
>
> And dost thou still regard
>   and cast a gracious eye
> on one so foul, so base, so blind,
>   so dead, so lost, as I?

Not surprisingly, it was the grief and sufferings of the Son of God in his death on behalf of sinners that became the constant theme of Hart's thankful lines. As he had once despised the cross as foolishness, he now saw in it an inestimable value. Perhaps more than any other hymn-writer, Hart would become the poet of the cross, and the word 'Gethsemane'[2] occurs time and again in his writings. The very first hymn he wrote sets the theme:

> Gethsemane, the olive press!
> (and why so called, let Christians guess)

> fit name, fit place! where vengeance strove
> and gripped and grappled hard with love.
>
> 'Twas here the Lord of life appeared
> and sighed and groaned and prayed and feared;
> bore all incarnate God could bear,
> with strength enough and none to spare.

He saw the whole cost of his salvation exacted on the Saviour as he knelt alone in anguish among those olive trees. And as the scenes in the garden gave place to the scenes on Calvary, Hart saw himself every bit as guilty as those who actually crucified the Saviour:

> They nailed him to the accursed tree:
> they did, my brethren — so did we:
> the soldier pierced his side, 'tis true;
> but we have pierced him through and through.
>
> O love of unexampled kind
> that leaves all thought so far behind!

Another long poem, stretching to twenty-three verses, is devoted to those same scenes enacted in that garden. Each verse concludes with the word 'Gethsemane'. All the burden of his years of searching for forgiveness seem to be crammed into such lines as these:

> Sins against a holy God;
>   sins against his righteous laws;
> sins against his love, his blood;
>   sins against his name and cause;
>   sins immense as is the sea —
>   hide me, O Gethsemane.

> Here's my claim, and here alone;
>> none a Saviour more can need;
> deeds of righteousness I've none,
>> no, not one good work to plead.
>>> Not a glimpse of hope for me,
>>> only in Gethsemane.

A hymn found in many modern hymn books, even today, begins on this same theme:

> Great High Priest, we view thee stooping,
>> with our names upon thy breast,
> in the garden, groaning, drooping,
>> to the ground with horrors pressed;
> weeping angels stood confounded
>> to behold their Maker thus;
> and can we remain unwounded,
>> when we know 'twas all for us?

For the next two years Hart gave himself to writing hymns. His earnest wish was to render some service to Christ and his church in view of the past years of damage and neglect that had characterized his life. Many of his hymns follow the church calendar with poems to mark Good Friday, Easter Sunday, Ascension Day, Whitsunday, Christmas, and other days he considered of particular note. Shortly after his conversion came the celebration of the gift of the Spirit at Pentecost and the hymn he wrote on this occasion, the fourth in his collected hymns, has become one of his most enduring:

> Come, Holy Spirit, come!
> Let thy bright beams arise;
> dispel the darkness from our minds,
>> and open all our eyes!

> Convince us of our sin,
> then lead to Jesus' blood;
> and to our wondering view reveal
> the secret love of God.
>
> Dwell, therefore, in our hearts;
> our minds from bondage free:
> then shall we know and praise and love
> the Father, Son and thee.

Like a number of Hart's hymns, this one was included by Augustus Toplady in his collection of hymns entitled *Psalms and Hymns,* published in 1776. Also, like many others in that collection, it was revised and improved by Toplady. In our modern hymn books it usually consists of six verses chosen from the nine that Hart wrote, and Toplady's alterations have been widely adopted.

Characterized by strong love for the Saviour, most of Joseph Hart's hymns also follow the tradition set by Isaac Watts. But having the advantage of seeing much of Charles Wesley's work, Hart employs a wider scope of metres than Watts used, frequently working in 7 7.7 7 metre and also 87.87. Hart generally used a close rhyming scheme and this could sometimes prove a stumbling block, reducing the quality of his verse. An example of one of his less happy compositions is based on the prayer of Jabez:[3]

> A saint there was in days of old
> though we but little of him hear,
> in honour high of whom 'tis told
> a short, but an effectual prayer.
> This prayer, my brethren, let us view
> and try if we can pray so too.

His use of dated language is a further reason why so few of Hart's hymns are sung today. But there is another possible explanation: many of them track paths unfamiliar to the majority of Christians. Despite the joy of his new-found assurance of forgiveness, Hart's spiritual life was by no means an even one. The pain of his previous pathway often seemed to pursue him. Depression of spirit would sweep over him in waves. At such times his only refuge was to go back to the gospel truths that had brought liberty to his soul:

> Nothing but thy blood, O Jesus,
>   can relieve us of our smart;
> nothing else from guilt release us;
>   nothing else can melt the heart...
>
> Jesus, all our consolations
>   flow from thee, the sovereign good;
> love and faith and hope and patience,
>   all are purchased by thy blood.

As a result of the constant fluctuations in his experience, Hart was forced to seek solace through ever-deepening communion with God. Consequently many of his hymns speak of things little known among Christians; like Charles Wesley, he soars to heights where most find it hard to follow. For this reason few of his one hundred or more hymns have become well known, although *Gadsby's Hymns*, first published in 1814, included a considerable number.[4] Yet all may readily identify with such words as:

> Come, ye sinners, poor and wretched,
>   weak and wounded, sick and sore;
> Jesus ready stands to save you,
>   full of pity, joined with power.
>   He is able,
>   he is willing; doubt no more!

> Let not conscience make you linger,
> nor of fitness fondly dream;
> all the fitness he requireth
> is to feel your need of him:
>   this he gives you;
>   'tis the Spirit's rising beam!

As we have seen, Joseph Hart had a strong desire to serve God, wishing in some way to make amends for the wasted years. He began to preach occasionally as he received invitations, and into his messages he poured all his aspirations that others might be rescued from the degradation he had known. Soon word of his powerful preaching spread around. One who heard him reported the fact to William Romaine, rector of St Ann's, Blackfriars. Inclined to be testy, Romaine exclaimed, 'What! That devil!' when he heard that Hart had been preaching. Joseph Hart soon received a report of the cynical comment. Instead of defending himself he wrote a poem which he entitled 'The Prodigal', and sent it to Romaine.

> The prodigal's returned;
> the apostate, bold and base,
> that all his Father's counsels spurned,
> and long abused his grace.

> What treatment since he came!
> Love tenderly expressed.
> What robe is brought to hide his shame?
> The best, the very best.

> Ye elder sons, be still;
> give no bad passions vent:
> my brethren, 'tis your Father's will,
> and you must be content.

> All that he has is yours:
> rejoice then, not repine!
> That love that all your state secures,
> that love has altered mine.

Certainly Romaine, who was always quick to apologize when he realized that he was in the wrong, would have been sorry for his over-hasty remark.

In 1759, two years after his conversion, Joseph Hart gathered up the various hymns and pieces of poetry he had written and prepared them for publication with the unpretentious title, *Hymns Composed on Various Subjects*. To this collection he affixed a preface which he described as 'The Author's Experience'. With candid honesty yet bitter regrets, he told the story of his long years of unbelief and detailed God's dealings with him. A masterly piece of prose, with numerous gems of quotable thoughts and a pathos of its own, it was instantly in demand, as were his hymns. The book became a common talking point, not only among churchgoers but also among literary men of all tastes. Some were repelled, others fascinated and still others became devoted readers. 'Hart is ungraceful and uncouth,' said one critic. His descriptions of

Title page of first edition
of *Hart's Hymns*

the physical sufferings of Christ against the backdrop of his own long rejection of the dying Saviour could leave none neutral:

> Mocked, spit upon and crowned with thorn,
>   a spectacle he stood;
> his back with scourges lashed and torn;
>   a victim bathed in blood.

Yet he never indulged in such descriptions without urging his readers to repent of their sins and find in that cross of Christ forgiveness and reconciliation with God.

> Come then, repenting sinner, come,
>   approach with humble faith;
> owe what you will, the total sum
>   is cancelled by his death.

Joseph Hart's name became a household word, and before long he had gathered a congregation eager to hear him preach. In 1760 he purchased a huge wooden chapel, situated in Jewin Street and recently vacated by the Particular Baptists. This would become the home of Joseph Hart's Independent congregation. With four spacious galleries it must have been a daunting place for any preacher, but especially for a man in Joseph Hart's position. Numerous hearers were attracted to the old building; Hart's long desire to serve the one to whom he owed so much was abundantly fulfilled. A second edition of Hart's hymns was called for three years after it had been published, and a year later a third, with a fourth and fifth in 1765 and 1767 respectively.

In 1763 Martin Madan, chaplain of the Lock Hospital, included as two four-line verses the last verse of one hymn, beginning 'No prophet nor dreamer of dreams', in his collection of *Psalms and Hymns*. The longer hymn is undistinguished, but how surprised Hart would have been had he known that this verse would become the best loved and known of all his hymns:

> How good is the God we adore,
>   our faithful unchangeable friend!
> His love is as great as his power,
>   and knows neither measure nor end!
>
> 'Tis Jesus, the first and the last,
>   whose Spirit shall guide us safe home;
> we'll praise him for all that is past,
>   and trust him for all that's to come.

Originally starting with the words 'This God is the God we adore', it has become a regular choice at church anniversaries and similar gatherings. Standing like a signpost on the path of life, the words point back to the faithfulness of God in the past and forward to an unknown but secure future. It underscores with absolute certainty that no eventuality can alter the divine purpose for the believer, and God's past goodness guarantees his future aid.

Joseph and Mary Hart were called upon to prove those confident words of faith in that same year of 1763 when they lost Daniel, their three-year-old son. Five years later, in 1768, their faith was tested even more: Mary was taken seriously ill with a condition that left her a semi-invalid for the rest of her life. Remembering that their eldest son suffered frequent epileptic fits, and their two other sons, eight and ten years of age, and a baby daughter all needed constant attention, we may appreciate the severity of such a trial. As if this were not hard enough, Joseph himself was far from well, experiencing continual pain. Soon it became obvious to family and congregation alike that Hart, still only fifty-six years of age, had not long to live. Unwilling to give in to the increasing weakness, he continued preaching; but as winter turned to spring his strength failed, and before long he could not rise from his bed.

'I know myself to be a child of God and an heir of glory,' said the dying poet, and these words were among his last, for on 26 May 1768 Joseph Hart was taken to serve his God more perfectly in a better country. Grief at the loss of such a man — one whose life as a true believer had spanned a mere ten years and yet whose influence had been widespread and profound — swept over the community. More than twenty thousand people attended his funeral, mingling among the graves at Bunhill Fields, the Nonconformist burial ground. Words of a funeral hymn written by Hart himself some years earlier were sung and as if from the grave itself Joseph Hart spoke yet again:

> Sons of God by blest adoption,
>   view the dead with steady eyes:
> what is sown thus in corruption
>   shall in incorruption rise...
>
> Jesus, thy rich consolations
>   to thy mourning people send;
> may we all with faith and patience
>   wait for our approaching end.

So in company with many great men and women of faith buried in Bunhill Fields — John Bunyan, Isaac Watts, John Owen, Thomas Goodwin, Susanna Wesley and countless others — Joseph Hart, the penitent poet, awaits that grand day of resurrection still to come. A tall obelisk now marks the original gravestone, and many from all parts of the world still visit the site, for wherever *Hart's Hymns* have travelled, the poet's name has been loved. On one side of the stone are quotations from two of his hymns:

O bring no price,
God's grace is free,
to Paul, to Magdalene and me.

None but Jesus
    can do helpless sinners good.

Joseph Hart's grave at
Bunhill Fields

Notes

1. Romans 6:1.
2. Literally 'the olive press'
3. 1 Chronicles 4:10.
4. The 1838 edition of *Gadsby's Hymns* contains many of Hart's hymns not included in the main part of the book, as Part IV of the collection. The 1965 edition keeps this arrangement. *Gospel Hymns*, first published in 1915, also contains a good number of them.

Augustus M. Toplady
(1740-1778)

'A sinner so signally loved'

A debtor to mercy alone,
of covenant mercy I sing;
nor fear, with thy righteousness on,
my person and offering to bring.
My name from the palms of his hands
eternity will not erase;
impressed on his heart it remains
in marks of indelible grace.

Augustus Toplady

Augustus M. Toplady
(1740-1778)

'A sinner so signally loved'

A young man of twenty-two was browsing in a second-hand bookshop in Lincoln's Inn, London. Soon to be ordained, Augustus Toplady was anxious to build up his personal library and, like many other candidates for the ministry since that day, had only limited resources at his disposal. Approaching his customer, the owner of the shop indicated that he had something to say to him. Together the two withdrew to the back of the shop. 'Sir, you will soon be ordained,' began the salesman in a low voice, 'I suppose you have not laid in a very great stock of sermons. I can supply you with as many sets as you please. All originals: very excellent ones, and they will come for a trifle.'

Shocked at the very thought of such a suggestion, Toplady answered indignantly, 'I shall certainly never be a customer to you in that way... How could you think of me buying ready-made sermons? A man who cannot or will not make his own sermons is quite unfit to wear the gown!'

'Nay, young gentleman,' retorted the other, 'do not be surprised, I assure you I have sold ready-made sermons to many a bishop in my time.' Such an incident, insignificant in many respects, acts as a window into the personality and character of Augustus Montague Toplady, one whose very name evokes strong reactions even today. Born in Farnham, Surrey, in 1740, Toplady would early reveal a disposition that was decisive, principled and unafraid to express his opinion. The youthful preacher set out on his ministry as he meant to continue, with deeply held convictions, and a sense of the high privilege and responsibility of such a calling.

The lives of Augustus and his mother Catherine were inextricably bound together. Born shortly after the death of her other child and only a few months before the death of her husband, this boy was all Catherine had. At the time of her child's birth, Richard Toplady, a military man, was far off in South America, and died in May 1741 during the Siege of Cartagena, not in battle but of a virulent infection — yellow fever. Augustus was six months old at the time and it appears that Catherine then settled in Exeter with her infant son.

Precocious and intense from early years, young Augustus may well have also been a little spoilt. While staying with one of his aunts and her family, the schoolboy complained that his aunt had 'cut me fat meat, though she knew I did not love it; no more don't her children, yet she makes 'em eat it. O the difference that there is between their mamma and mine!' Of another aunt the twelve-year-old could write, 'She is so vastly quarrelsome; in short, she is so fractious, captious and insolent that she is unfit for human society.' We wonder if his beloved 'mamma' reproved her son for expressing such sentiments.

In 1749, when Augustus was nine years of age, Catherine Toplady moved from Exeter to London, renting accommodation for herself and her son in Petty France, not far from Westminster. This was to enable Augustus to attend Westminster School. Catering mainly for the sons of the nobility, Westminster was considered a school that offered a superior education, and the headmaster at the time, a Dr Nicholls, was a kindly man. A diary which the young Toplady kept for a period during

his schooldays reveals both his schoolboy troubles and his
sensitivity of conscience. 'Had a rash bad slap from my usher,'
he records on one occasion, and in a written prayer asks God
to 'grant that I may not have any anger for Mr Nicholls ... also
that I may not have any quarrels with my school fellows'. At
another time he prays, 'Blessed be thy name, O most righteous
Lord... Make me not to err as some other schoolboys do ...
grant that I may keep a watch over myself, never to perpetrate
any crime. Grant that I may never fall from thee, nor leave
so kind, so bountiful, so faithful a Master as thou art.' Clearly
an able child, Augustus Toplady was beginning to show the
characteristics which would mark him out in later years as a
man of extraordinary talent, tenderness of conscience and
sharpness of conviction.

Catherine Toplady's poor health left her son in constant
anxiety lest he should also lose his mother, and references to
this fear creep into his private diary during these years. He
tried to prepare his mind for such an event: 'I must beware of
impatience, that is, murmuring at her death, and despairing
of God's lifting me up again; therefore I must keep a heart
of thanksgiving and faith: thanksgiving, in praising him for
sparing the life of Mamma so long...' Sometimes he expressed
his thoughts in verse. An early poem, written when he was
fourteen and one which 'came all flop into my head without
studying', expresses his sense of spiritual need:

> Whilst I am thine, I dread no fierce assault
>   which Satan, earth or any foe can give;
> renew my heart and rectify each fault;
>   cleanse me from sin and every want relieve.

In 1755, when Augustus was not quite fifteen, he
matriculated from Westminster and, like his father before him,
became a student at Trinity College, Dublin. Meanwhile his

mother, who had an estate to settle in Ireland, made a home for him in County Wexford. His first summer vacation there in August 1756 was one he would never forget. In a place named Cooladine the young student had joined a few Irish peasants in a simple service of worship held in a barn. And there the head knowledge of the truths of the Christian faith with which he had long been familiar was turned to true heart experience, as Toplady himself was later to describe:

> That sweet text Ephesians 2:13 was particularly delightful and refreshing to my soul and the more so as it reminded me of the days and months that are past... It was from that passage that Mr [James] Morris preached on that memorable evening of my effectual call by the grace of God. Under the ministry of that dear messenger, and by that sermon, I was, I trust, brought nigh by the blood of Christ in August 1756. Strange that I, who had sat so long under the means of grace in England, should be brought nigh in an obscure part of Ireland, amidst a handful of God's people, met together in a barn!... Surely it was the Lord's doing and it was marvellous!

From early years Toplady had chosen to express his thoughts and spiritual aspirations in verse. We are not surprised, therefore, to find lines that speak of his search for forgiveness, together with the joys of assurance and gratitude to God, among an early collection of his poems which he published in 1759 when he was just nineteen years of age and still a student at Trinity. Seeking to know that God had accepted him, he wrote:

> If my Lord himself reveal,
>   no other good I want;
> only Christ my wounds can heal
>   or silence my complaint;

> he that suffered in my stead,
>> the Lamb, shall my physician be;
> I will not be comforted
>> till Jesus comforts me.

Or again, he pleads,

> Pilot of the soul awake,
> save us for thy mercy's sake;
> now rebuke the angry deep,
> save, O Lord, thy sinking ship.
>
> Be, thou, our haven of retreat,
> a Rock to fix our wavering feet;
> teach us to own thy sovereign sway,
> whom the winds and seas obey.

The imagery that depicts Christ as a Rock for his people, springing directly from Scripture itself, is one that often features in Toplady's early verse. As a child he had known little security: with no father and a mother whose health was in constant jeopardy, it is natural that he should find comfort in such a concept — one that would come to fruition in later years with his outstanding hymn 'Rock of Ages, cleft for me'.

There is a simplicity of expression in much of Toplady's early verse which is rarely found in his later compositions. Published under the title *Poems on Sacred Subjects,* the material was divided under five separate headings, and contained more than a hundred pieces from his childhood and student days. Although none of these early poems is used as a hymn today, as many as twenty-seven were to be found in collections in regular use during the nineteenth century. C. H. Spurgeon included at least a dozen in *Our Own Hymn Book*, which he compiled and published in 1866 for use in the Metropolitan Tabernacle.

Converted under a sermon from a Wesleyan lay preacher, it is not surprising that young Toplady should initially embrace Arminian tenets of faith and be prejudiced against a Calvinistic interpretation of Scripture. It also becomes evident on reading these early hymns that, although he accepted John Wesley's teaching that a Christian could be freed from all known sin in this life, he found the standard impossible to attain. Some later editors of Toplady's work were embarrassed to discover references to these views in the hymns of so ardent a Calvinist and removed such 'objectionable' expressions from his early poems.

While Toplady remembered throughout life the joy of his conversion in 1756 and the debt he owed to James Morris, another date also stood out in his mind as formative for his entire spiritual life. In September 1758 he came across a work by the Puritan writer, Thomas Manton — perhaps in another second-hand bookshop. It was an exhaustive tome of sermons on John 17,[1] and Toplady read it eagerly. Manton's teaching on the sovereignty of God in salvation, beginning with his electing love in eternity and stretching down to his final presentation of his people perfect and secure at the last, gripped the young Toplady and revolutionized his thinking:

Though awakened in 1756, I was not led into a full and clear view of the doctrines of grace till 1758 when in the goodness of God, my prejudices received an effectual shock in reading Dr Manton's sermons on John 17. I shall remember the years 1756 and 1758 with gratitude and joy in the heaven of heavens to all eternity.

The relief and sense of spiritual security that Toplady now knew is echoed in such words as:

Immovable our hope remains,
within the veil our anchor lies;
Jesus, who washed us from our stains,
shall bear us safely to the skies.

Strong in his strength, we boldly say,
for us Immanuel shed his blood;
who then shall tear our Shield away,
or part us from the love of God?

The winds may roar, the floods may beat;
the rain, impetuous, descend;
yet will he not his own forget,
but love and save them to the end.

Toplady graduated from Trinity College with a BA degree in the summer of 1760 and both he and his mother left Ireland for good. His diary also concluded that summer, with no other personal record surviving apart from one covering twelve months begun seven years later. From the pages of this first diary we learn that, even as a youth, Toplady suffered indifferent health. It is peppered with references to his ailments and the remedies tried — details that have led his biographers to wonder if he was already beginning to suffer from tuberculosis, a condition that would eventually cut short his effective ministry. His own condition led him to think on the sufferings of the Saviour and to measure anything he experienced in that light:

The pangs which my weak nature knows
are swallowed up in thine;
how numberless thy ponderous woes,
how few, how light are mine.

> Make me, O Lord, thy patient son;
> thy language mine shall be;
> Father, thy gracious will be done,
> I take this cup from thee.

Following his ordination as deacon on 5 June 1762, when he was still eighteen months short of the accepted age stipulated in the Church of England protocol, Augustus Toplady was offered a small country curacy in Blagdon, Somerset, a village nestling under the Mendip Hills. Little is known of the two years he spent there, or why he moved on to Farleigh Hungerford, eight miles south of Bath two years later. This lack of information may be due to the fact that at the end of his life he insisted on many of his personal diaries being destroyed.

Although the first powerful impact of the eighteenth-century evangelical revival had passed by this time, the early 1760s were years that saw a renewed work of God up and down Britain and in Ireland. It is evident that Toplady's ministry, particularly at Farleigh, was touched with the flame of divine blessing; even though he spent little more than a year there. Possibly his uncertain health lay behind his short stay or perhaps the vicar disapproved of his curate's strong evangelicalism. Certainly it appears that his people loved him. Describing his last Sunday at Farleigh, Toplady wrote:

> I administered the Lord's Supper to a number of weeping communicants; nor do I remember whether that ordinance was ever accompanied with so signal a blessing to my own soul. The gracious melting seemed to be general; and the overpowering flame of holy love was I believe caught from heart to heart... When all was over we bid a personal and particular *adieu* to each other, though with many tears... There was something in their manner

which seemed to say, 'We shall meet again'. And so I trust we shall, in that place of love where ministers and people part no more but are for ever with the Lord and with each other.

Now twenty-five years of age, and recently ordained as priest, it may well be that Augustus Toplady hoped for some more influential pulpit. But after a period in London, a time when he developed friendships with some of the best-known preachers of the day, he was appointed as vicar of two even more remote villages, this time in Devonshire: Harpford and Venn Ottery, a few miles inland from the coastal resort of Sidmouth. Although the villages had only a combined population of 300, with Harpford the larger of the two, Toplady's preaching soon began to draw the people from many miles around.

Little has changed since the days of Toplady; these hamlets with their thatched roof cottages give the visitor the impression that he has stepped back in time and at any moment may meet members of Toplady's congregation wending their way down the narrow lanes to the parish church. With the advantage of the further diary mentioned above which Toplady began in December 1767, we have a remarkable window into the effectiveness of his ministry in this insignificant outpost, but more importantly into the depth and closeness of his communion with God. On Sunday 6 December, he records, 'In the morning read prayers and preached here in Fen-Ottery to a very attentive congregation. In the afternoon the congregation at Harpford was exceedingly numerous.' Four days after this entry Toplady records that 'in my chamber before I went to bed was much comforted while singing praise to the great Three-One, the Author of all the blessings I enjoy'. In all probability the hymn Augustus Toplady was singing that night was one of his own that he entitled 'A Chamber Hymn', beginning 'A

sovereign protector I have'. Three weeks later, as he reviewed
the closing year, he copied down in his diary some lines from
that same hymn:

> Kind Author and ground of my hope,
>   thee, thee for my God I avow;
> my glad Ebenezer set up,
>   and own thou hast helped me till now.
> I muse on the years that are past,
>   wherein my defence thou hast proved;
> nor wilt thou relinquish at last
>   a sinner so signally loved.

Like Charles Wesley, Toplady sometimes chose to write in
anapaestic metre, as in the lines above. This metre has often
been used for light-hearted or frivolous verse[2], but Toplady
charged it with weight and seriousness, employing it for a
number of his later hymns.

Venn Ottery, or Fen-Ottery as it was then known, was
well named because of the fen-like quality of the area, with
its damp, heavily overgrown lanes. Unfortunately Toplady
had chosen to live there rather than in Harpford, and it soon
proved detrimental to his already indifferent health. In turn this
constant illness often led the young preacher to be dejected in
spirit, fearing that God had cast him off because of his sins:

> Encompassed with clouds of distress,
>   just ready all hope to resign,
> I pant for the light of thy face,
>   and fear it will never be mine.
> Disheartened with waiting so long,
>   I sink at thy feet with my load;
> all-plaintive I pour out my song,
>   and stretch forth my hands to my God.

> Shine Lord, and my terror shall cease;
>   the blood of atonement apply;
> and lead me to Jesus for peace,
>   the Rock that is higher than I...
> While harassed and cast from thy sight,
>   the tempter suggests with a roar,
> 'The Lord has forsaken thee quite,
>   thy God will be gracious no more.'

But such gloomy fears were soon replaced by renewed confidence in God as he looked away from himself to Christ and reminded himself of his perfect righteousness:

> From whence this fear and unbelief?
> Has not the Father put to grief
>   his spotless Son for me?
> And will the righteous Judge of men
> condemn me for that debt of sin,
>   which, Lord, was charged on thee?
>
> Turn then, my soul, unto thy rest;
> the merits of thy great High Priest
>   have bought thy liberty;
> trust in his efficacious blood,
> nor fear thy banishment from God,
>   since Jesus died for thee.

Early in 1768 Toplady realized that he must move from Venn Ottery for the sake of his health. At times his chest and throat had become so affected that he could scarcely preach. Nine miles further north lay the quiet village of Broadhembury, and before long Toplady was able to arrange an exchange of parishes with Francis Luce who was willing to take charge of Harpford and Venn Ottery. The final exchange took place in

April 1768 and here he would be based, at least nominally, for the rest of his life, although his actual period of residence was not more than a few years.

The picturesque village of Broadhembury presented a total contrast to the damp overgrown lanes of Venn Ottery. As its name suggests, it had a broad main street, lined with thatched cottages. With its bright sparkling stream running through the village, little has changed over the centuries, and it remains an idyllic spot even today. Although the village, comprising mainly farmsteads, had only some one hundred and sixty families, Toplady continued to record congregations that were 'exceedingly great indeed'. The reason for this, although he did not intend the connection, lies in his next sentence, 'I was all on fire for God; and the fire I verily believe caught from heart to heart.' This comment would indicate the manifest presence of God among the people and, added to Toplady's outstanding gifts as a preacher, explains why the villagers flocked in such numbers to Broadhembury.

During these Broadhembury years of his life, Toplady wrote and published a further twenty-eight hymns — and it is these, together with some later ones, for which he is largely remembered today. They were printed in *The Gospel Magazine*, a journal 'designed to promote experimental religion' which had first been published in 1766. Although it represented the Calvinistic wing of the Church of England, it was also favoured by many Dissenters. In 1775 Toplady took over the editorship of the magazine, but his hymns had begun to appear as early as 1771, with 'A debtor to mercy alone' among the first.

The truths that Toplady held dear shine out again and again in this hymn of confident assurance. Once more in anapaestic metre, he wrote:

> My name from the palms of his hands
> eternity will not erase;

> impressed on his heart it remains
>   in marks of indelible grace.
> Yes, I to the end shall endure,
>   as sure as the earnest is given;
> more happy, but not more secure,
>   the glorified spirits in heaven.

Fifteen other poems were also published in that same year, and although none other has survived as a hymn, clear Toplady characteristics were beginning to emerge. We note his ability to create an arresting opening line — for example: 'Jesus, immutably the same', or 'Awake, sweet gratitude, and sing', or even 'Happiness, thou lovely name'. Another feature of his verse is his use of polysyllabic words. A typical example is found in these words:

> Fountain of never-ceasing grace,
>   thy saints' *exhaustless* theme,
> great object of immortal praise,
>   *essentially* supreme.

Words such as *imputatively, efficacious, unchangeably, mediatorial, distinguishing* and others are scattered throughout his compositions. Unlike Charles Wesley, who is able to use such words with dynamic effect, Toplady's use can give his hymns a heavy feel. Combined with intensive theological concepts crammed into every line, and 'no padding, nor even any breathing space',[3] this characteristic has led some to dismiss his work. As a result a number of excellent hymns have fallen into disuse. John Julian deals unkindly and undeservedly with Toplady in allowing an article into his *Dictionary of Hymnology* which demeans the preacher and includes such comments as 'He is no poet or inspired singer. He climbs no heights. He sounds no depths… He is a fervent preacher, not a bard.' In contrast a modern writer can give a far different estimate:

> Toplady maintains that a good hymn can 'only be written by a spiritual person under the impressions of spiritual influence'. All his own hymns bear that stamp. They have a divine unction upon them, and carry a beauty, pathos and warmth of spiritual experience which strikes a chord in the believer's heart.[4]

To suggest that Toplady 'sounds no depths' in his hymns flies in the face of facts. It is their very 'depth' of theological and experimental content that sometimes makes them hard to sing. The concepts covered in words such as these provide an irrefutable example:

> In him we have a righteousness
>   by God himself approved,
> our rock, our sure foundation this,
>   which never can be moved.
> Our ransom by his death he paid,
>   for all his people given;
> the law he perfectly obeyed,
>   that we might enter heaven.

To demonstrate his poetic gift we may cite one of Toplady's early poems, altered and improved in later years, and seldom matched for lyrical beauty. Based on verses in Revelation 7, he begins, 'I saw, and lo! a countless throng'. And as he looks he muses on the happiness of those who have already entered heaven and exult in the untold blessings of that state. He realizes that some whom he calls his 'junior saints' had been converted later than he, yet had already overtaken him, and had reached the glory first:

Little once I thought that these
would the summit gain
and leave me far behind, slow journeying through the plain.
Loved while on earth; nor less beloved though gone,
think not I envy you your crown;
no; if I could, I would not call you down.
Though slower is my pace,
to you I'll follow on,
leaning on Jesus all the way,
who, now and then, lets down a ray
of comfort from his throne.
The shinings of his grace
soften my passage through the wilderness,
and vines, nectareous, spring where briars grew;
the sweet unveilings of his face
make me at times near half as blest as you.

It was such 'sweet unveilings of his face' that made Toplady what he was, although some may think of him solely in terms of the bitter controversies that sprang up in the late 1760s and early 1770s between the Arminians and Calvinists. True to the intensity and impetuosity of his character, he wrote and gave expression to unacceptable comments about John Wesley. Yet an understanding of the nature of the 'pamphlet wars' that broke out from time to time in the eighteenth century, coupled with the ardent convictions that Toplady held, can in part excuse him. It was not so much at Wesley as a person that he aimed his poisoned barbs, but at what he deemed to be Wesley's betrayal of the truth and of the Church of England. 'Let it not be supposed that I bear them the least degree of personal hatred. God forbid! I have not so learned Christ,' he declared on one occasion, adding, 'the very men that have my opposition have my prayers also.' Called paradoxically the 'saintly sinner', Toplady clearly failed at this point. By not controlling those natural traits that led to such outbursts, he became guilty of invective, even of slander. It must be said, however, that the abuse he received from Wesley and his followers was equally inexcusable.

In contrast we find a pastoral tenderness in Toplady's verse gleaned from his own spiritual experience; he understands the bleakness of the believer's heart when he fears that Christ is not present with him:

> When we in darkness walk
> nor feel the heavenly flame,
> then is the time to trust our God,
> and rest upon his name.
>
> Soon shall our doubts and fears
> subside at his control;
> his loving-kindness shall break through
> the midnight of the soul.

Yet all that Augustus Toplady wrote pales before the supreme effect of his best-known hymn, 'Rock of ages, cleft for me'. Published in 1776, it appeared in its full form in *The Gospel Magazine*. Even his critics allow that this is a great hymn and, as one grudgingly admitted, it 'expresses the profoundest needs of the spirit': the cleansing of the conscience through the saving work of Calvary and the security of the ransomed soul in the extremity of death and final judgement. Often painfully aware of his own sins and shortcomings, Toplady knew where to find cleansing for the troubled conscience:

> Nothing in my hand I bring,
> simply to thy cross I cling;
> naked, come to thee for dress;

> helpless, look to thee for grace;
> foul, I to the fountain fly;
> wash me, Saviour, or I die.

Since his anxious childhood, and through a life of uncertain health and disappointments, Toplady himself had found a secure standing on the Rock of ages. As he expressed it to a parishioner in 1765, 'the water floods shall not overflow thee ... the rock of ages lies at the bottom of the brook; and God will give you a firm footing all the way through.' Several legends have arisen regarding the original circumstances of this hymn. Although Toplady would clearly have been familiar with the awesome cleft rock at Burrington Coombe, near Blagdon, there is no evidence for the tale that he wrote it on a playing card while sheltering there from a storm — an anecdote traced to a Somerset landowner seventy years after Toplady's death.

As we have seen, the reference to Christ as a Rock is scriptural, prefigured in the Old Testament, particularly in the reference to a 'cleft of the rock' in Exodus 33, where God hid Moses. It becomes more apparent in the New Testament, where, referring to the Israelites' desert wanderings, we read that they drank of 'that spiritual Rock that followed them, and that Rock was Christ'.[5] It may well be, however, that Toplady was also familiar with an extract from one of John Wesley's abridged classics quoted in the preface to a 1745 selection of Communion hymns. In it he cited the following words from Dr Daniel Brevint's *The Christian Sacrament and Sacrifice:*

> O Rock of Israel, Rock struck and cleft for me, let those two streams of blood and water which once gushed out of thy side bring down pardon and holiness into my soul; and let me thirst after them now as if I stood ... near the cleft of that rock, the wounds of my Lord.[6]

The similarity between such words and those of Toplady's masterpiece is evident:

> Rock of Ages, cleft for me,
> let me hide myself in thee;
> let the water and the blood,
> from thy riven side which flowed,
> be of sin the double cure,
> cleanse me from its guilt and power.

In 1775, when Augustus Toplady was thirty-four, his broken health convinced him that he needed to leave Devonshire and seek a period of respite. With the arrival of a curate at Broadhembury to care for his people, he set out for Bath to 'take the waters'. There he met the redoubtable Selina, Countess of Huntingdon. After a little persuasion he agreed to serve her chapels, particularly in Brighton where the sea air would have a restorative effect. After ten months of itinerant preaching for the Countess, the opportunity of a London pulpit at last became a reality. In April 1776 Toplady began his ministry at Orange Street Chapel — originally erected some eighty years earlier to meet the needs of the French Huguenots, fleeing persecution in their own land. Quickly the chapel became packed as the people thronged to hear the tall, though slight and pale-looking preacher, whose fiery words soon drove every other thought from their minds. At last Toplady had an outlet for his ministry which his exceptional gifts well merited. Celebrities of the calibre of David Garrick the actor, and the painter Joshua Reynolds, could be seen listening attentively. When he was able, he still spent time in Broadhembury, and the Countess continued to send urgent requests for his services.

Despite the many calls on his time and strength, Toplady undertook the editorship of *The Gospel Magazine* in December 1775, and also prepared sermons and other treatises for the press. More than this he compiled a hymn book entitled *Psalms*

and Hymns for the use of the Orange Street congregation.
'Hymn singing', he declared, 'has proved a converting
ordinance to some, a recovering ordinance to others, and a
comforting ordinance to all; and one of the divinest means of
communion with God.' Among the four hundred and nineteen
hymns chosen, he included half a dozen of his own, and the
book was published in 1776 to 'help Zion's travellers on their
way to the Mount of God'. With a high hand Toplady modified,
edited and improved the compositions of other hymn-writers,
mainly for theological reasons but sometimes for faulty
grammatical constructions, or obscure and banal phraseology.
His alterations were not always an improvement, and have
been called 'hymnological vandalism', particularly when he
dealt with Wesley's verse.

Despite this plethora of activity, Toplady was a sick man.
Evidences of tuberculosis became increasingly obvious, and
death came as no unexpected visitor. His preparation of mind
stretched back over many years, and when he faced the reality,
he was unafraid. Some years earlier he had written a poem to
a dying friend that echoed his own feelings:

> Shudder not to pass the stream:
> venture all your care on him;
> him whose dying love and power
> stilled its tossing, hushed its roar…
> Not one object of his care
> ever suffered shipwreck there.
> See the haven full in view!
> Love divine shall bear you through.
> Trust to that propitious gale,
> weigh your anchor, spread your sail.

In April 1778 his physician urged him not to attempt to
preach again, but regardless of his advice, Toplady made a
brave effort. Too ill to do anything except give out his text,

he had to be helped out of the pulpit and back to his home. Apart from one other brief pulpit appearance, his days of public ministry were over. But another ministry was about to begin — an example to Christians of all time of how a true believer may die in confident faith. In the custom of the times, his friends wrote down some of the expressions which they caught in those remaining weeks of his life: 'I cannot tell you the comforts I feel in my soul,' he confessed to one, 'they are past expression. The consolations of God to such an unworthy wretch are so abundant that he leaves me nothing to pray for. I enjoy a heaven already in my soul.'

Just an hour before he died on 11 August 1778, the thirty-seven-year-old preacher and hymn-writer, weeping tears of sheer joy, was heard to say, 'It will not be long before God takes me, for no mortal man can live after the glories which God has manifested to my soul.' His confidence however, as for any other dying Christian, lay not in any special disclosures of God's presence but in the sacrifice of Jesus Christ for sinners. As he had written:

> While I draw this fleeting breath,
> when my eyelids close in death,
> when I soar through tracts unknown,
> see thee on thy judgement throne,
> Rock of Ages, cleft for me,
> let me hide myself in thee.

Notes

1. Republished Banner of Truth Trust, 1959.
2. Two unstressed syllables, followed by a stressed one, as in the limericks of Edward Lear (1812-88).
3. Eric Routley, *I'll praise my Maker*, p.273.
4. Paul E. G. Cook, 'The Saintly Sinner', Evangelical Library Annual Lecture, 1978.
5. 1 Corinthians 10:4.
6. Quoted by J. R. Watson, *An Annotated Anthology of Hymns*, p.213.

John Newton
(1725-1807)

Grace so amazing

Let us love and sing and wonder,
let us praise the Saviour's name!
He has hushed the law's loud thunder,
he has quenched Mount Sinai's flame;
he has washed us with his blood,
he has brought us nigh to God.

John Newton

John Newton
(1725-1807)

Grace so amazing

A seventeen-year-old sailor awoke suddenly from an alarming dream. For some days after, he could neither eat, sleep nor work satisfactorily, so troubled was he by all he had dreamt.

In his dream John Newton had been standing on the deck of his ship as it sailed out of Venice harbour. A stranger unexpectedly appeared and offered him the gift of a ring. As long as he kept the ring in safety, all would be well with him, the stranger assured him; but if he should lose it, nothing but trouble and disaster would be his lot. Confidently the young man accepted the ring, satisfied that he could fulfil the conditions. Then the stranger disappeared. Just at that moment a second figure appeared and, noting the ring on John's finger, began to persuade him that he was being deceived. The thing was worthless, and the sooner he flung it over the side of the ship into the depths below the better. Sceptical at first, the dreamer was at last convinced by such insinuations and plucking off the ring cast it overboard. No sooner had it touched the water than flames lit up the skyline. The distant Alps were all on fire.

Then the second stranger, none other than the devil himself, told John that the ring he had just jettisoned represented all the mercy of God reserved for him. Now it was gone for ever. All that remained was fiery judgement and John must accompany him immediately to the burning mountains. At that moment of horror and despair, the first stranger reappeared. When he heard the sorry tale, he reprimanded the young man for his folly. Would he be more careful if he had the ring back? Scarcely could he give an answer before the stranger vanished into the sea and soon returned bringing the ring with him. As John joyfully stretched out his hand to take it back, the stranger said, 'If you should be entrusted with this ring again, you would very soon bring yourself into the same distress. You are not able to keep it, but I will preserve it for you and whenever it is needful will produce it on your behalf.'

In later years John Newton could see that this dream mirrored his subsequent experiences and had been sent by God as a warning of the consequences of his present reckless and unbelieving way of life. But after the initial alarm had worn off, Newton managed to put such thoughts from his mind. Born in 1725, John had a godly mother whose influence both spiritually and intellectually had been wholly beneficial. But when she died in 1732, shortly before the boy's seventh birthday, the loss spelled disaster for the child. His father, a remote and austere figure, was himself a sea captain and could give little time to his son. Despite several attempts to reform his ways during his teenage years, John had gradually drifted first into a careless lifestyle and then into agnosticism.

At the age of nineteen, as he was idling away his time, the young man was press-ganged into the navy. With war threatening, the country needed an effective naval force, and this was one method regularly used to obtain it. The *Harwich* on which Newton was compelled to serve was bound for the distant East Indies and he was desperate to avoid such a trip. Two years earlier he had met and fallen in love with Mary Catlett, the fourteen-year-old daughter of old family friends. The thought of a prolonged sea voyage, with its necessary separation from the girl he loved, seemed insufferable. But his efforts to obtain his release or escape from the ship proved futile and only resulted in savage punishment.

As Newton watched the English shoreline fade into the distance, he was forced to accept the inevitable separation. Through a variety of circumstances, however, he managed to exchange ships and, instead of sailing to the East Indies, joined a merchant ship bound for the west coast of Africa. But soon after his arrival he fell under the power of a slave owner named Clow and his black mistress, until he had become little more than a slave himself. During the months that followed, John Newton was to endure intense cruelty and privation. Starving and ill, he would creep out at night and pull up roots in the plantation, eating them raw and making himself sick as a consequence. But the hardness of the natural heart apart from God's grace is demonstrated in this sorry chapter of Newton's life, for these experiences and others equally gruelling left him as unbelieving and cynical as before. Well could he confess:

> In evil long I took delight,
> unawed by shame or fear...

Only the thought of Mary, and the remote possibility that one day he might be able to return to England to claim her for his own, kept hope alive in those dark days. To preserve his mind from collapsing beneath such conditions, Newton studied the only book he had in his possession, the theories of Euclid, the third-century Greek mathematician, tracing out the geometrical diagrams in the sand with a stick. Writing to his father whenever a ship was returning to England, Newton urged him to forward the purchase price for his freedom and to commission a captain of some vessel to find him and bring him home.

A change in his situation, however, enabled the young Englishman to enter the service of another trader, bringing a significant improvement in his prospects. When at last a ship commissioned by John's father to search for his son sailed along the coast, it happened to pass the remote beach where John was standing. Seeing an English vessel, John lit a fire and sent out a smoke signal, causing the captain to dispatch a small boat to shore. There he discovered the very man he was looking for; but he also found that Newton was now not so eager to return home. Conjuring up a false story about a legacy that had been left to John, the captain lured Newton to come aboard the vessel and then resumed his journey. After some months of further trading along the coast, the captain set his ship on her homeward course.

Although John Newton still had no thought for God nor for his eternal destiny — indeed he was not even convinced that man did not perish like the animals — God's time for him was approaching. He had been glancing casually through a copy of a work by Thomas à Kempis, *The Imitation of Christ,* which he discovered on board. This caused him to reflect on his life, but one night, as Newton turned into his bunk as usual, disaster struck. A violent storm hit the vessel. Powerful waves ripped away the boarding, and the ship was fast sinking. Life expectancy for all on board seemed now only a question of hours — for some, only moments — as they were dashed from the ship into the raging sea. Strapping himself to the rigging, Newton attempted to bale out the water rushing into the ship. He toiled endlessly although the endeavour seemed hopeless. After many hours, exhausted and numb, the young man offered a half-prayer, the first for many years: 'If this will not do, the Lord have mercy on us.' His prayer was a surprise even to himself. Mercy? How could he expect mercy? It would be better if he perished in the waves, because if God did exist he would have to send him to hell. Perhaps some thought of the lost ring of his dream came back to his mind. Words he later wrote express his thoughts:

> The case is too plain,
>> I had my own choice;
> again and again
>> I slighted his voice;
> his warnings neglected
>> his patience abused,
> his gospel rejected,
>> his mercy refused.

But God did have mercy on John Newton. Battered and leaking, the ship eventually weathered the storm and limped to haven on the Irish coast. For Newton himself, now twenty-three years of age, these events proved the beginning of his quest for salvation. In the coming weeks and months he read the Scriptures, prayed earnestly and step by step turned from his profanity and unbelief, casting himself on the mercy of a forgiving God. As at the dawn of day, light gradually grows stronger and brighter, so the truth increasingly illumined Newton's mind: morally awakened, he was now concerned to please God, while still remaining a stranger to true saving faith and the power of the indwelling Spirit.

Understandably Newton lost little time before he visited Mary who lived in Chatham, Kent. To his joy he discovered that she was still free and not averse to continuing a friendship, but was not yet ready to commit herself to him. Before long Newton set out on another voyage bound for the coast of West Africa, but this time in the position of ship's mate. As he mingled with godless company once more, the strong spiritual impressions grew fainter and by the time the ship reached its destination he had to confess, 'I seemed to have forgot all the Lord's mercies … and was, profaneness excepted, almost as bad as before.'

But God intervened yet again, this time by allowing the young sailor to succumb to a serious fever. With his life hanging in the balance Newton, no longer hardened as before, realized how seriously he had spurned God's mercies. Was all hope gone for ever?

> Weak and almost delirious, I arose from my bed and crept to a retired part of the island; and there I found a renewed liberty to pray. I durst make no more resolves but cast myself before the Lord, to do with me as he should please. I do not remember any particular text … but in general I was able to hope and believe in a crucified Saviour. The burden was removed from my conscience and not only my peace but my health was restored… And from that time, I trust, I have been delivered from the power and dominion of sin.

John Newton was now a new man in Christ. Problems and inconsistencies there still were, but he now had an inner strength and motivation to deal with them. Well could he write:

> O, can I e'er that day forget,
>   when Jesus kindly spoke!
> Poor soul, my blood has paid your debt,
>   and now I break your yoke.

In 1750 John Newton at last married Mary Catlett. For eight long years he had loved her: she was now twenty-two and John was twenty-five. Fourteen more years would elapse before Newton, after overcoming many obstacles, would eventually enter the ministry of the Church of England. But these intervening years formed an essential period in his life for he had much to learn about the Christian gospel and much to unlearn as well — remnants of his previous lifestyle. Of his new desires to please God, he could say:

Saved by blood, I live to tell
    what the love of Christ has done:
he redeemed my soul from hell,
    of a rebel made a son.
O! I tremble still to think
    how secure I lived in sin;
sporting on destruction's brink
    yet preserved from falling in!

During this period Newton spent six years as captain of slave-trading vessels that plied their trade to and from the west coast of Africa. At first he appeared to see little amiss in so grotesque an activity, but gradually began to be 'shocked with an employment that was perpetually connected with chains, bolts and shackles'. In 1754, however, a sudden illness spelt the end of Newton's seafaring days. For the next nine years he was employed as the Tide Surveyor for the port of Liverpool. An important task, it involved, in part, a diligent search of incoming vessels for contraband, and over the period of the Seven Years War from 1756 to 1763 the safety of shipping using Liverpool harbour rested on the Tide Surveyor's powers of detection. 'I have a good office, with fire and candle, and fifty or sixty people under my direction,' wrote Newton.

Ever since he had written mocking rhymes for the ship's crew to sing in order to deride the captain of one of the vessels in which he sailed, John Newton had shown remarkable facility to express himself in verse. With a heart renewed by the Spirit of God, he continued to write, but to a far different strain. The sense of Christ's presence now became all-important to him:

When my Saviour, my Shepherd, is near,
    how quickly my sorrows depart!
New beauties around me appear,
    new spirits enliven my heart.

His presence gives peace to my soul,
    and Satan assaults me in vain;
while my Shepherd his power controls,
    I think I no more shall complain.[1]

These years were strategic in Newton's life, for during this
period God gave him some Christian friends whose influence on
him was wholly beneficial. He also met some of the outstanding
men of the evangelical revival, including George Whitefield,
the Wesley brothers and William Grimshaw. Grimshaw's
friendship came at a crucial juncture in Newton's life, as he
himself declared in a tribute written many years later:

> I number it amongst the many great mercies of my life
> that I was favoured with his notice, edified (I hope) by his
> instruction, and encouraged and directed by his advice
> at a critical time when my own mind was much engaged
> with a desire of entering the ministry.

The two men met only twice, the first occasion being in 1758
after Newton recorded 'an indifferent journey the weather
being rough' across the Pennines. He would, however, have
received a warm welcome from the rugged curate of Haworth.
They had much to share, for both grieved over an ungodly
past. It was Newton who first gave to the Christian public an
extended account of Grimshaw's life and ministry. And we may
well suppose that it was the curate of Haworth who encouraged
Newton to write an account of his own experiences, which he
did shortly after this visit — an account that would be much
used in the purposes of God.[2]

    With a strong desire to serve his generation and to
compensate as he was able for the wasted years, Newton
confided to Grimshaw his wish to enter the Christian ministry.
Encouraged by his new friend, he tried to obtain ordination
but was refused by the bishops. His identification with the

Methodists, coupled with his lack of formal education, were probable contributory factors. When Lord Dartmouth[3] was shown Newton's *Authentic Narrative*, still only in manuscript form, he was deeply impressed and used his considerable influence with the bishops to gain ordination for Newton, also offering him an appointment to a country curacy in Olney, Buckinghamshire, where he himself owned property. Newton saw the providence of God in all these things:

> And since his name we knew,
>   how gracious has he been!
> What dangers has he led us through,
>   what mercies have we seen!
>
> Our lot in future years
>   unable to foresee,
> he, kindly to prevent our fears,
>   says, 'Leave it all to me.'

The living to which Newton had been appointed in 1764 was not well endowed, yielding only a meagre income of £50 a year, £20 of which had to be paid to the previous incumbent. Apart from the help of generous friends like Lord Dartmouth and John Thornton, Christian businessman and philanthropist,[4] John and Mary Newton would have often been in need. His own experiences are reflected in his words:

> The birds without barn
>   and storehouse are fed;
> from them let us learn
>   to trust for our bread:
> his saints what is fitting
>   shall ne'er be denied,
> so long as it's written,
>   'The Lord will provide.'

Gratitude for God's provision, mingled with wonder at his unexpected mercy, can be found as the backdrop to almost all the verses which John Newton composed:

> Determined to save,
>   he watched o'er my path
> when, Satan's blind slave,
>   I sported with death:
> and can he have taught me
>   to trust in his name,
> and thus far have brought me
>   to put me to shame?

Not long after his arrival in Olney, Newton began to establish several regular gatherings for prayer in the parish. In January 1765 he noted in his diary, 'We now have a fixed little company who come to my house of sabbath evening after tea. We spend an hour or more in prayer and singing...' Hymn-singing — whether his own hymns or those of others, we do not know — played an important part in Newton's early ministry and it was at these home gatherings that hymns were sung, for they were not yet permitted in the stated services of worship in the Established Church. Before long a regular meeting for prayer and ministry had been introduced on a Tuesday evening, one that proved particularly popular, and for these occasions Newton had begun composing hymns related to his messages and to the theme of prayer.

In 1767, three years after he had begun his ministry in Olney, a highly significant event occurred in Newton's life. A small and recently bereaved family unit arrived in the town, having rented a home close by the vicarage. Mary Unwin, her two children and their lodger, a friend of the family, moved from their home in Huntingdon following the death of Mary's husband Morley. The lodger, none other than the poet William Cowper, was to form a lifelong friendship with Newton — a friendship that would immeasurably enrich Christian hymnody.

Discovering his new friend's poetic talent, Newton stimulated Cowper into helping him to compose hymns for these Tuesday meetings. Before long the numbers wishing to attend each week had increased to such an extent that alternative accommodation became necessary. In 1769 the meeting was transferred to the 'Great House', as the locals called the home of Lord Dartmouth that stood not far from the church. For the first prayer gatherings in the 'Great Room' Newton composed the words:

> Great Shepherd of thy people, hear,
>   thy presence now display;
> as thou hast given a place for prayer,
>   so give us hearts to pray.
>
> Show us some token of thy love
>   our fainting hope to raise;
> and pour thy blessing from above,
>   that we may render praise.

Originally beginning with the words 'O Lord, our languid souls inspire', it ended with an aspiration of yet greater blessing on the preaching of the gospel:

> And may the gospel's joyful sound
>   enforced by mighty grace,
> awaken many sinners round,
>   to come and fill the place.

A number of different hymnals had been published during the 1750s and 1760s: Joseph Hart's collection in 1759, Martin Madan (a cousin of William Cowper) brought out his *Psalms and Hymns* in 1763 and Selina, Countess of Huntingdon's

Olney Church

first collection came in 1765. Newton and Cowper had both already published specimens of their verse in such periodicals as *The Gospel Magazine*; and certainly by 1771 Newton was contemplating the possibility that his contributions, together with Cowper's, might be collected together and published as a hymn book, initially for the use of his Olney parishioners. Two men more different in temperament it would be hard to find, but they complemented each other; and although Cowper had the superior talent, in the opinion of John Julian in his *Dictionary of Hymnology*, the best work of both is equally rich. Julian adds, 'A comparison of both will show no great inequality between them. Amid much that is bald, tame and matter-of-fact, Newton's rich acquaintance with Scripture, knowledge of the heart, directness and force, and a certain sailor imagination, tell strongly.'

The book, known as *Olney Hymns,* was not, in fact, published until 1779. The delay, as Newton explained in his preface, was caused by Cowper's long depressive illness, which began in January 1773. 'My grief and disappointment were great,' he wrote, 'I hung my harp upon the willows, and for some time thought myself determined to proceed no further without him.' But at last he overcame his reluctance, and even though he had only sixty-eight hymns by Cowper to include in comparison to two hundred and eighty-one of his own, he proceeded to publication.

Openly acknowledging his debt to Isaac Watts whose tradition he aimed to follow, Newton emulated him in a number of ways. Even the layout of *Olney Hymns* bears striking resemblance to Watts' own collection of *Hymns and Spiritual Songs* published in 1709. Both are divided into three books; both begin with hymns on selected passages of Scripture, a hundred and forty-one items in the case of *Olney Hymns.* Both have a second book of 'free compositions', *Olney Hymns* including a further one hundred on subjects as diverse as the Day of Judgement and an allegorical comparison between the spider and the bee. Only in the third book do the two collections differ markedly. Watts includes mainly doxologies and hymns suitable for the Lord's Supper, where Newton and Cowper provide a further one hundred and seven items dealing with all aspects of the Christian life, from warnings to the unrepentant, to conversion, consolations and glory to come.

Newton would later describe himself as an able versifier rather than a poet; but he underestimated his gift, for his words flow naturally and rhythmically, touching the heart and experience of the believer. Frequently making use of the first person singular in his lines, he spoke not only for himself but for all who would sing his hymns. 'The workings of the heart of man and of the Spirit of God are in general the same in all who are the subjects of grace,' he states in the preface, adding that the convictions his hymns conveyed were 'the fruit and expression of my own experience'.

Newton believed, however, that hymn-writing differed from poetry in one or two essential elements. First, its meaning had to be immediately apparent to the singer, especially as few would have copies of the words, and many of his first parishioners were illiterate in any case. Each line or couplet would need to be complete in itself to facilitate the practice of giving out the hymns line by line. To make this easier still, Newton employed largely monosyllabic words, as in a hymn like:

> Show me what I have to do;
>   every hour my strength renew;
> let me live a life of faith;
>   let me die thy people's death.

The effectiveness of the following verse lies in the simplicity of the words Newton chooses:

> One there is above all others,
>   well deserves the name of Friend;
> his is love beyond a brother's,
>   costly, free and knows no end:
> they who once his kindness prove,
> find it everlasting love.

In addition, because a hymn was intended for use in public worship, Newton believed that it should be stripped of flights of fanciful language so dear to poets, keeping the use of metaphors and other imagery to a minimum. He recognized that this represented self-denial on the poet's part, but with his own 'mediocrity of talent' he said this did not present him with much of a problem. With his rhymes strong and accurate, he hoped his hymns would satisfy the poetically sensitive, but his primary aim was always usefulness to the church of Jesus Christ.

Like Watts, the metres Newton employed were generally short metre, long metre and common metre and the majority of his hymns were in four-line verses, either in rhyming couplets or rhyming alternate lines. To these he added the 87.87 metre, often using it doubled as in such hymns as 'Glorious things of thee are spoken/Zion, city of our God'. But he would also adopt less common structures to fit the mood of his words. Unusual for Newton, or indeed for any hymn-writer, was the three-line verse, but he was able to use the arrangement to good effect in 'Why should I fear the darkest hour?' A distinct pattern may be traced in many of the verses. In the first line he states his problem, in the second he exhorts his own soul on the basis of truths from God's Word, and in the third adds a further biblical incentive to encourage himself:

> Though sin would fill me with distress
> the throne of grace I dare address,
> for Jesus is my righteousness.

> Though faint my prayers and cold my love,
> my steadfast hope shall not remove,
> while Jesus intercedes above.
>
> Against me earth and hell combine;
> but on my side is power divine;
> Jesus is all, and he is mine.

Sometimes he would experiment with a 55.55.65.65 metre in a hymn in which he wished to present a strong argument either to himself or to others:

> Begone, unbelief,
>   my Saviour is near,
> and for my relief
>   will quickly appear:
> by prayer let me wrestle,
>   and he will perform;
> with Christ in the vessel,
>   I smile at the storm.

This bright anapaestic beat, favoured also by Toplady in such hymns as 'A debtor to mercy alone', forms an effective medium for this aspect of Newton's skill. In a number of his hymns he presents a reasoned argument, almost a storyline, that might well echo the thoughts and perplexities of the believer:

> 'Tis a point I long to know,
>   oft it causes anxious thought —
> Do I love the Lord, or no?
>   Am I his, or am I not?

He then lists all the reasons that cause him to doubt his spiritual position, followed by all the signs, however small, of grace in the heart, and then concludes:

> Lord, decide the doubtful case!
>> Thou who art thy people's sun;
> shine upon thy work of grace,
>> if it be indeed begun.

In addition to this narrative style, Newton often uses direct speech to make his point. A well-known example is found in the following lines:

> I asked the Lord that I might grow
>> in faith and love and every grace,
> might more of his salvation know,
>> and seek more earnestly his face.

He then tells of the strange way in which his prayer was answered, not in extra measures of blessing, but by trials and pains:

> 'Lord, why is this?' I trembling cried,
>> 'Wilt thou pursue thy worm to death?'
> ''Tis in this way,' the Lord replied,
>> 'I answer prayer for grace and faith.'

At the close of the hymn God reveals that this is indeed an answer to his prayer:

> 'These inward trials I employ,
>> from self and pride to set thee free,
> and break thy schemes of earthly joy,
>> that thou mayst seek thy all in me.'

Such lines, so helpful to Christians, are clearly more suitable for private meditation.

Newton also employs what has been called 'the argument of faith' in which he reasons with himself, or even with Satan,

arguing that in God's greater mercies we may find a guarantee
for every lesser mercy:

> If he shed his precious blood
>   to bring me to the fold,
> can I think that meaner [lesser] good
>   he ever will withhold?
> Satan, vain is thy device!
>   Here my hope rests well assured,
> and in that grand redemption price
>   I see the whole secured.

Newton could never forget the debt he owed to the grace of
God. Even when he wrote hymns on prayer he remembered
the burden of a guilty conscience from which Christ had liber-
ated him:

> Approach, my soul, the mercy-seat,
>   where Jesus answers prayer;
> there humbly fall before his feet,
>   for none can perish there.
>
> O wondrous love, to bleed and die,
>   to bear the cross and shame;
> that guilty sinners, such as I,
>   might plead thy gracious name.

He made use of his own experiences of God's mercy as an encouragement to himself and to others to persevere in the difficult
exercise of prayer. Again he employs 'the argument of faith':

> Once a sinner near despair
> sought thy mercy-seat by prayer;
> mercy heard and set him free:
> Lord, that mercy came to me.

> Thou hast helped in every need,
> this emboldens me to plead;
> after so much mercy past,
> canst thou let me sink at last?
>
> No! I must maintain my hold;
> 'Tis thy goodness makes me bold:
> I can no denial take
> when I plead for Jesus' sake.

There is a note of confident faith in Newton's hymns, a vigour and gladness that marked his whole personality. The man or woman who recognizes the power of the blood of Christ to cleanse from all the guilt of past sin cannot but celebrate God's mercy:

> Let us love and sing and wonder,
>   let us praise the Saviour's name!
> He has hushed the law's loud thunder,
>   he has quenched Mount Sinai's flame;
>   he has washed us with his blood,
>   he has brought us nigh to God.
>
> Let us wonder; grace and justice
>   join, and point to mercy's store;
> when through grace in Christ our trust is,
>   justice smiles, and asks no more.
>   He who washed us with his blood
>   has secured our way to God.

To convey the spirit of his theme, Newton chose to use a fast-moving trochaic metre, as he did for a number of his other hymns. When the strong beat is placed on the first syllable of each word, as in this metre, it is not as easy to find suitable rhymes; but Newton generally succeeds admirably, although 'trust is'/'justice' and 'before us'/'chorus' are not so well matched.

Not only did the hymn-writer rejoice, but he wanted the worshippers to rejoice with him, and so he wrote:

> Rejoice, believer, in the Lord,
>   who makes your cause his own;
> the hope that's built upon his word
>   can ne'er be overthrown.
>
> As surely as he overcame
>   and triumphed once for you;
> so surely you that love his name
>   shall triumph in him too.

John Newton had studied well both his own heart and the hearts of his people and knew how to counsel despondent or anxious Christians who feared that their sins and failures might exclude them from God's mercy. Calling upon his own experience, he could write such words as:

> True, I've been a foolish creature,
>   and have sinned against his grace!
> But forgiveness is his nature,
>   though he justly hides his face:
>   ere he called me, well he knew
>   what a heart like mine would do.

The concepts covered in Newton's hymns are straightforward and strike a chord in every Christian's heart. 'Amazing grace' has become a front runner in terms of popularity for this very reason, but also because of its lilting folksy tune — there can be few Christians who are unfamiliar with such words as:

> Through many dangers, toils and snares
>> I have already come;
> his grace has brought me safe thus far,
>> and grace will lead me home.

A close competitor, and perhaps equally widely used, is Newton's well-loved hymn on the names of Christ:

> How sweet the name of Jesus sounds
>> in a believer's ear!
> It soothes his sorrows, heals his wounds,
>> and drives away his fear.

Another favourite, also written in trochaic metre, is his masterpiece on the church and the privileges of the Christian:

> Glorious things of thee are spoken,
>> Zion, city of our God!
> He, whose word cannot be broken,
>> formed thee for his own abode.
> On the Rock of Ages founded,
>> what can shake thy sure repose?
> with salvation's walls surrounded
>> thou may'st smile at all thy foes.

Drawing his thoughts from many different portions of Scripture, Newton glories in the benefits of the redeemed people of God, and encourages every disheartened believer to lift up his head and rejoice in his heritage both here and in the world to come:

> Saviour, if of Zion's city
>> I through grace a member am,
> let the world deride or pity,

I will glory in thy name:
fading is the worldling's pleasure,
        all his boasted pomp and show;
solid joys and lasting treasure
        none but Zion's children know.

The majority of verses in *Olney Hymns* are not, in fact, strictly hymns at all. Whether some were ever sung as such is doubtful. A number consist of a straight retelling of a Scripture text, as in the story of Naaman the leper:

Before Elisha's gate
the Syrian leper stood,
but could not brook to wait —
he deemed himself too good…

But always in these hymns based on Scripture narrative Newton would bring out some application of the text to the circumstances of those who read or sung his lines. After recounting the miracle of the raising of Jairus' daughter he writes:

Fear not, then, distressed believer,
        venture on his mighty name;
he is able to deliver,
        and his love is still the same.

Sometimes Newton would weave parables from natural phenomena. In a piece entitled 'The Thaw', he writes:

The ice and snow we lately saw,
which covered all the ground,
are melted soon before the thaw,
and can no more be found.

And turning the theme to spiritual profit, Newton continues:

> Jesus, we in thy name entreat,
> reveal thy gracious arm;
> and grant thy Spirit's kindly heat,
> our frozen souls to warm!

In 1780 John Newton accepted a call to a London pulpit, that of St Mary Woolnoth, and with regret left Olney after sixteen years. He was then fifty-five years of age and for the next twenty-five years or more ministered to a far different congregation from the one made up of his rural parishioners in Olney. Politicians, noblemen and well-heeled Londoners could now be found among his hearers.

Newton experienced many sorrows in his long life. Without any children of their own, John and Mary took in Mary's two nieces, Betsey Catlett and Eliza Cunningham, both of whom had lost their parents. They loved them as if they were their own daughters. Eliza died at the age of fifteen and Betsey suffered a mental breakdown which meant a spell in 'Bedlam', the infamous mental institution of the day. But no sorrow was more acute than the loss of his dearly loved wife Mary in 1790 after forty years of marriage. Speaking of his grief, John confessed, 'the world seemed to die with her'. These things encouraged Newton to keep his eyes steadfastly on a better world. As he had written many years before in *Olney Hymns,* he was like a tired traveller who views his destination from the top of some hill:

> Thus when the Christian pilgrim views,
> by faith, his mansion in the skies,
> the sight his fainting strength renews,
> and wings his speed to reach the prize.

> The thought of home his spirit cheers,
>   no more he grieves for troubles past;
> nor any future trial fears
>   so he may safe arrive at last.

In 1807 the grand old preacher and hymn-writer came to the end of his pilgrimage. Deaf and nearly blind, he had been urged by his friends to give up preaching. 'What!' he roared, 'I cannot stop. Shall an old African blasphemer stop while he can talk?' When he died on 21 December 1807 at the age of eighty-two, his epitaph, which he himself composed, read in part as follows:

JOHN NEWTON

Clerk

ONCE AN INFIDEL AND LIBERTINE,

A SERVANT OF SLAVES IN AFRICA,

WAS

BY THE RICH MERCY

OF OUR LORD AND SAVIOUR

JESUS CHRIST

PRESERVED, RESTORED, PARDONED,

AND APPOINTED TO PREACH THE FAITH

HE HAD LONG LABOURED TO DESTROY.

Notes

1. Written in 1763 — one of the earliest hymns Newton wrote.
2. *An Authentic Narrative of some Remarkable and Interesting Particulars in the Life of John Newton*, first published 1764.
3. Lord Dartmouth, evangelical peer, converted through Whitefield's preaching at the home of Selina, Countess of Huntingdon, was soon to be appointed to the Privy Council and later became President of the Board of Trade. His support for evangelical causes was highly significant in the revival.
4. John Thornton, one of the richest men in the land, donated more than £3,000 to provide for the Newtons during their time at Olney.

William Cowper
(1731-1800)

'God is his own interpreter'

My song shall bless the Lord of all,
my praise shall climb to his abode;
thee, Saviour, by that name I call,
the great supreme, the mighty God.

William Cowper

William Cowper
(1731-1800)

'God is his own interpreter'

My mother! When I learn'd that thou wast dead,
say, wast thou conscious of the tears I shed?
Hovered thy spirit o'er thy sorrowing son,
wretch even then, life's journey just begun?
Perhaps thou gav'st me, though unseen, a kiss;
perhaps a tear, if souls can weep in bliss...

Such words, written by William Cowper when he was almost sixty years of age and a national poet, carry their own story of the depth of sorrow a six-year-old child experienced when his mother died. Ann Cowper, who came from a well-established Norfolk family, had been a tender and loving mother, and her death at the age of thirty-four, a few days after the birth of her seventh child John left a permanent scar on William's life. Born in November 1731, William was Ann's fourth child. His father, John Cowper, sprang from one of the large land-owning families of England and served as rector of Berkhampsted, in Hertfordshire.

Details of William Cowper's childhood days may be gleaned from further lines in this poem which he entitled, 'On the Receipt of my Mother's Portrait out of Norfolk'. Insignificant details they may be: the biscuit or sugar plum his mother pressed into his hand as he set off for school dressed in a warm red coat; the last-minute checks on her young son at night to see he was safely settled in bed... The loss of such a mother was irreparable and particularly for a child with a disposition as sensitive as William's. Nor was this the only sorrow of his childhood days. Two of his siblings died in infancy and three more failed to reach adult

Cowper's mother

years. Apart from William himself, only John, whose birth had precipitated his mother's death, reached maturity, and a close bond of affection existed between the two remaining brothers.

Bullying at school was as much an eighteenth-century problem as it is today. When the six-year-old was sent to a boarding school shortly after his mother's death, probably by a father too distraught to be able to care adequately for his young family, William was an obvious target for such torment. In sharp contrast with the joys he had so recently lost, Cowper records some of the 'barbarities' he suffered at the hands of a fifteen-year-old:

> It will be sufficient to say that he had, by his savage treat-ment of me, impressed such a dread of his figure upon my mind, that I well remember being afraid to lift up my eyes upon him higher than his knees; and that I knew him by his shoe buckles, better than any other part of his dress. May the Lord pardon him and may we meet in glory!

Yet even such circumstances were not without spiritual value to the boy. He records that one day as he was sitting alone on a school bench, dreading the approach of his tormentor, a verse of Scripture flashed into his mind, 'I will not be afraid. What can man do unto me?'[1] 'Instantly,' he recorded, 'I perceived in myself a briskness of spirits, and a cheerfulness which I had never before experienced; and took several paces up and down the room with joyful alacrity — his gift in whom I trusted.'

Soon after this he suffered such a severe eye inflammation that he was taken from the school, and went to live with a leading oculist who could give the necessary treatment. It would seem that his trouble cleared up and at about ten years of age William was sent to Westminster School. Here he worked well, excelling not only in academic subjects, but also in sport, becoming adept at both cricket and football. On leaving school the eighteen-year-old youth was articled for three years to a London solicitor, and went to live in Ely Place, prior to his admittance to the Middle Temple in 1752.

As many as thirty biographies and biographical sketches have been written dealing with the fascinating and often sad life of William Cowper. In addition there have been numerous academic dissertations and critical studies of his verse. It would be a mistake, however, to imagine a pall of sadness resting over the youth from his earliest days — a concept for which Cowper himself may be partly to blame, by describing himself in the poem quoted above, as a 'wretch even then, life's journey just begun'. Like many other young men, he would enjoy the company of his peers and with a number of former Westminster boys set up the 'Nonsense Club' which met weekly and, true to its name, existed for 'trivial pursuits'. Some of Cowper's early verse shows a strong element of humour in his make-up:

> William was once a bashful youth;
>   his modesty was such,
> that one might say (to say the truth),
>   he rather had too much…
>
> Howe'er, it happened, by degrees,
>   he mended and grew perter;
> in company was more at ease,
>   and dressed a little smarter.

Although the Cowper family had produced outstanding lawyers and politicians, law was a discipline for which William was unfitted both by temperament and inclination. Describing his mental state during his apprenticeship, he wrote, 'I was struck with such a dejection of spirits as none but they who have felt the same can have the least conception of. Day and night I was upon the rack, lying down in horror and rising up in despair.' Despite this, in the summer of 1754 Cowper completed his training and was called to the Bar.

Although averse to his lot in life, William's days were brightened by frequent visits to his cousins, Harriet and Theodora Cowper, who lived nearby. With them he relaxed, spending his time 'giggling and making giggle instead of studying the Law'. Before long a strong affection sprang up between William and Theodora. His subsequent engagement to her, followed in 1756 by the harsh manner in which Theodora's father insisted that the relationship should be terminated, has been well chronicled. Ashley Cowper had noted his nephew's depressive tendencies — a family trait which Theodora shared — and perhaps feared that the marriage of cousins would accentuate the characteristic. This circumstance left a deep scar on William's sensitive nature. Over the years he wrote a number of poems addressed to 'Delia' (his pseudonym for Theodora) that express the depth of his grief:

> But now, sole partner in my Delia's heart,
>> yet doomed far off in exile to complain,
> eternal absence cannot ease my smart,
>> and hope subsists but to prolong my pain.

Theodora, for her part, never married nor forgot her early affection for William. Throughout her life she sent anonymous gifts to him through her sister Harriet, who retained a warm friendship with the poet. It is hard to believe that William did not guess the source of such generous provision. She treasured up his early poems to her, sealing them in an envelope, only to be opened after her death.

Not only did Cowper suffer the loss of Theodora at this time but also two deaths affected him, first that of his father, followed by that of a close friend, William Russell, who was drowned while bathing. These events were clearly related to the onset of Cowper's subsequent stormy experiences and mental distress as he prepared to proceed to Chambers at the Inner Temple in 1759. But despite his periods of black depression, Cowper's attractive personality meant that he was never short of friends who were willing to help him and even provide for him financially, for he had little idea how to manage his slender resources.

His situation deteriorated dramatically early in 1763 when Ashley Cowper attempted to 'settle' his nephew in life by procuring an opportunity for him to fill a vacant post as clerk to the committee of the House of Lords. Intensely shy, lacking in confidence and given to prolonged self-analysis, Cowper was unhappy about a number of circumstances surrounding this offer and felt quite unable to face the interviews with the necessary speeches and appearance at the Bar of the House. As the appointed time for his presentation drew closer, he endured increasing mental anguish, and finally a nervous collapse leading to several desperate and farcical attempts to take his own life.

William Cowper might have wished to terminate his miserable existence, but God had other plans for this man — plans that have lifted many others to new trust and faith in God's wise overruling purposes in times of distress. Nor was Cowper without thoughts of God at this time, but they were misguided and seriously flawed. His distorted judgement suggested, 'Surely, you must have committed the unforgivable sin and final damnation will soon be your portion.' Even hell seemed too good for him … and so he wrote:

> Man disavows, and Deity disowns me,
> hell might afford my miseries a shelter;
> therefore, hell keeps her ever-hungry mouth all
>   bolted against me.

But help was at hand. First, his brother John did all in his power to alleviate William's suffering. Then, in his need, William asked to see another cousin of his, Martin Madan, whose conversion under the preaching of John Wesley had shaken the legal world in which he had already made a mark some years earlier. Madan spoke to him of forgiveness of sins, through the cleansing blood of Christ, and of his power to heal the wounded spirit. William was comforted but still far from well. His brother, together with another close friend, made arrangements for him to be placed under the care of the evangelical Dr Nathaniel Cotton, a well-reputed and kindly physician of the mentally ill, who kept a home in St Albans.

As the months passed under Cotton's wise supervision, the darkness enveloping Cowper gradually began to lighten. Hearing that his brother's condition was improving, John, now an ordained man living in Cambridge, came to visit him, but was disappointed to find William still talking about imminent judgement which must surely fall on him. John, who did not hold evangelical beliefs, protested stoutly against the delusion of such a notion. Bursting into tears, William proclaimed with a mixture of doubt and hope, 'If it be a delusion then am I the happiest of all beings.' And at the back of his mind a voice kept sounding, 'Yet there is mercy; yet there is mercy.' Indeed there was. Not many days later, as he was wandering in the garden of the home in St Albans, Cowper found an open Bible left on a seat. There he read of Christ's sorrow over the death of his friend Lazarus, and William's hope in the same merciful, pitying Saviour grew stronger. Some days later, as he opened his own Bible at random, his eyes alighted on Romans 3:25.[2] God's moment of healing, both spiritual and mental, had come for William Cowper. He tells us what happened next:

> Immediately I received strength to believe, and the full beams of the Sun of Righteousness shone upon me. I saw the sufficiency of the atonement he had made, my pardon sealed in his blood, and all the fulness and completeness of his justification. In a moment I believed and received the gospel.

Lines he wrote at the time express his new understanding:

> All my chains at once were broken,
>   from my feet my fetters fell,
> and that word in pity spoken,
>   snatched me from the gates of hell.
> Grace divine, how sweet the sound,
>   sweet the grace that I have found!

Still not secure enough to leave Nathaniel Cotton's compassionate care, Cowper remained a further year in St Albans, but by 1765 felt well enough to venture out. Naturally, the only place he wanted to be was within easy distance of his brother in Cambridge and so he moved to lodgings in nearby Huntingdon. Resigning his position at the Bar, Cowper now had no source of income and depended on the generosity of his relatives and friends, especially upon an anonymous donor, almost certainly Theodora.

Shy as he was, Cowper settled quickly among the Christians who met for worship in Huntingdon, feeling 'full of love to all the congregation'. Many were attracted to the genteel yet quixotic young man who had just arrived, and particularly one family — the Unwins. Cowper's friendship with this family of four, Morley and Mary Unwin, their son William, and daughter, eighteen-year-old Susanna, was such that it was not long before they invited him to move in with them as a permanent lodger. He enjoyed rich spiritual fellowship with the family and particularly with Mary Unwin, eight years his senior, who would act the part of a mother for most of the poet's life. Their relationship belongs to the realm of God's timely and perfect provisions for his people, and especially for a man like Cowper whose loss of a mother's care had left serious wounds.

These days were among the happiest of the poet's life. With new-found spiritual joys and few domestic cares, he had leisure to enjoy Christian fellowship all day long. They prayed together, walked together, read Christian books and sermons. Then they would join in singing hymns from a collection gathered by his cousin, Martin Madan, while Mary Unwin accompanied the singing on the harpsichord. But it was an abnormal sort of life and we cannot be surprised that he would recall those days with a degree of nostalgia:

> What peaceful hours I once enjoyed,
> how sweet their memory still!
> But they have left an aching void
> the world can never fill.

After only eighteen months an incident occurred which changed everything for the Unwin family and their lodger. Morley Unwin, who had established a warm friendship with Cowper, was killed when his horse panicked and threw him to the ground. Shortly before the accident he had specifically told his wife that if anything were to happen to him she must not feel obliged to ask their lodger to leave. Morley had held a number of responsibilities in connection with the congregation that met in Huntingdon, but in recent days the family had been less happy with the ministry they were receiving. This bereavement released them from any sense of obligation to remain in the town. They began to look around for a place to live where they could receive the sort of ministry which they felt they needed.

When the vicar of Olney in Buckinghamshire, John Newton, whose remarkable career we have already followed, called to offer his condolences to Mary and her family, an immediate rapport was established. And it was not long before the Unwin family and their lodger were packing up their Huntingdon home, ready to move to

Cowper's summer house

Olney to be under Newton's ministry. Here William Cowper could foresee a useful role for himself as Newton's unofficial assistant, and for Mary a part in supporting Mrs Newton would be equally important.

The Unwins and their lodger arrived in November 1767, and John and Mary Newton kindly accommodated them until their new home, Orchard Side — only separated from the vicarage by an orchard behind the two properties — was ready for them. But hardly had they settled in before Mary Unwin fell seriously ill. The strains she had endured had been too much for her. Cowper thought she was dying: it seemed that yet another whom he dearly loved was being removed. He describes his feelings:

> My dear friend Mrs Unwin whom the Lord gave to me to be a comfort to me in that wilderness from which he has just delivered me, has been for many weeks past in so declining a way … that I have hardly been able to keep alive the faintest hope of her recovery… Her illness has been a sharp trial to me — O that it may have a sanctified effect, that I may rejoice to surrender up to the Lord my dearest comforts…

With this letter to his aunt Cowper enclosed some verses he had just written, expressing his desires in that crisis. The words are now among the best known of his hymns:

> O for a closer walk with God,
>   a calm and heavenly frame,
>   a light to shine upon the road
>   that leads me to the Lamb!

We may more easily understand the significance of the fifth verse in the light of these testing circumstances:

> The dearest idol I have known,
> whate'er that idol be,
> help me to tear it from thy throne,
> and worship only thee.

> So shall my walk be close with God,
> calm and serene my frame,
> so purer light shall mark the road
> that leads me to the Lamb.

Although Cowper's faith was being severely tried, God did not require him to surrender this one on whom he relied and gradually Mary Unwin regained strength. During the following few years he devoted his energies to helping Newton in pastoral work. Together they would walk to outlying areas visiting scattered parishioners, and the Unwin family would join John and Mary Newton in times of warm Christian fellowship, singing hymns and sharing spiritual experiences.

Clearly aware of his new friend's troubled past, John Newton kept a watchful eye on Cowper. In 1769 William's brother John became ill and appeared to be dying — a circumstance that took a heavy toll on the poet's emotional strength. Perhaps it was this situation that caused Newton to ask Cowper to use his poetic gifts to help him compose hymns, initially for the gathering for prayer on Tuesday evenings. When the meeting outgrew its accommodation and was transferred to the Great Hall, in the home of Lord Dartmouth, Cowper contributed a hymn which has become a favourite and is immediately more understandable in the light of the specific circumstances:

> Jesus, where'er thy people meet,
> there they behold thy mercy seat;
> where'er they seek thee, thou art found,
> and every place is hallowed ground.

Dear Shepherd of thy chosen few,
thy former mercies here renew;
here to our waiting hearts proclaim
the sweetness of thy saving name.

Here may we prove the power of prayer
to strengthen faith and sweeten care,
to teach our faint desires to rise,
and bring all heaven before our eyes.

In 1770 John Cowper died, a significant loss to William. Perhaps noticing signs that his friend might be descending into another spiral of depression, Newton had a further suggestion to make. He proposed that the hymns they had both written, some of which had already been published in various periodicals, should be collected together and they should jointly compile a hymn book for the use of both Olney parishioners and the wider community. Although there was a marked distinction between Newton's brisk outgoing hymns, with their challenge and joyful spirit, and Cowper's gentle, pensive, and often wistful poems with their inward looking, self-doubting musings, the two complemented each other. Cowper's introspective, self-analytical temperament can be traced in many of his hymns. This factor has limited their usefulness for general congregational singing, but increased their value for private meditation. A sensitive woman such as Anne Brontë could write:

Sweet are thy strains, Celestial Bard,
   and oft in childhood's years
I've read them o'er and o'er again
   with floods of silent tears.

The language of my inmost heart
   I traced in every line —

> my sins, my sorrows, hopes and fears
> were there, and only mine.

As we have seen, *Olney Hymns* was divided into three sections, the first covering biblical passages and the second diverse subjects, both doctrinal and didactic. It is significant that over half of Cowper's contribution to the book is to be found in the last section, devoted to the trials, sorrows and consolations of Christian experience. This contrasts markedly with the far smaller proportion from his pen in the rest of the book, in fact only one in seven in the previous two sections. We may easily discover his spiritual autobiography from his hymns:

> I was a grovelling creature once,
> and basely cleaved to earth...

is his description of his condition before his conversion. Awakened to his need and his failure to please God he writes:

> How long beneath the law I lay
> in bondage and distress!
> I toiled the precept to obey,
> but toiled without success.
>
> Then to abstain from outward sin
> was more than I could do...

Many tried to help and lead him:

> Friends and ministers said much
> the gospel to enforce;
> but my blindness still was such,
> I chose a legal course.

> Much I fasted, watched and strove,
>> scarce would show my face abroad,
> feared almost to speak or move,
>> a stranger still to God.

At last came the day of God's mercy:

> Then my stubborn heart he broke,
>> and subdued me to his sway,
> by a simple word he spoke —
>> 'Your sins are done away!'

and now he was able to rejoice:

> What thanks I owe thee, and what love,
>> a boundless, endless store,
> shall echo through the realms above,
>> when time shall be no more!

The majority of Cowper's work is written in the style of Watts with four-line verses, in short metre, long metre or common metre, sometimes in rhyming couplets or in alternate rhyming lines. Verses such as these are typical:

> Lord, we are few, but thou art near,
> nor short thine arm, nor deaf thine ear;
> O rend the heavens, come quickly down,
> and make a thousand hearts thine own!

Or we may choose:

> My soul rejoices to pursue
>> the steps of him I love,
> till glory breaks upon my view,
>> in brighter worlds above.

He also experimented with a variety of other metres, probably the most common being 7.6.7.6. Doubled, as in some evocative lines from a poet given to melancholia:

> Lord, my soul with pleasure springs
>   when Jesus' name I hear;
> and when God the Spirit brings
>   the word of promise near:
> beauties too in holiness,
>   still delighted I perceive;
> nor have words that can express
>   the joys thy precepts give.

The relationship between the writing of poetry and hymn-writing is one that is discussed fully in Professor J. R. Watson's work, *The English Hymn*.[3] Critics have attempted to dismiss the hymn form as mere versification, but a close study of hymnology makes such a view unsustainable. A good hymn-writer should most certainly possess a poetic gift, but his work demands a divergent discipline from that of the secular poet. He is under the taxing strictures of working to an exact metre and in regular stanzas, for the end-product is intended primarily for congregational singing. If the stress is thrown on a different syllable or an extra beat is added, the hymn becomes difficult to sing. Such constant regularity, however, rarely makes good poetry. Many of today's popular hymn-writers avoid this problem by the creation of a flexible tune to fit variants in the length of verse and line, a tune that will not be suitable for any other hymn. Cowper is perhaps the only hymn-writer who still receives national recognition as a poet, excelling in both disciplines, poet and hymn-writer, and has been called the 'poet laureate' of the Evangelical Revival. James Montgomery and Henry Lyte were also recognized as poets in their own day, but it is their hymns which live on. Watts and Wesley, on the other hand, laid their poetic genius on the altar of devotion to

Christ, deliberately choosing to serve the people of God rather than their own reputations.

With all the ease of a natural poet, Cowper introduces into a number of his hymns an element of conversation — an expedient that few others could copy or achieve with success. A well-known example of this occurs in a hymn such as 'Hark, my soul, it is the Lord'. Here a conversation between the believer and his Saviour follows, as Christ demonstrates his changeless love for the 'poor sinner':

'Can a woman's tender care
cease towards the child she bare?
Yes, she may forgetful be,
yet will I remember thee.

'Mine is an unchanging love,
higher than the heights above,
deeper than the depths beneath,
free and faithful, strong as death.'

At last the believer replies,

'Lord, it is my chief complaint
that my love is weak and faint;
yet I love thee and adore;
O for grace to love thee more!'

The scriptural content of Cowper's hymns is striking, revealing his own detailed knowledge of the Bible. In a hymn entitled 'Prayer for Patience' — a little-known contribution to *Olney Hymns* — he makes references to Old Testament narratives that might leave many of today's worshippers baffled:

Man should not faint at thy rebuke,
like Joshua falling on his face,

> when the accursed thing that Achan took
>   brought Israel into just disgrace.
>
> Perhaps some golden wedge suppressed,
>   some secret sin offends my God;
> perhaps that Babylonish vest,
>   self-righteousness, provokes the rod.

In another hymn dealing with the privileges and difficulties of prayer Cowper draws on several biblical narratives, beginning with Jacob's dream in Genesis 28:

> Prayer makes the darkened cloud withdraw,
> prayer climbs the ladder Jacob saw,
> gives exercise to faith and love,
> brings every blessing from above.

This is followed by a reference to an incident recorded in Exodus 17 when Moses interceded for Israel as Joshua led the people into battle against Amalek:

> When Moses stood with arms spread wide,
> success was found on Israel's side;
> but when through weariness they failed,
> that moment Amalek prevailed.

The hymn ends with a quaint thought that removes all excuses for neglecting prayer, again introducing the conversational style:

> Have you no words? ah, think again!
> Words flow apace when you complain,
> and fill your fellow-creature's ear
> with the sad tale of all your care.

> Were half the breath thus vainly spent
> to heaven in supplication sent,
> Your cheerful song would oftener be —
> 'Hear what the Lord has done for me.'

Throughout his hymns Cowper reveals this same perceptive knowledge of the Bible. Clearly he had studied its pages with diligent care. One of our better-known hymns on the subject of the Scriptures comes from his pen:

> The Spirit breathes upon the word,
>   and brings the truth to sight;
> precepts and promises afford
>   a sanctifying light.
>
> A glory gilds the sacred page,
>   majestic like the sun;
> it gives a light to every age;
>   it gives, but borrows none.

Since his first severe breakdown, Cowper's mental health had never been robust, but the stability afforded by Mrs Unwin's motherly care and John Newton's pastoral concern kept him from any serious deterioration. From the time that the two men started to compile *Olney Hymns* it would be a further two years before his health finally crumbled and with it his spiritual assurance. It would be wrong, therefore, to interpret all Cowper's contributions to *Olney Hymns* in the light of this impending disaster or even anachronistically as if it had already taken place. Cowper's tentative and often diffident personality finds expression in many of his hymns, but this is not the same as despair. In his otherwise excellent chapter on the poet in *I'll Praise my Maker: Studies in English Classical Hymnody,* Erik Routley most certainly gives this false impression. He writes: 'Cowper urges the worshippers to a hopefulness which he was not able to compass. This discrepancy between his words and his experience we shall notice many times.' But a man who could write:

> A cheerful confidence I feel,
>   my well-placed hopes with joy I see;
> my spirit glows with holy zeal,
>   to worship him who died for me,

must certainly be one who at that moment actually felt a strong assurance of God's love and grace. In fact, many of Cowper's hymns present a robust, even confident faith; a prime example would be the well-known hymn based on Zechariah 13:1, 'There is a fountain filled with blood':

> The dying thief rejoiced to see
>   that fountain in his day;
> and there have I, though vile as he,
>   washed all my sins away.
>
> E'er since, by faith, I saw the stream
>   thy flowing wounds supply,
> redeeming love has been my theme,
>   and shall be till I die.

Cowper might not always enjoy such moments of strong assurance, but here it was evidently his experience. People often wonder why this hymn has a weak ending. Instead of a bold triumphant note, it apparently concludes with a negative thought:

> Then in a nobler, sweeter song
>   I'll sing thy power to save,
> when this poor lisping, stammering tongue
>   lies silent in the grave.

But Cowper's original had two further verses, now regrettably omitted — verses that led beyond the grave to the anticipation of heaven, and gave his lines a joyful, positive ending:

> Lord, I believe thou hast prepared
>   (unworthy though I be)
> for me a blood-bought free reward —
>   a golden harp for me!

> 'Tis strung and tuned for endless years,
>   and formed by power divine,
> to sound in God the Father's ears
>   no other name but thine!

There is evidence, nevertheless, that throughout 1771 and 1772 Cowper passed through times of spiritual uncertainty, so it is not surprising that we should find tell-tale indications of such conflict scattered among his hymns, almost all of which were written in this period. But he could still find the path that led to spiritual comfort:

> Trials must and will befall;
>   but with humble faith to see
> love inscribed upon them all —
>   this is happiness to me.

> Trials make the promise sweet;
>   trials give new life to prayer;
> trials bring me to his feet,
>   lay me low and keep me there.

Sometimes the storm was so severe that it was harder to find the haven:

> The billows swell, the winds are high,
> clouds overcast my wintry sky;
> out of the depths to thee I call,
> my fears are great, my strength is small.

> Amidst the roaring of the sea,
> my soul still hangs its hope on thee;
> thy constant love, thy faithful care
> is all that saves me from despair.

> Though tempest-tossed and half a wreck,
> my Saviour through the floods I seek;
> let neither winds nor stormy main
> force back my shattered bark again.

As so often happens, the Christian's great adversary, Satan, took advantage of the situation to cast his fiery darts of doubt and falsehood at Cowper:

> My soul is sad and much dismayed;
>   see, Lord, what legions of my foes,
> with fierce Apollyon at their head,
>   my heavenly pilgrimage oppose!

> Their fiery arrows reach the mark,
>   my throbbing heart with anguish tear,
> each lights upon a kindred spark,
>   and finds abundant fuel there.

Yet even in that dark hour, faith still triumphed as the poet prayed:

> Come then, and chase the cruel host,
>   heal the deep wounds I have received!

> Nor let the powers of darkness boast
>   that I am foiled and you are grieved.

And then he would experience a renewing of faith, hope and a peaceful trust in God:

> When darkness long has veiled my mind,
>   and smiling day once more appears,
> then, my Redeemer, then I find
>   the folly of my doubts and fears.

But it was a lesson he found difficult to bring to mind in times of temptation:

> Sweet truth, and easy to repeat!
>   But when my faith is sharply tried,
> I find myself a learner yet,
>   unskilful, weak, and apt to slide.

As 1772 wore to its close there were further troubling signs that all was not well with Newton's poet friend. 'Dear Sir Cowper is in the depths as much as ever,' he wrote in a letter to his wife Mary in July 1772. But despite these periods of depression, there were still bright moments — moments that inspired such words as:

> Sometimes a light surprises
>   the Christian while he sings;
> it is the Lord who rises
>   with healing in his wings:
> when comforts are declining,
>   he grants the soul again
> a season of clear shining,
>   to cheer it after rain.

With a prolonged reference to the end of Habakkuk 3, he concludes with a verse that has cheered many other believers since Cowper's day:

> Though vine nor fig-tree neither
>   their wonted fruit shall bear;
> though all the field should wither,
>   nor flocks nor herds be there;
> yet God the same abiding,
>   his praise shall tune my voice;
> for, while in him confiding,
>   I cannot but rejoice.

A further factor endangering Cowper's fragile condition at this time was the increasing gossip that sometimes reached his ears regarding his relationship with Mary Unwin, and not merely from village wags, but from those whom Cowper held in high regard. William Unwin had left the family home and in the summer of 1772 Susanna was engaged to be married. This would leave Cowper and Mrs Unwin alone together. What could he do? The thought of trying to set up a home on his own was too demanding for a nervous system so finely balanced as Cowper's. He was wholly dependent on Mary's wise motherly care. Only one option remained. They must marry. But the relationship had never been a conjugal one, and although Cowper now proposed to Mary and she accepted, the prospect of marriage brought increased pressure on his already faltering health.

As 1772 turned to 1773 Cowper morbidly called to mind what had happened just ten years earlier in 1763, when his mental stability had collapsed. And on New Year's Day as he walked alone in the fields near Olney, probably under a sullen wintry sky, he experienced a strange premonition that a darkness was about to envelop him. Storm clouds were gathering, possibly literally, certainly metaphorically, as the poet hastened back to his home. There he wrote one last hymn — a courageous testament of faith in the purposes of God:

> God moves in a mysterious way
>   his wonders to perform;
> he plants his footsteps in the sea
>   and rides upon the storm...
>
> Ye fearful saints, fresh courage take,
>   the clouds ye so much dread
> are big with mercy, and shall break
>   in blessings on your head.

Entitled 'Light Shining out of Darkness', these words are the best known of all Cowper's hymns. Every line except two in the fifth verse finds its way into *The Oxford Dictionary of Quotations,* and some of the expressions have become interwoven with the warp and woof of our English phraseology. The hymn has received a variety of comments, depending on the perspective of the writer. To Erik Routley it was 'a grim and tragic summary of Cowper's outlook', displaying 'an unnatural calm, a dangerous lucidity'. He draws attention to the fact that there is no mention of Christ throughout and concludes, 'to call this a hymn of triumph, optimism or even adoration is merely fanciful'.[4]

Yet despite such comments it remains a hymn that Christians struggling to cope with painful situations have turned to, reread or sung, and have received profound consolation and new faith in the purposes of God. J. R. Watson takes a very different view of it. To him it is a 'delightful hymn on the wonders of God'. To suggest that this is a cry of despair is in his view far from the truth. 'It is the Christian's duty and joy to interpret the signs of God's providence... Belief is needed and then God, who is the great Interpreter, will make everything clear... The hymn is therefore one of truth and hope.'[5] We might add that this hymn stands as a shining beacon casting its rays of light far into the darkness that was about to engulf the poet, and it is by these words we must judge his true spiritual state, however much he might deprecate himself and his own standing before God.

> Judge not the Lord by feeble sense,
>> but trust him for his grace;
> behind a frowning providence
>> he hides a smiling face.
>
> His purposes will ripen fast,
>> unfolding every hour;
> the bud may have a bitter taste,
>> but sweet will be the flower.
>
> Blind unbelief is sure to err,
>> and scan his work in vain;
> God is his own interpreter,
>> and he will make it plain.

Although Cowper finds God's ways mysterious as he starts this hymn, by the time he reaches the last line that mystery has become 'plain' as he views it through the eyes of faith.

Little more than three weeks after Cowper had written these words, the cloud he had so much dreaded — a cloud of mental darkness — broke over him. Newton records in his diary for 24 January 1773: 'A very alarming turn roused us from our beds and called us to Orchard Side [Cowper's home] at four in the morning. I stayed there till eight before which time the threatening appearance went entirely off.' Though his reason might temporarily have fled, yet Cowper still clung to his hope and faith in God. But soon a worse circumstance overtook him. Little more than a month later he had a dream — a dream so fearful that it all but destroyed the stricken man. He never divulged the exact contents of that dream, which can only have been injected into his troubled mind by the Evil One himself, but by it he understood that he was utterly forsaken by God, with all hope of salvation gone for ever. Robbed in a moment of all that had sustained his spirit since his conversion eight years earlier, the poor man was reduced to a frightening degree of irrationality.

When he had recovered mental balance some years later he could describe his condition: 'I was suddenly reduced from my wonted rate of understanding to an almost childish imbecility ... I believed that everybody hated me, and that Mrs Unwin hated me most of all; was convinced that my food was poisoned...' Far from hating him, his friends showed an astonishing degree of self-sacrificing love. John and Mary Newton invited the patient, along with Mary Unwin, to stay at the vicarage where he was tenderly watched, restrained from many attempts to end his life and gradually nursed back to health. Early biographers, understanding little of Newton's personality and even less of the faith that had upheld Cowper, have blamed both Newton and his doctrinal position for the poet's malady, ignoring the fact that his earlier severe breakdown had occurred before his conversion.

It is beyond the scope of a sketch such as this to recount in any detail the rest of Cowper's life. We are mistaken, however, if we picture his depression dominating the remaining years. After his recovery he found fulfilment in writing poetry and by his most famous poem, 'The Task', achieved astonishing fame, with a public clamouring to read his work. He would eventually be offered the position of Poet Laureate. Although depression was never far away, much of the time he was quietly cheerful, enjoying a wide correspondence, many rich friendships and the delights of rural life.

It would seem, however, that he never recovered his assurance of salvation. He did not deny the faith; he believed the promises of God; all were true, but he maintained that they

did not apply to him. He alone of all the elect children of God
was to be cast aside; why this should be he did not pretend
to know. 'Nature revives,' he wrote gloomily, 'but a soul once
slain lives no more... There is a mystery in my destruction and
in time it shall be explained.'

Although the spiritual darkness rarely lifted, it was possibly
not as intense nor as continuous as he himself sometimes
suggested. One poem in particular would imply this:

> I was a stricken deer that left the herd
> long since; with many an arrow deep infixt
> my panting side was charged, when I withdrew
> to seek a tranquil death in distant shades.
> There was I found by One who had himself
> been hurt by th'archers. In his side he bore,
> and in his hands and feet, the cruel scars.
> With gentle force soliciting the darts,
> he drew them forth and heal'd and bade me live.

Towards the end of his life Cowper nursed his well-loved
friend and companion Mary Unwin through a long declining
illness that included several strokes. Almost blind and semi-
paralysed, Mary could now do little to help either herself or
'Mr Cowper', as she invariably had called him. Cowper was to
write a most beautiful poem of devotion entitled 'My Mary':

> Thy spirits have a fainter flow,
> I see thee daily weaker grow;
> 'twas my distress that brought thee low,
>   My Mary!

> Thy silver locks, once auburn bright,
> are still more lovely in my sight,
> than golden beams of orient light,
>   My Mary!

> Partakers of thy sad decline,
> thy hands their little force resign,
> yet gently press'd, press gently mine,
>   My Mary!

Soon it became evident that neither Cowper nor Mrs Unwin was in any state to look after each other, and in 1795, a young relative of Cowper's, John Johnson, wisely and compassionately moved the couple to Norfolk, where he had arranged for them to be accommodated and cared for. Mary Unwin died late in 1796, and four years later Cowper also, now at Johnson's own home in East Dereham, drew near to the end. Still convinced that he was 'a castaway' — the subject of his last sad poem — Cowper died on 21 April 1800 at the age of sixty-nine. But there is one ray of hope. Johnson, who was present when Cowper died, noticed that after death his 'expression ... was that of calmness and composure, mingled as it were with holy surprise'. What could it be that surprised William Cowper at the moment of death? It is not fanciful to suppose that the 'holy surprise' that marked his expression was due to the discovery that he was no castaway after all but a beloved child of God. It had indeed proved true that:

> God is his own interpreter,
> and he will make it plain.

Notes

1. Psalm 56:4.
2. 'Whom God has set forth to be a propitiation through faith in his blood, to declare his righteousness for the remission of sins that are past, through the forbearance of God.'
3. OUP, 1995.
4. *I'll Praise my Maker*, p.109.
5. *An Annotated Anthology of Hymns*, J. R. Watson, OUP, 2002, p.221.

James Montgomery
(1771-1854)

'Psalms and hymns and songs of praise'

Songs of praise the angels sang,
Heaven with hallelujahs rang,
when creation was begun,
when God spoke and it was done.

Saints below, with heart and voice,
still in songs of praise rejoice,
learning here, by faith and love,
songs of praise to sing above.

James Montgomery

James Montgomery
(1771-1854)

'Psalms and hymns and songs of praise'

The pupils at the Fulneck Moravian school, near Leeds in Yorkshire, were on their best behaviour. Lord Monboddo, a fiery, if eccentric, Scottish judge, was visiting the school. But as the name of each pupil was announced in turn, Lord Monboddo showed little interest. With eyes to the floor he appeared to be counting the nails in the floorboards instead. 'Here is James Montgomery,' announced the master in charge, 'one of your own countrymen.' Suddenly alert, the old judge looked up, reached for his horsewhip and, brandishing it over the apprehensive boy's head, roared, 'I hope he will take care that his country will never be ashamed of him!' Young James Montgomery never forgot those words.

Although James Montgomery's parents were Scottish by birth, they had lived most of their lives in Ballymena, Co. Antrim, in the north of Ireland. Not long before James was born in November 1771, they had moved to Irvine in Ayrshire to take pastoral charge of a small Moravian community there. When the child was just five years of age, however, the family had returned to Ballymena. Little more than twenty years earlier John Cennick, Moravian preacher and friend of George Whitefield, had forged an entrance for the gospel among a hostile population in that town, often at the risk of his life. Before Cennick's early death in 1755, he had established many Societies in the area where the converts of his ministry could worship together. Grace Hill was one such Moravian settlement and here James' father, who had himself been converted through Cennick's preaching, temporarily resumed the ministry he had been conducting before his transfer to Irvine five years earlier.

Not many months after the family had returned, six-year-old James found himself crossing the Irish Sea once more as he was sent to the Moravian settlement in Fulneck for his education. Never again was James to know any settled home life, for not long afterwards his parents sailed as missionaries to Barbados in the West Indies — numbered amongst the earliest pioneers of the gospel to that land. James never saw them again. There, far from home, both were to die while their son was still a teenager.

His teachers at Fulneck found James a difficult pupil. With a policy of isolating the children from the local people, the Moravian community was an inward-looking group with a tendency to regard any pupil's individual expressions of imagination and gifts with deep suspicion, even as a manifestation of the depravity of human nature. With an imaginative, poetical temperament, James inwardly rebelled against the strictures of his education. While his teachers were endeavouring 'to drive him like a coal ass' through the monotonous routines of his Greek and Latin primers, James was secretly scribbling screeds of verse, trying to improve on the odd rhyming schemes he discovered in the Moravian hymn book. The boy could frequently be found under hedgerows indulging his imagination in the delights of the adventures of *Robinson Crusoe* or moved to the depths by some of the great epic poems of the day. In his heart James determined that some day he too would be a poet, however much the school tried to regularize and constrict his talents.

By the time James was thirteen he had filled a notebook with his verses, to the despair of his teachers. The boy was lazy and unmanageable, they decided. Never would he make a Moravian pastor as his missionary parents had wished. The only hope for him was to leave school and do something useful for a while. Perhaps after that he would be less of a visionary and the school would then be able to make him into a man of more useful endowments. Soon after his fourteenth birthday, therefore, James was apprenticed to a baker in Mirfield, not far from Leeds, where the Moravians also had a settlement. With time on his hands and little to stimulate his imaginative gifts, James was restless and dissatisfied. Music became a delight filling his leisure hours, but still his great passion was the composition of poetry.

After eighteen months the boy could tolerate his situation no longer. When his master returned from worship at the local Moravian church one day, he discovered that his apprentice had absconded. With pockets crammed with his poetic endeavours and his earnings of three shillings and sixpence in his hand, James was on the road seeking his fortune. As many others before him, he discovered the world to be a hostile place and had not gone far before hunger and homelessness convinced him that he must seek further employment. At Wath upon Dearne, near Rotherham, he engaged himself as an assistant in a small general store.

For some time Montgomery served his new master well. The standards of honesty and morality that he had been taught at Fulneck had moulded the youth's character and restrained him from the wild excesses of many of his contemporaries. But still he was restless. He wished to make his mark in the world as a poet, and there was only one place where he could achieve such a goal — London. With increasing maturity James, who was now eighteen, decided to ask his employer for permission to leave his service in order to try his fortune in the capital.

This time he set off with letters of commendation in his pocket together with his bundles of poetry stuffed in his bag. A year later he was back, dejected but more realistic. Although a number of London publishers and critics had spoken encouragingly to the young poet, none had been prepared to publish his material. Kindly his old employer received him back again.

In April 1792 when Montgomery was still only twenty years of age he noticed an advertisement for a post as clerk and bookkeeper in the offices of a Sheffield newspaper, *The Sheffield Register*. A far cry from the poetical career he had envisaged, this position would at least bring him into contact with the literary world, and who could tell? Perhaps it would lead to a more satisfying occupation than shopkeeping. His new employer, Joseph Gales, appeared to combine the various functions of newspaper proprietor, printer, journalist and bookseller all at the same time. Montgomery now found himself involved in journalism in fast-changing and dangerous times. War with France seemed imminent and the horrors of the French Revolution were a frightening reality to the English aristocracy. Industry and agriculture were in flux as the Industrial Revolution gained momentum and land workers poured into the towns desperately seeking a livelihood.

Joseph Gales soon found himself in trouble for the controversial opinions expressed in the columns of *The Sheffield Register* and, with the Sheffield police at his heels, was forced to flee the country. After just two years with Gales, Montgomery, still only twenty-three years of age, bought over the presses and business, changing the name of the paper to *The Sheffield Iris*. More circumspect and far more gifted than his master, he succeeded at first, but soon his terse and logical articles drew the attention of a wary authority to his printing press. It was fast becoming the outlet for progressive views written by a wide spectrum of thinkers. But when he reprinted a ballad in the pages of the paper commemorating the Fall of the Bastille in 1789 (written not by Montgomery but by a hopeful young man on whom he had taken pity), Montgomery found himself at the sharp end of the law. Tried and found guilty of 'seditious libel', he was fined £20 and sentenced to three months' imprisonment in York Castle.

The Iris,
Montgomery's newspaper

'A guilty verdict cannot make an innocent man guilty,' Montgomery declared as he began his sentence. Accepting his imprisonment philosophically, he used the hours of confinement to write more poetry, and a number of his poems of this period have survived. On 'The Pleasures of Imprisonment' he could write,

> In this sweet place where freedom reigns
> secured by bolts and snug in chains,
> where innocence and guilt together
> roost like two turtles of a feather...
> Here each may as his means afford
> dine like a pauper or a lord...

Released after three months, Montgomery returned to his office, more wary of avoiding controversy. But two years later when a riot in Sheffield was suppressed with unnecessary cruelty and bloodshed, he could not avoid some cryptic and indignant comments in the columns of *The Sheffield Iris*. Once more he was accused of publishing 'seditious libel'. This time the fine was £60 with six months in prison. No longer able to face his sentence with a light heart, Montgomery's spirits sank, and as the days of his sentence dragged by he became emaciated and depressed. He wrote poetry and novels, but destroyed this work.

Beyond the mere loss of liberty, a deeper disquiet was gnawing at his peace. Since his school days at Fulneck, Montgomery had resolutely turned his back on the values and teachings of the Christian gospel. Rarely had he attended a place of worship; he had been ambitious for fame and recognition, and his friendships with men of agnostic attitudes had further undermined the early foundations of faith taught in his home and school. He was an apostate, of that he was sure, and he knew well the final destiny of apostates. He looked back on his life with profound regrets:

> I left the God of truth and light,
>   I left the God who gave me breath,
> to wander in the wilds of night
>   and perish in the snares of death.
>
> I wooed ambition, climbed the pole,
>   and shone among the stars — but fell
> headlong in all my pride of soul,
>   like Lucifer from heaven to hell.
>
> Heart-broken, friendless, poor, cast down,
>   where shall the chief of sinners fly,
> Almighty vengeance, from thy frown?
>   Eternal justice, from thy eye?

Writing to a friend from prison he unburdened his heart: 'What can I do? I am tossed to and fro on a sea of doubts and perplexities: the further I am carried from that shore where once I was happily moored, the weaker grow my hopes of ever reaching another where I may anchor in safety.' His friend, a man of Socinian persuasion, was unable to help.

On his release from prison James Montgomery might be seen slipping into a local Methodist church. At this very time William Bramwell had been exercising a powerful ministry in Sheffield and almost two thousand men and women had been brought to faith within a two-year period. Whether Montgomery listened to the searching words of that anointed preacher we do not know, but slowly he was brought, sin-burdened and miserable, to the Saviour he had long rejected. A sermon he read by John Cennick, whose ministry had been held in honour in his childhood home, affected him deeply. Now he could write in growing confidence:

> My suffering, slain and risen Lord,
>   in sore distress I turn to thee;
> I claim acceptance of thy word,
>   my God, my God, forsake not me.
>
> Prostrate before thy mercy-seat,
>   I dare not, if I would, despair;
> none ever perished at thy feet,
>   and I will lie for ever there.

His Moravian friends at Fulneck did not verbally chastise him for the wayward years, rather they received him back with joy. Words written by Montgomery express his gratitude:

> Lonely I no longer roam,
>   like the cloud, the wind, the wave;
> where you dwell shall be my home,
>   where you die shall be my grave.

> Mine the God whom you adore,
>   your Redeemer shall be mine;
> earth can fill my heart no more:
>   every idol I resign.

The way back was long and hard, and throughout his life Montgomery experienced periods of depression and the deep-seated fear that he might fail his God at the last. But gradually, steadily, the evidences of a true conversion were becoming obvious, first to a small circle of those close to him and then to his wider public — the readers of *The Sheffield Iris*. For almost thirty years Montgomery retained the editorship of this weekly journal, submitting articles to which his name was attached; and increasingly presenting through its columns news and comment on national and international affairs from a Christian perspective.

Meanwhile Montgomery's reputation as a poet was steadily growing. Lord Byron (whose poetic brilliance was beyond question, even if his morals were not) spoke of him as 'a man of considerable genius'. Percy Shelley, whose early death at the age of thirty-two deprived the English language of one of its greatest poets, was another who highly regarded Montgomery's work. But although his poetic works ran to four volumes, they are scarcely remembered today, while his hymns live on and place their writer high in the esteem of those who value the heritage left us by our hymn-writers. Erik Routley called him 'the greatest of Christian lay hymn-writers', and John Julian was full of praise in his magisterial *Dictionary of Hymnology:*

> With the faith of a strong man he united the beauty and simplicity of a child. Richly poetic, without exuberance, dogmatic without uncharitableness, tender without sentimentality ... richly musical without apparent effort, he has bequeathed to the Church of Christ wealth which can only have come from a true genius and a sanctified heart.

In a letter to a friend written in 1807 Montgomery unintentionally suggests a reason why his hymns remain so highly valued: he did not merely decide to compose a hymn; instead, as he commented, 'I lie in wait for my heart and when I can string it to the pitch of David's lyre, I will set a psalm "to the Chief Musician".' As with all true poets, his pen followed the inspiration of his heart.

In 1817 an event occurred which was to be of lasting significance, not only for Montgomery, but for the Established Church in particular. In that year Thomas Cotterill arrived in Sheffield as Perpetual Curate of the downtown church of St Paul's — soon sparking off a controversy within his church. Seven years earlier Cotterill had compiled and produced a *Selection of Psalms and Hymns* which he had used in his previous churches, but without the approval of the Establishment. This selection contained work by Wesley, Watts, Newton and others, but when he tried to introduce his book at St Paul's there was trouble. His indignant congregation took the matter to the Consistory Court at York. Archbishop Harcourt examined Cotterill's collection, and instead of banning it outright suggested that he improve it and return it to him. James Montgomery agreed to help Cotterill by contributing a number of his own hymns and so, with weaker material omitted, Cotterill returned to the archbishop. The Church of England had long held out against such 'innovations' in worship as hymn-singing — viewing it with in-built suspicion as a characteristic of both Dissenting and Methodist services. Harcourt wisely saw, however, that the changes brought about by the evangelical revival of the previous century meant that hymn-singing had become a permanent feature of Christian worship. He gave permission for the use of Cotterill's collection of hymns at St Paul's, suggesting that it should be dedicated to himself. 1820 therefore marks an important date in the story of the progress of hymnody because permission from an archbishop gave tacit approval for the general acceptance of hymns throughout the Established Church, overthrowing the sanctions that had previously permitted only the singing of psalms and other responses.[1] Cotterill, who was also the writer of a number of hymns, went on to produce a further edition of his *Selection of Psalms and Hymns*. This too included a number of Montgomery's compositions.

James Montgomery wrote over four hundred hymns, although only a handful of these have survived the passage of time. His ear for rhythm was sensitive and accurate and his use of rhyme so skilled that the singer is left with the impression that no other word in the English language could be more fitting in the context than the one Montgomery has chosen — yet it also happens to rhyme:

> In the hour of trial
>   Jesus pray for me,
> lest by base denial
>   I depart from thee;
> when thou see'st me waver,
>   with a look recall,
> nor for fear or favour
>   suffer me to fall.

The predominant use of single-syllable words in many of his hymns gives Montgomery's lines a terse strength. His poetic gift also means that those who attempt to edit his work to any significant extent do so at their peril. As Josiah Conder, writing in the following century, would remark: 'He must be a bold man, if not a wise one, who would attempt to improve the compositions of Mr Montgomery.' Montgomery himself was highly displeased with any such alterations, yet he was not averse to modifying the hymns of others! Augustus Toplady's hymn, 'Rock of Ages, cleft for me', is a case in point. Although our modern hymn books have largely reverted to Toplady's original version, they have retained one of Montgomery's many alterations: the introduction of the line 'When my eyelids close in death' in place of Toplady's 'When my eyestrings break in death'.

In 1825 Montgomery published *The Christian Psalmist* or *Hymns Selected and Original.* In his introductory essay to this work, described by J. R. Watson as 'the finest essay that has ever been written on hymns',[2] Montgomery laid down exacting rules for would-be hymn-writers, listing common faults that should be avoided. Among them he placed inverting word construction within a line in order to achieve a rhyming word. Lines such as these would not have pleased him:

> The troubles that afflict the just
>   in number many be;
> and yet at length out of them all
>   the Lord doth set him free.

His list continues with such things as 'barbarous abbreviations that make our beautiful English horrid even to the eye, and bad rhymes or no rhymes where rhymes are expected'. Extra words should not be added for the sake of the rhyme or in order to achieve the correct number of beats in a line; nor should new concepts be introduced unrelated to the original theme at the dictate of the rhyming scheme. His extensive list of faults is inclusive enough to discourage even the most gifted from venturing into the hymn-writing arena; but Montgomery was unrepentant, suggesting that if secular poets strive after the highest possible standards for their work, a Christian poet ought to be prepared to take equal pains.

On the positive side Montgomery suggested guidelines for good hymn-writing: a hymn should have a beginning, a middle and an end; it should deal with a single subject, developed throughout, each line and stanza building on the last, with the whole brought to a firm and satisfying conclusion. A good hymn should leave a strong impression on the singer, so that he recalls it with a sense of joy and delights to sing it again and again. He cites Watts, Wesley and Newton as prime examples of composers of such hymns.

Of the 562 hymns in *The Christian Psalmist*, one hundred were by Montgomery. He readily admits that to have laid down stringent guidelines for others invites criticism of his own work. In fact some of it falls short of elements of his own criteria and has not stood the test of time. Those hymns that live on have significantly enriched the Christian Church since Montgomery's day, forming a valuable contribution even into the twenty-first century. In his 1825 collection he introduced a number of paraphrases based on the Psalms. Although less venturesome than Watts or Wesley in his 'Christianizing' of the Psalter, Montgomery frequently augments his rendering by bringing in other Scriptures as part of his interpretation. We notice this in his version of Psalm 63:

> O God, thou art my God alone:
>> early to thee my soul shall cry;
> a pilgrim in a land unknown,
>> a thirsty land whose springs are dry.

> Yet through this rough and thorny maze
>> I follow hard on thee, my God;
> thine hand unseen upholds my ways;
>> I safely tread where thou hast trod.

Then in the fourth verse he turns to Psalm 73:25 and continues:

> Better than life itself thy love,
>> dearer than all beside to me;
> for whom have I in heaven above,
>> or what on earth, compared with thee?

Paraphrasing Psalm 27, he writes:

> God is my strong salvation;
>   what foe have I to fear?
> in darkness and temptation
>   my light, my help is near.

But Montgomery's paraphrase of Psalm 72 must take pride of place among these renderings:

> Hail to the Lord's Anointed,
>   great David's greater Son!
> Hail, in the time appointed,
>   his reign on earth begun!
> He comes to break oppression,
>   to set the captives free,
> to take away transgression,
>   and rule in equity.

He writes with burning compassion for the 'poor and needy' — which had placed him behind bars twice — expressing his fierce denunciation of the slave trade; then he changes to a gentler strain as he recognizes the blessings of Messiah's reign:

> He comes with succour speedy
>   to those who suffer wrong;
> to help the poor and needy
>   and bid the weak be strong;
> to give them songs for sighing,
>   their darkness turn to light,
> whose souls, condemned and dying,
>   were precious in his sight.

First written in 1821, this hymn appeared in *The Evangelical Magazine* the following year, and remains among the best known of Montgomery's hymns.

With a sensitive temperament, easily elated, easily cast down, Montgomery suffered periods of depression throughout his life. We may detect this particularly in some of his paraphrases of the Psalms. In his version of Psalm 63 he finds in his God strength to continue through the 'rough and thorny maze' of life, and in his version of Psalm 77, he writes:

> In time of tribulation
>   hear, Lord, my feeble cries.
> With humble supplication,
>   to thee my spirit flies.
> My heart with grief is breaking;
>   scarce can my voice complain;
> mine eyes with tears kept waking,
>   still watch and weep in vain.

And God heard his cry:

> I call to recollection
>   the years of his right hand;
> and, strong through his protection,
>   again through faith I stand...

A further feature of Montgomery's verse is found in the strong final lines he chooses to conclude his hymns. His rendering of parts of Psalm 91 gives an excellent example of this: beginning, 'Call Jehovah thy salvation,/rest beneath the Almighty's shade', then, in a triumphant ending, he proclaims:

> Here for grief reward thee double,
>   crown with life beyond the grave.

We find a further instance of such a robust conclusion in Montgomery's well-known hymn beginning 'Songs of praise the angels sang'. He traces the progress of that mighty anthem of praise that arises to God from the heavenly hosts, and leads us on to the duty and privilege of his people on earth to unite in that song:

> And shall man alone be dumb,
> till that glorious kingdom come?
> No! the church delights to raise
> psalms and hymns and songs of praise.

But one day we too will join heaven's jubilant song of praise:

> Borne upon their latest [final] breath,
> songs of praise shall conquer death;
> then, amidst eternal joy,
> songs of praise their powers employ.

Although Montgomery first published his popular nativity hymn 'Angels from the realms of glory' in his newspaper *The Sheffield Iris* on Christmas Eve 1816, it was not until 1825 that he eventually included it in his selection of hymns and psalms. In each verse the poet called on a different category of those who witnessed the birth of the Saviour to join in worship: angels, shepherds, sages (or wise men) and saints (a reference to Simeon and Anna). In contrast to the 'saints' of the fourth verse, in the fifth verse 'sinners' are also called to worship the newly born Saviour. Some have disliked this last verse, feeling it inappropriate for the festive season, and have either omitted it or inserted another in its place, but Montgomery's purpose was to bring to a climax the saving purposes of God behind Christ's birth in a manger:

> Sinners wrung with true repentance,
> doomed for guilt to endless pains,
> Justice now revokes your sentence,
> Mercy calls you, break your chains:

come and worship,
worship Christ the new-born King.

Montgomery showed a close interest in missionary work and his desire to see the worldwide spread of the gospel found frequent expression in his hymns. Often he would speak with pride of his own parents who had laboured and died far from family and home. 'I am the son of missionaries,' he would declare. Such hymns as 'O Spirit of the living God' convey his aspirations:

O Spirit of the Lord, prepare
all the round earth her God to meet;
breathe thou abroad like morning air,
till hearts of stone begin to beat.

His vision for the ultimate triumph of the kingdom of God could not be hidden:

Baptise the nations; far and nigh
the triumphs of the cross record;
the name of Jesus glorify,
till every kindred call him Lord.

Meditations on the believer's communion with God, as he seeks his face in prayer, are expressed in some of the poet's most enduring lines. A hymn described by Professor J. R. Watson as 'the greatest of all hymns on the difficult subject of prayer' is the one beginning 'Prayer is the soul's sincere desire'.[3] Each of the first six verses gives an added portrayal of the nature of true prayer. It can be spoken or unspoken; perhaps just a glance heavenward, a sigh, a tear. In a surprising study in opposites, he continues:

> Prayer is the simplest form of speech
>> that infant lips can try;
> prayer the sublimest strains that reach
>> the Majesty on high.

More than this, prayer stands at the beginning of the Christian experience as the voice of the penitent turning from his sins, it sustains him along the way, and at the close it becomes the dying believer's 'watchword' as he enters the gates of heaven. Little wonder then that Montgomery should end such a hymn on prayer with a cry for divine help:

> O thou by whom we come to God,
>> the Life, the Truth, the Way,
> the path of prayer thyself hast trod:
>> Lord, teach us how to pray.

Like all Montgomery's hymns there is not a word too many, nor a word too few. He said that he had received more appreciation for this one piece than for any other. In a further hymn on prayer, the poet would appear to take up the theme with which he closed this last one, as he begins, 'Lord, teach us how to pray aright'. Loosely basing his words on David's heart-broken prayer of penitence in Psalm 51, he writes:

> Lord, teach us how to pray aright,
>> with reverence and with fear;
> though dust and ashes in thy sight,
>> we may, we must, draw near.

> Burdened with guilt, convinced of sin,
>> in weakness want and woe,
> fightings without and fears within,
>> Lord, whither shall we go?

> God of all grace, we come to thee
>   with broken contrite hearts;
> give what thine eye delights to see,
>   truth in the inward parts.

In common with other believers, Montgomery found that even his most earnest prayers sometimes seemed unavailing. But he must pray on, and therefore asked God for:

> Patience to watch and wait and weep,
>   though mercy long delay;
> courage our fainting souls to keep,
>   and trust thee though thou slay.

In the final verse he picks up all these strands of thought and weaves them into a satisfying conclusion that links up with his prayer at the outset:

> Give these, and then thy will be done;
>   thus strengthened with all might,
> we through thy Spirit and thy Son,
>   shall pray, and pray aright.

Temptations and trials are common to the Christian life and Montgomery had experienced many, but he had discovered that prayer is the pathway to deliverance:

> Go to dark Gethsemane,
>   ye that feel the tempter's power;
> your Redeemer's conflict see;
>   watch with him one bitter hour;
> turn not from his griefs away;
> learn of Jesus Christ to pray.

As he follows the Saviour from Gethsemane to the judgement hall and on to Calvary, he does not merely grieve over the sufferings Christ endured, but points in the last couplet of each verse to the lessons a believer may learn as he contemplates the scene:

> Follow to the judgement hall;
>> view the Lord of life arraigned.
> O the wormwood and the gall!
>> O the pangs his soul sustained!
> Shun not suffering, shame or loss:
> learn of him to bear the cross.

The cross stands at the heart of Christian experience and in his communion hymns Montgomery leads the believer to Calvary where he may contemplate Christ's sufferings:

> When to the cross I turn my eyes,
>> and rest on Calvary,
> O Lamb of God, my Sacrifice!
>> I must remember thee…

> Remember thee, and all thy pains,
>> and all thy love to me:
> yes, while a breath, a pulse remains,
>> will I remember thee.

Another hymn, moving in its intensity and economy of words, is frequently sung at the Lord's Supper. In his original version Montgomery compares Mount Sinai, representing the demands of the law of God, with Calvary where that law was satisfied. Only the final two verses are commonly used:

When on Calvary I rest,
God in flesh made manifest
shines in my Redeemer's face,
full of beauty, truth and grace.

Here I would for ever stay,
weep and gaze my soul away;
thou art heaven on earth to me,
lovely, mournful Calvary.

James Montgomery did not marry, but lived in Sheffield all his life, giving his time to the editorial work of his press and to the writing of poetry. Numerous cantos of verse flowed from his ready pen: some to be greeted with enthusiasm, much to fall under the censure of the critics of his day. Finally in 1825, when he was fifty-four years of age, he sold *The Sheffield Iris* with its presses and copyright in order to concentrate on his other writings. By this time he had gained a national reputation as both a journalist and poet. But it is as a writer of some of these, our best-loved hymns and psalms, that the Moravian poet is still remembered today.

'All my hymns embody some portion of the joys and sorrows, the hopes and fears of this poor heart,' said James Montgomery when he was in his eighties and knew he had not long to live. All his long life he had struggled with doubts and fears, and it is those conflicts etched on his memory and expressed in his hymns that still strike a chord in the hearts of Christians, even though one hundred and fifty years have elapsed since the poet's pen was laid aside in death. In his own day the popularity of his inspiring hymn beginning 'For ever with the Lord' was second only to his hymn on prayer:

My Father's house on high,
    home of my soul, how near
at times to faith's foreseeing eye

> thy golden gates appear!
> Ah! then my spirit faints
>   to reach the land I love,
>   the bright inheritance of saints,
>   Jerusalem above.

With the imagery of the apostle Paul, who spoke of the physical body as a tabernacle or tent, Montgomery takes up the picture in striking words:

> Here in the body pent,
>   absent from him I roam,
> yet nightly pitch my moving tent
>   a day's march nearer home.

The final verse is a cry of triumph in which Montgomery brings the believer full circle back to where he began:

> So when my latest [final] breath
>   shall rend the veil in twain,
> by death I shall escape from death
>   and life eternal gain.
> That resurrection word,
>   that shout of victory:
> once more, 'For ever with the Lord!'
>   Amen, so let it be!

With such words as these Montgomery sought to lift the spirits of his fellow Christians as they approached those 'golden gates'. Yet he himself often looked to the future with a degree of foreboding, lest his sins, his weakness and his wasted years should disqualify him or at least dismay him as the end drew near. Old and failing in health, he asked a friend to read him some of his earlier hymns, and in those words written long years before, he found consolation.

Be thou at my right hand,
then can I never fail;
uphold thou me, and I shall stand;
fight, and I must prevail.

But, in the event, the final passage was easy, for James Montgomery died in his sleep after only a few hours of illness. He was eighty-three. The people of Sheffield erected a statue in his honour: it depicts the poet standing wrapped in thought, with a bard's script at his side and the Bible under his arm.

Notes

1. He must have known that hymns were already being used in numerous individual Anglican churches.
2. J. R. Watson, *The English Hymn*, OUP, 1995, p.305.
3. *Christian Hymns* places this verse second, beginning and ending with Montgomery's final verse.

Henry Francis Lyte
(1793-1847)

'Who like me his praise should
sing?'

Praise, my soul, the King of heaven,
 to his feet thy tribute bring;
ransomed, healed, restored, forgiven,
 who like me his praise should sing?
 Praise him! Praise him!
 Praise the everlasting King.

Henry Francis Lyte

Henry Francis Lyte
(1793-1847)

'Who like me his praise should sing?'

Henry Francis Lyte was born in 1793 at Ednam, near Kelso in the Scottish Borders. A sensitive and delicate child, Henry was the second of three boys born to Anna and Thomas Lyte. Doubtless his father had chosen the village of Ednam, nestling on the banks of the Eden, a tributary of the Tweed, as a home for his family because of his own love of fishing and hunting. And in these pursuits he spent his days, neglecting his duties to his family, both as a father and as a breadwinner. Anna found herself left to fend for the family.

At last a day came when the relationship between Thomas Lyte and his wife became so strained that Thomas abandoned home altogether and travelled far off to Jersey in the Channel Islands. Before he left, however, he made arrangements for the two older boys to attend a school in Enniskillen, south-west of Omagh, Northern Ireland, even though Henry was little more than seven at the time. With her husband and older sons far away, Anna took the youngest boy and went to London in search of employment. There she began work as a nurse but before long her child died. Worn with suffering, Anna too had not long to live.

Meanwhile, Henry and his older brother knew nothing of these things. Homesick and lonely, Henry wondered why his mother did not come to him, or even write him a letter. She had been the only stabilizing influence in his young life and had taught him the truths of the Bible from an early age. No one told the child — possibly no one knew — that Anna had died. One of Henry Lyte's earliest poems expresses his desolation at his mother's unexplained absence:

> Stay, gentle shadow of my mother, stay;
> thy form but seldom comes to bless my sleep.
>
> Ye faithless slumbers, flit not thus away,
> and leave my wistful eyes to wake and weep…
> Light of my heart and guardian of my youth,
> thou com'st no more to fancy's slumbering bed,
> to aggravate the pangs of waking truth…

When no further financial support was provided for Henry and his brother it seemed that the boys would have to be placed in the Poor Law Institution. Dr Burrowes, headmaster of the Royal Portora School and a kindly man, was concerned about the future of his two pupils. Henry was showing uncommon abilities, and to abandon the boys to the institution would spell the end of any academic opportunities they might have had. Generously he decided to become their legal guardian and to fund the rest of their education himself.

Dr Burrowes, himself a clergyman of the Church of Ireland, impressed on Henry the importance of a strict adherence to his studies — perhaps a hard task for a dreamy eight-year-old, but one the boy did his best to fulfil, realizing that with no home support his future was dependent upon it. Idyllically situated on the banks of Loch Erne, the Royal Portora School provided constant stimulus to Henry's developing poetic gifts. Spring

flowers would carpet the banks of the Loch and verses that
Henry composed at just sixteen years of age illustrate his early
love of nature. Describing the delicate beauty of the primrose,
he wrote:

> Hail, lovely harbinger of Spring!
> Hail, little modest flower,
> fanned by the tempest's icy wing,
> dusted by the hoary shower…
> Thy gems are strewn in every place,
> on every bank they fling
> an early wreath, with artless grace
> around the brows of Spring…
> No plundering grasp, no heedless bruise
> shall harm one bud of thine,
> and, gaudier sweets while others choose,
> the primrose shall be mine.

Shortly before his sixteenth birthday, in May 1809, Henry
Lyte began his university course at Trinity College, Dublin,
hoping to enter the medical profession. Tall, good-looking and
with a boundless store of natural energy, he became a popular
figure during his college days, making lifelong friendships and
winning a number of university prizes for his poetry. But by the
time of his graduation in 1815, Henry had decided to enter
the Christian ministry rather than to follow a medical career.
After his ordination that same year he began parish duties at
the village church of Taghmon, nine miles from Wexford in the
south of Ireland.

Serious and diligent though he was, there is no evidence as
yet that Lyte had any personal experience of the grace of God.
But the young clergyman was lonely. The sudden change from
all the stimulus of university days to the solitude of a village
rectory with no one to challenge or engage him intellectually

left him depressed and vulnerable. Possibly in an attempt to counter this situation, Lyte gave himself to a variety of 'worldly pursuits' which, at his own confession, resulted in a long inner battle with sceptical and unbelieving thoughts, and even a measure of rebellion against God's ways.

These were the days when a widespread work of God was being felt in many parts of England and in Ireland too. Methodist churches founded by John Wesley and his preachers in the previous century were being quickened into new life. But Lyte was unimpressed: 'Methodist enthusiasts, weak simpletons, unable rationally to defend their beliefs,' was the way he described these local preachers. He did, however, form a close friendship during his time in Taghmon with the vicar of a nearby church — an 'upright, benevolent and sensible man', in Lyte's judgement.

When this friend was taken seriously ill, he turned to Lyte both to support him in his weakness and to make arrangements for his wife and young family if he should die. Henry Lyte spent much time with him and it soon became evident that his condition was deteriorating rapidly. Then the dying man asked a crucial question, 'How can I be sure of a happy eternity?' Lyte was stunned into silence as his friend went on to declare that they were both leading their people astray. In studying the Scriptures, he told Lyte, he had discovered that only the death and sufferings of Christ could atone for sin. Nothing else could fit him to spend eternity in the presence of God. When his friend died happy in this newly gained assurance that his sins were forgiven, Henry Lyte knew that he too would have to rethink the entire basis of his life and understanding.[1]

The loss of his friend, the loneliness of his situation, but more than all, his spiritual crisis, brought on a major breakdown in Lyte's health. Never strong constitutionally, his chest was affected and soon he began to show signs of the dreaded condition of tuberculosis. A long break was imperative. Taking leave of his congregation, the young clergyman travelled to France to convalesce. Here the warmer climate proved beneficial, and as he recovered strength, Lyte gave many hours to studying the Scriptures. He meditated on the experience of John Wesley, who like himself had begun to preach before he knew the inner assurance of forgiveness of sin. Before he left France, Henry Lyte was a changed man and could testify with Wesley that 'Christ has taken away my sins, even mine, and saved me from the law of sin and death.'

On his return to England in 1817 an appointment in the Cornish parish of Marazion, near Penzance, became available and here Henry Lyte, now twenty-five years of age, began a new ministry. Here too he met and fell in love with Anne Maxwell, who had come to Cornwall for a holiday. Unknown to Henry when he began to court Anne was the fact that she was heiress to a considerable fortune. Anne's father, rector of a parish in Bath, had once been on familiar terms with both John Wesley and George Whitefield. This did not mean, however, that Dr Maxwell in any way approved when his daughter began associating herself with a Methodist Society — far from it. After Anne, whose own mother had died shortly after her birth, was converted, her father was privately annoyed, while her stepmother displayed her disapproval openly. When Anne became engaged to a young clergyman with obvious 'Methodist views' the antagonism was even more marked.

Anne Maxwell and Henry Lyte were married the following year, 1818, and a very happy marriage it proved, although Anne's stepmother could still scarcely tolerate Henry; so much so, that at one time Anne was in danger of forfeiting her inheritance. It is thought that Henry had this situation in mind when he wrote the words of a hymn that was once among his most popular:

> Jesus, I my cross have taken,
>   all to leave and follow thee;
> destitute, despised, forsaken,
>   thou from hence my all shalt be.
> Perish every fond ambition
>   all I've sought, and hoped and known;
> yet how rich is my condition!
>   God and heaven are still my own.

Even though he faced the loss of income on which he relied owing to his indifferent health, he could continue in a verse omitted from our hymn books:

> Go, then, earthly fame and treasure;
>   come disaster, scorn and pain;
> in thy service pain is pleasure,
>   with thy favour loss is gain.
> I have called thee 'Abba, Father',
>   I have set my heart on thee;
> storms may howl, and clouds may gather,
>   all must work for good to me.

Commenting on the early days of his marriage, Henry wrote, 'In the evenings we are always together and very swiftly and happily do they glide away in conversation and reading.' Five children were born to the couple, although their second daughter died in infancy. Following the death of her father the year after the marriage Anne was, in fact, granted an annual income of £400 — a generous allowance in days when many clergyman struggled to support families on £60 or less. When her stepmother died twenty years later the whole of the family fortune was settled on Anne. This was a providence for Henry whose recurring ill-health called for long periods of recuperation in warmer climates such as the South of France or Italy.

Meanwhile, the climate of south-west Cornwall proved detrimental to Henry Lyte's uncertain health and soon his lung trouble flared up again. The only answer seemed to be to resign his parish duties and move further inland until he had regained some stability. This he did in 1821. A cottage in the New Forest in Hampshire proved an ideal location, and in this quiet wooded spot Henry gave time to writing verse. When he published *The Poet's Plea*, in which he urged the critics of his day to deal kindly with a young poet's work, he was rewarded with many accolades from the reviewers. The editor of *Blackwood's Magazine* compared the spirit and style of the poet to both William Wordsworth and Oliver Goldsmith; while *The Encyclopaedia Britannica*, commenting on such lines as:

> Deal gently with the poet. Think that he
> is made of finer clay than other men
> and ill can bear rough handling…
> A stony look, a lip of scorn may crush
> his young aspirings…

went further, comparing the lines with Gray's *Elegy*, and declaring:

> The poetry of Lyte is marked by refinement, pathos and beauty of thought. He also possesses great imaginative power. There are few poems in the English language that contain a greater wealth of it than this classic entitled *The Poet's Plea*.

But Henry Lyte's call to the ministry was strong and as soon as his health was restored he looked for another parish. In 1823 the thirty-year-old preacher moved once again, this time to Charlton, not far from Plymouth. During his time there George Canning, an eminent politician of the day and later to become prime minister, was deeply impressed after hearing Henry Lyte preach on the words of the apostle Paul, 'without God in the world'. Little more than eighteen months after Lyte's settlement at Charlton, George Canning used his influence with the king to nominate the preacher for the pulpit of the parish of Brixham — a fishing village whose rapidly rising population had now reached 4000.

Perched on the side of the cliff, a new church had been built the previous year to meet the needs of the people. Here Lyte was to conduct a ministry that would last the rest of his life. Brixham, situated on the southernmost point of Torbay, was the scene of constant activity as the fishing vessels came and went. The rough fishing community warmly accepted the young family and soon the new church, seating seven hundred, was crowded to hear Henry Lyte's pointed messages.

Many of the fishermen's homes were hewn out of the sides of the cliffs, and Henry Lyte would toil up the steep paths as he visited his scattered parishioners — no easy assignment for a man of his uncertain health. As he stood before his congregation each Sunday, he knew well that when the men set off for the fishing grounds, some would never return. To the skipper of each vessel he gave a copy of the Bible, urging him to read it both privately and to his men. So greatly was Henry Lyte respected that these hardened seafaring men voted that each time the ships set out the men would all come, ready clad in their heavy protective garments, to listen to a final sermon before their departure.

Anne Lyte shared in all the joys and sorrows of their parish, visiting the sick and using her means to bring consolation and relief, especially when a young family was left destitute by some disaster at sea. Yet despite all this, her early loyalty to the Methodists remained strong. Each Sunday morning the vicar and his family could be seen driving in their chaise to the door of the Methodist chapel. Dismounting, Henry would give Anne a hand down and she would enter the Methodist church and worship there, while her family proceeded to All Saints. In the evenings Anne attended the parish church with Henry.

During his years in Brixham, Lyte was concerned to enrich every part of the worship of the people and in this period he wrote many of his best-known hymns. Critics were less kind when he published his *Poems Chiefly Religious* in 1833, which contained most of the hymns that have subsequently come into widespread usage. Many sound a wistful note, perhaps reflecting the poet's constant struggle with ill health. John Julian in his *Dictionary of Hymnology* speaks of their 'sadness, tenderness and beauty'. Such words as these are typical:

> In thee I place my trust
> on thee I calmly rest;
> I know thee good, I know thee just,
> and count thy choice the best.

> Whate'er events betide,
> thy will they all perform;
> safe in thy breast my head I hide,
> Nor fear the coming storm.

> Let good or ill befall,
> it must be good for me;
> secure of having thee in all,
> of having all in thee.

In 1834 he published *The Spirit of the Psalms,* a loose paraphrase of sixty-six of the psalms — verses which Erik Routley in his classic *Hymns and Human Life* describes as 'magnificent'. In times of sickness and need Lyte himself had often drawn consolation from the experiences of David and others in former days. So now he wished the worshippers at All Saints to share the same benefits. Outstanding among them is his rendering of Psalm 103:

> Praise, my soul, the King of heaven,
>   to his feet your tribute bring;
> ransomed, healed, restored, forgiven,
>   who like me his praise should sing?
>   Praise him! praise him!
>   Praise the everlasting King.

Written in trochaic metre, the strong beat at the beginning of every line gives the hymn a robust, even joyful note. 'Ransomed, healed', 'Slow to chide', and 'Angels help us…' are examples of this. On several occasions Lyte inverts the word order of the second line of a couplet, adding significance to the first:

> Frail as summer's flower we perish:
>   *blows the wind* and it is gone.

Or:

> Sun and moon, bow down before him,
>   *dwellers all* in time and space.

With a wistful reference to the qualities of fatherhood that he himself had never known, he writes:

> Father-like he tends and spares us,

and then again inverts the word order in the following line:

> *well our feeble frame* he knows.

The jubilant exhortation to praise God at the close of each verse is not a mere repetition of words, for each final line extols a different aspect of the character of God, whom Lyte acclaims as everlasting, faithful, merciful, changeless and gracious.

> Praise him! Praise him!
> Praise with us the God of grace.

This hymn has found a place in British national life, being among those sung during at least two significant royal weddings, those of George VI and of Elizabeth II. More recently it formed the opening hymn for the Jubilee thanksgiving service held to commemorate the fifty years of the reign of Elizabeth II in St Paul's Cathedral in June 2002. And far away in a Japanese prisoner-of-war camp this great hymn was sung, not by well-attired guests at some royal occasion, but by emaciated and ragged prisoners: British, American, Australian and Dutch men who bore in their bodies the marks of torture and disease. As news of VJ Day (15 August 1945) came across the crackling wireless, the men spontaneously wished to praise God for their deliverance, and this was the hymn they sang together as they gathered for an impromptu service. The opening note for the hymn was pitched by an ex-East London barman:

> Praise him for his grace and favour,
> to our fathers in distress,
> praise him still the same for ever,
> slow to chide and swift to bless.
> Praise him! Praise him!
> Glorious in his faithfulness.

How little could Henry Lyte have anticipated such events!

As with all his Psalm versions, 'Praise, Lord, for thee in Zion waits' is an interpretation of Psalm 65 rather than a paraphrase; and is therefore more accurately described as being 'based on' the psalm. As Lyte traces the believer's cry to God, 'the sinner's friend', he is carried forward in his thought to the plentiful provision that the Creator makes for his people both in the world of nature and in the realm of grace. He ends with

a prayer that, as the natural world is renewed in spring, so God
would refresh and revive his church:

> Lord, on our souls thy Spirit pour;
> the moral waste within restore;
> O let thy love our spring-tide be,
> and make us all bear fruit to thee.

In his paraphrase of Psalm 18, Lyte depicts in dramatic language
the believer's experience of the help of God out of deep distress.
Basing his words of David's great song of deliverance from his
enemies, his poetic genius finds full expression:

> The storm upon us fell,
>   the floods around us rose;
> the depths of death and hell
>   seemed on our souls to close;
> to God we cried in strong despair;
> he heard, and came to help our prayer.
>
> Above the storm he stood,
>   and awed it to repose;
> he drew us from the flood,
>   and scattered all our foes.
> He set us in a spacious place,
> and there upholds us by his grace.

A rendering of Psalm 67, found in most modern hymnals, has
also proved of lasting worth:

> God of mercy, God of grace
> show the brightness of thy face;
> shine upon us, Saviour shine;

> fill thy church with light divine;
> and thy saving health extend
> unto earth's remotest end.

With a skilful use of opposites and reversal of word order in the last verse, Lyte creates a memorable conclusion:

> God to man his blessing give,
> man to God devoted live:
> all below, and all above,
> one in joy and light and love.

Constant illness, coupled with the instability springing from the loss of his childhood home, frequently turned Lyte's mind to the security of the heritage and home awaiting believers in the life to come. Even his secular poems echoed this theme:

> There is change in all below;
>   nought sure beneath the sky:
> suns rise and set, tides ebb and flow
>   and man but lives to die.

Yet as a Christian, Lyte could not end on such a dismal note, so continues:

> And let them pass — each earthly thing —
>   while, Lord, 'tis mine to stand
> on thy eternal word, and cling
>   to thy almighty hand.

His rendering of Psalm 84 picks up this theme. Even though he experienced the comforts of his home and family, he looked for a more permanent joy:

> Pleasant are thy courts above,
> in the land of light and love;
> pleasant are thy courts below,
> in this land of sin and woe.
>
> O my spirit longs and faints
> for the converse of thy saints,
> for the brightness of thy face,
> for thy fulness, God of grace.

As he meditates on the joys of those who arrive at last in that 'land of light and love' he concludes with a prayer that he too may attain to those joys:

> Lord, be mine this prize to win;
> guide me through a world of sin;
> keep me by thy saving grace;
> give me at thy side a place.

Without the alleviation of modern drugs, Henry Lyte's asthma and bronchitis proved a serious handicap, making even walking difficult at times. But he had one privilege that eased many days of illness for the poet-preacher: his beautiful garden at Berry Head House not far from Brixham. At one time a military hospital, the magnificent structure, with views over Torbay and out across Dartmoor, had fallen into disuse after the defeat of Napoleon in 1815. Opened first as a rest home in 1831, Berry Head House then became Anne and Henry's home in 1832 and remained so until the end of Henry's life. A welcome place of retreat, he had the gardens laid out, transforming the rambling wasteland to a delightful haven with unusual species of plants and trees. Here too he built up a library, so comprehensive that when his son came at last to sell it after his father's death, the sale at Sotheby's lasted for seventeen days.

But even the gardens of Berry Head House could not supply the health that Lyte needed for his labours among the fishermen of Brixham. At last in 1839 when he was forty-six his doctor warned him that unless he travelled to a more congenial climate during the winter months, his life expectancy would be brief at best. A sensitive man and a lover of family and home, Henry postponed the decision as long as he dared. In days when travel was slow and amenities restricted, there could be no possibility of uprooting his family each winter that they might accompany him on his travels. So from 1840 onwards he braced himself for the long separations from Anne and his children. From some remote though lovely spot in Naples, he wrote sadly:

> Stern Britain, why a home deny
> to one who loves as well as I,
> who woos thee with as warm a zeal
> as sons for tenderest mothers feel...
> and would this moment rather share
> your homely fireside converse there,
> and smile with you 'neath wintry skies
> than reign in this fair paradise?

Added to the pain of these regular partings, Lyte faced the distress of seeing his All Saints congregation divided and weakened by the rise of the Plymouth Brethren movement. Although he was not unsympathetic to the ideals of the movement, Lyte felt that the divisive effect on many well-established and united congregations could only be a retrograde one.

His visits to France, Switzerland and Italy proved beneficial to some extent, but Lyte was frequently unwell, even as he travelled: 'I have been too ill to visit or take any interest in the various attractive objects around me,' he wrote to Anne from Italy. 'I enjoyed the blue mountains close by Mont Blanc that ennobled our voyage down the Rhône and I gasped or tottered through a palace or two...' He then drew the conclusion that Anne must secretly have guessed, 'I sometimes think that I am near the end of my journey altogether, but I hang on the goodness and mercy of God and amid the watches of the night enjoy some comfortable meditations on his pardoning love, his restoring grace and his protecting providence.'

When Henry Lyte returned home in the spring of 1847, he knew it would probably be his last summer with his family at Berry Head House. The ministry at All Saints was now mainly undertaken by his son-in-law and Henry only preached when he felt able. Much of his time he spent in the quietness of his gardens, and there was one particular spot where he could often be found: a seat at the far end overlooking the sea. Here he would meditate, watching the play of sun on water.

A serious illness towards the end of the summer months only confirmed what Henry and Anne already knew: that his work on earth was almost done. Sitting one evening on his customary seat during his period of convalescence, he was watching the sun set across the sea. As twilight slowly gave place to darkness, he began to meditate on God's unchangeable nature in contrast to the uncertainty of all created things. He then began to think on the Scripture narrative of the disciples on the road to Emmaus after the crucifixion. 'Abide with us,' they had said, 'for it is toward evening.' Translating his thoughts to verse, he began:

> Abide with me, fast falls the eventide.
> The darkness deepens; Lord, with me abide.

The words immediately take on an autobiographical character. We can almost hear the child Henry calling out in the dark for his mother to stay with him. The second line is a repetition of the first, except for the reversal of word order, emphasizing the gathering gloom as night approaches; the reference to his childhood becomes yet clearer in the following two lines:

> When other helpers fail and comforts flee,
> help of the helpless, O abide with me.

But now his days were fast slipping away for, like the ebbing of the sea, nothing in this life remains changeless and stable:

> Swift to its close ebbs out life's little day;
> earth's joys grow dim, its glories pass away.
> Change and decay in all around I see:
> O thou who changest not, abide with me.

He recalled the time when he had lived in unbelief:

> Thou on my head in early youth didst smile,
> and, though rebellious and perverse meanwhile,
> thou hast not left me, oft as I left thee;
> on to the close, O Lord, abide with me.

For much of his life Lyte had feared death, but not long before, in conversation with a friend, he had been given a new appreciation of Christ's conquest over this last enemy:

> I fear no foe, with thee at hand to bless;
> ills have no weight, and tears no bitterness:
> Where is death's sting? Where, grave, thy victory?
> I triumph still, if thou abide with me.

Many of these lines contain a dramatic pause, a caesura, usually after the first four syllables — an arrangement that compels us to focus on the solemnity of the words we are singing. Lyte uses this arrangement of his thought many times over, and particularly in the first verse.

As night at last closed in, Lyte left his seat and returned to the house. Here he wrote out the words of this hymn for his wife. A few weeks before this he had written a long poem describing the thoughts of a believer who knows that he will shortly leave this earth. One wish above all he had expressed in those lines, not for fame or some elaborate memorial:

> But might I leave behind
> some blessing for my fellows, some fair trust
> to guide, to cheer, to elevate my kind
> when I am in the dust.
> Might verse of mine inspire
> one virtuous aim, one high resolve impart,
> light in one drooping soul a hallowed fire,
> or bind one broken heart —
> Death would be sweeter then...

And in 'Abide with me', a hymn dubiously classified in many hymnals as an evening hymn, Lyte's wish was abundantly fulfilled. 'Abide with me', wrote Erik Routley, 'ranks with the classics in every sense. In it this obscure and humble curate has ministered to a parish as wide as the English-speaking world.'

With the coming of autumn, Lyte prepared to leave the country once more but on 4 September 1847, the Sunday before he was due to travel, he astonished his family by announcing at the breakfast table that he would like to preach that morning. Preparations were hastily made and his congregation watched with joy and apprehension as the emaciated figure of their pastor slowly mounted the pulpit steps. Describing himself as 'one alive from the dead' the preacher seemed to be buoyed up by an inward vigour that overcame his weakness. With full heart he preached, exhorting and warning his people for what seemed certain to be the last time. As he set out the following day the streets of Brixham were lined with rugged fishermen, their wives and children, who waited to see his carriage pass, and many were the tears that were shed as they waved their last goodbye.

Crossing the Channel, Lyte and his party drove on. Through breathtaking scenery they passed, with autumn colours glowing against snow-capped mountains. But as they neared Nice, Lyte was taken ill with 'flu, a fatal condition for a man with his chest complaint. And there in a hotel room in Nice, far from home and family, it quickly became apparent that Henry Lyte was dying. 'I glory not save in the cross of our Lord Jesus Christ,' he whispered as the end drew near. 'O there is nothing terrible in death,' exclaimed the man who had long feared its approach, 'Jesus Christ steps down into the grave before me... Blessed faith! Today piercing through the mist of earth; tomorrow changed to sight! Abiding for ever with the Lord.' It was even as he had written:

> Hold thou thy cross before my closing eyes,
> shine through the gloom and point me to the skies;
> heaven's morning breaks and earth's vain shadows flee:
> in life, in death, O Lord, abide with me.

And on 20 November 1747 the light of heaven shone through the gloom as the eternal morning broke for Henry Lyte. He was fifty-four. His last words were 'Peace... joy...'

Notes

1. Some accounts of the life of Henry Lyte place these events a few years later during his Brixham ministry, but a biography by a friend of the family has recorded them during his period in Taghmon.

Horatius Bonar
(1808 –1889)

Prince of Scottish hymn-writers

I heard the voice of Jesus say,
'Behold, I freely give
the living water — thirsty one,
stoop down, and drink, and live!'
I came to Jesus, and I drank
of that life-giving stream;
my thirst was quenched, my soul revived,
and now I live in him.

Horatius Bonar

Horatius Bonar
(1808-1889)

Prince of Scottish hymn-writers

The young assistant minister of St John's in Leith, not far from Edinburgh, was troubled. Recently licensed by the Edinburgh Presbytery of the Church of Scotland, the twenty-five-year-old Horatius Bonar had been placed in charge of a district of Leith and given particular responsibility for the children's work. But things were not going very well. In a small red notebook he had entered the names of almost three hundred children who attended the services on a Sunday. But they appeared bored and listless. As they sang the metrical psalms and paraphrases of Scripture they were disinterested and easily distracted. What could he do to arrest their attention and so gain a hearing for the message of the Christian gospel?

Then one day Horatius Bonar made a discovery — a discovery that would have lifelong implications, for the young people, certainly, but more so for himself. He noticed that as these same children were playing in the streets or walking home from school they were singing, and delighting to sing, many of the popular tunes of the day — which of course had secular words. What if he could compose Christian words to these tunes which they clearly enjoyed? Would that create a response, he wondered? It seemed an experiment worth trying.

And before many days had passed he had begun to teach the children some new words set to one of their favourite tunes:

> I lay my sins on Jesus,
>   the spotless Lamb of God;
> he bears them all and frees us
>   from the accursed load.
> I bring my wants to Jesus,
>   to wash my crimson stains
> white in his blood most precious,
>   till not a spot remains.

The response was remarkable. The young people soon showed a new interest in the services. And so he tried another composition, one that began 'The morning, the bright and the beautiful morning/is up'... and in the final verse he urged the young singers to yield the early morning of their lives to the Saviour:

> O now let us haste to our heavenly Father
>   and ere the fair skies of life's dawning be dim,
> let us come with glad hearts, let us come altogether,
>   and the morning of youth let us hallow to him.

Horatius Bonar had begun his life work.

Born in Edinburgh on 19 December 1808, Horatius was one of a family of eleven. Two of his brothers, Andrew and John, would also enter the Christian ministry. The family was brought up in days when 'moderatism', with its deadening effects on the souls of the people, was widespread in the Church of Scotland. As the Scottish church historian Thomas McCrie wrote, those were days when 'to deliver a gospel sermon or to preach to the hearts and consciences of dying sinners, was as completely beyond their power as to speak in the language of angels'. However, the Bonar family were privileged beyond most.

They attended the Lady Glenorchy Church in Edinburgh, and were brought up listening to the warm evangelical preaching of Thomas Snell Jones, who had been trained as one of the first students at Trevecca College, founded by the Countess of Huntingdon in 1768. Horatius was to record in verse his gratitude to God for these things:

> I thank thee…
> for seeds of truth and light and purity
> sown in this heart from childhood's earliest age;
>> for word and church and watchful ministry,
>> the beacon and the tutor and the guide.

As a student at Edinburgh University, Horatius, who had early experienced a true work of grace in his life, quickly began to associate with an influential group of like-minded friends, particularly men such as Robert Murray M'Cheyne. His period of study under Thomas Chalmers, Professor of Divinity from 1828 onwards, also proved a dominant influence in the life of the young Horatius Bonar.

Like most poets, Bonar had begun to express his thoughts in verse at a young age. At nineteen he published his first poem, one that depicted the desolation of an old man left without family or friends:

> He stood bewildered on his lonely hearth;
> sadness was written on his fixèd brow…
> proudly he stood, yet sorrowfully too,
> the latest leaf upon the topmost bough
> of a tall oak that lately threw
> its hundred leafy arms when summer days were new.

After four years as an assistant missioner in Leith, Horatius Bonar was ordained in 1837 and appointed as the minister

of North Church, Kelso, in the Scottish Borders. Full of zeal
and desire to influence his Kelso congregation, Bonar sounded
one clarion note above all others: 'You must be born again.'
Surprised by the starkness of his approach, some of his hearers
were offended, but with others the message went home to
their hearts; many were converted and the church built up.
Commenting later, Bonar expressed the opinion that the reason
why the gospel often seems to make so little progress may well
be traced to a lack of clarity at this very point — the paramount
importance of the new birth.

Reticent by nature, Horatius Bonar, in common with many
Scotsmen, was reserved about his personal and private thoughts.
But in his poetry he found an emotional outlet. Addressing his
'lute', as he termed his muse, he wrote:

> Thou art the lute with which I sung my sadness,
> when sadness like a cloud begirt my way;
> thou art the harp whose strings gave out my gladness
> when burst the sunshine of a happier day.

But when he married Jane Lundie in 1843, he found a
partner who understood him and was well suited to his poetic
temperament. Jane too wrote verse and several of her hymns
are found among Horatius' early collections.

1843 was also a momentous year for the Church of
Scotland. At last there came a parting of the ways known as the
Disruption. The issue of patronage of the church by the state
was the catalyst that brought it about; but in essence the new
spiritual life expressed in the ministry of such men as Robert
M'Cheyne, William Burns, Andrew, John and Horatius Bonar,
with that of many others, could no longer co-exist with the
moderatism of the Church of Scotland. Under the leadership
of Thomas Chalmers, over four hundred and fifty men were
prepared to sacrifice home, stipend and church buildings for

the sake of spiritual freedom and the gospel truths they valued. So began the Free Church of Scotland with which Bonar and his Kelso church identified.

Scottish hymnody was in its infancy when Horatius Bonar started his ministry. During the evangelical revival of the previous century, hymn-singing had become increasingly popular as Charles Wesley in England and William Williams in Wales gave the people the great truths of the gospel in song. As we have seen, the Church of England only authorized the singing of hymns in a service of worship in 1820, more than thirty years after Charles Wesley's death. But north of the border, psalmody remained the order of the day, together with a few Scripture paraphrases, for many years longer; hymns were not regarded in a favourable light until after 1861 when a small collection of eighty-nine hymns gained official approval in the Church of Scotland. Despite such restrictions, Horatius Bonar had been writing both poems and hymns ever since his first ministry in Leith. One of his earliest compositions to have survived the years was designed to encourage his fellow-workers:

> Go, labour on, spend and be spent,
>   your joy to do the Father's will;
> it is the way the Master went;
>   should not the servant tread it still?

> Toil on, faint not, keep watch and pray;
>   be wise the erring soul to win;
> go forth into the world's highway,
>   compel the wanderer to come in.

Crammed into small notebooks were ideas which Bonar began to jot down for his hymns and poems. Sometimes he would write an entire script. Glancing at a few of these early manuscripts, photographed and later published by his son after his father's death, it is apparent that Bonar would compose a complete hymn virtually in its final form. He then returned and polished up his work. Some words were crossed out and sometimes entire lines replaced with a variant written either in the margin or above the original. Clearly, though, the initial poem was the result of the elevated thought or inspiration of the moment.

In that same momentous year of 1843, Bonar published his first small selection of hymns called *Songs of the Wilderness,* mainly intended for the use of children. It included only two or three of his own compositions. Two years later he produced a more substantial book of hymns that he had collected together, this time containing some three hundred pieces. Entitled *The Bible Hymn Book*, this second volume included sixteen or seventeen of his hymns, but with nothing to indicate that Bonar had written them. In this second collection we find a hymn considered by many to be the best Bonar ever wrote:

> I heard the voice of Jesus say,
>   'Come unto me and rest,
> lay down, thou weary one, lay down
>   thy head upon my breast.'
> I came to Jesus as I was,
>   weary and worn and sad,
> I found in him a resting place
>   and he has made me glad.

This hymn has been described as unique in hymnody for its unusual construction. Each verse contains in its first four lines an invitation from the Saviour, followed in its second four lines by a response from the one addressed. In the third and final verse, the words mount to a crescendo of mercy on the one hand and an answer of confident joy on the other:

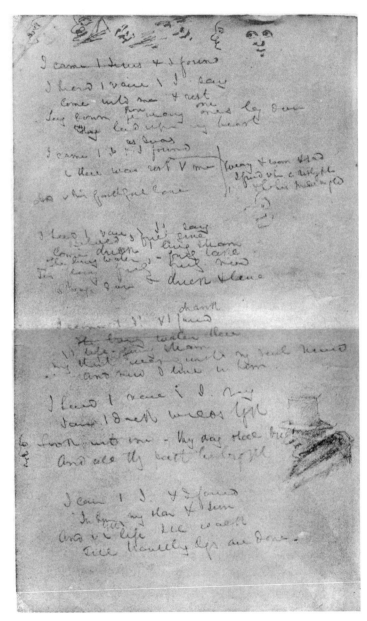

Pencil ms of Bonar's hymn

I heard the voice of Jesus say,
'I am this dark world's light;
look unto me, thy morn shall rise
and all thy days be bright.'
I looked to Jesus and I found
in him my star, my sun;
and in that light of life I'll walk
till travelling days are done.

One commentator on hymns and their background stories asserts that in his view only the Last Day will reveal the hundreds who will be able to testify to the part that this hymn played in their conversion.

During the following twenty years Bonar wrote numerous hymns and poems reflecting his personal experiences, his convictions and his future hopes. At last in 1857 the first of three volumes, each to be entitled *Hymns of Faith and Hope*, was published, this first containing a hundred and fifteen hymns, but now with Bonar as the named author. Four years later a second volume was in circulation, with a further one hundred and twenty-three compositions; five years after that, in 1866, came the last of the trilogy with another one hundred hymns and a number of psalms set to verse. The total number of hymns written by Bonar would eventually rise to more than 600.

The great themes of the Christian gospel dominated Bonar's thought and can be found throughout his hymns: sin, judgement, Christ's atoning death, his righteousness imputed to the believer, the Christian life with its joys and trials, the hope of heaven, and the prospect of Christ's second coming. As a typical Victorian, Bonar tended to write in a style at once too flowery, too emotional, for modern taste. Many of his hymns lack the sturdy reality of compositions from the previous century: hymns that sprang from a background of persecution and resurgent spiritual life, like those of Charles Wesley. Although the hymnologist John Julian, writing in 1909, could then count nearly a hundred of Bonar's hymns in common use, in our own day that number has shrunk to a mere handful, with modern collections containing only some ten to fifteen. In his *Dictionary of Hymnology* Julian writes of Bonar's hymns, 'They win the heart by their tone of tender sympathy, they sing the truth of God in ringing tones', and it is this, together with a warmth and simplicity of expression, that gives those that are left their enduring value. The singer may readily identify with such words as:

> Not what these hands have done
> can save this guilty soul;
> not what this toiling flesh has borne
> can make my spirit whole.

> Thy work alone O Christ,
> Can ease this weight of sin;
> thy blood alone, O Lamb of God,
> can give me peace within.

And on a similar theme:

> Thy death, not mine, O Christ,
> has paid the ransom due;
> ten thousand deaths like mine
> would have been all too few.
> To whom save thee,
> who can alone
> for sin atone,
> Lord, shall we flee?

The strength, beauty and simplicity of such words as:

> I hear the words of love,
> I gaze upon the blood,
> I see the mighty sacrifice,
>   and I have peace with God

will always find an echo in the Christian's experience.

The wide range of metres and stanza length chosen by Bonar for his work indicates that many of his pieces were written as poems and not initially intended for public singing. Some needed tunes specially composed to accompany them, as for example the tune *Berwyn*, set to:

> Light of the world, for ever, ever shining,
>   there is no change in thee;
> true light of life, all joy and health enshrining,
>   thou canst not fade or flee.

A specific tune, appropriately named *Kelso*, was set to 'No blood, no altar now, the sacrifice is o'er'. But the verses Horatius Bonar wrote as hymns and set to regular metres would seem to be the ones that have best survived the years. Such words as these have an undying quality:

> Fill thou my life, O Lord my God,
>   in every part with praise,
> that my whole being may proclaim
>   thy being and thy ways.

Or:

> I bless the Christ of God,
> I rest on love divine,
> and with unfaltering lip and heart
>   I call this Saviour mine.

Or again:

> All that I am while here on earth,
>   all that I hope to be,
> when Jesus comes and glory dawns,
>   I owe it, Lord, to thee.

A hymn, or perhaps more strictly a poem, which Bonar himself regarded as one of his favourites, was based on Solomon's prayer at the dedication of the temple. Beginning 'When the weary, seeking rest, to thy goodness flee', Bonar describes all the situations of need in which men and women might find themselves. He depicts how such people turn to their God in their distress and ends each verse with the prayer:

> Hear then, in love, O Lord, the cry,
> in heaven, thy dwelling place on high.

In the final verse he returns to a favourite theme: the longing of the believer for Christ's second coming:

> When thy widowed, weeping church,
>   looking for a home,
> sendeth up her silent sigh,
>   'Come, Lord Jesus, come!'
> Hear then, in love, O Lord, the cry,
> in heaven, thy dwelling place on high.

Few of Bonar's hymns carry any date or indication of the circumstances in which they were written. One exception is the well-known communion hymn, 'Here, O my Lord, I see thee face to face'.[1] This was written in October 1855 at the request of his brother John. Each year Horatius would attend the annual Communion Season at his brother's church in

Greenock to help with the administration. This hymn, speaking clearly of the imputed righteousness of Christ, still finds a place in modern hymn books:

> Mine is the sin, but thine the righteousness;
>   mine is the guilt, but thine the cleansing blood!
> Here is my robe, my refuge and my peace —
>   thy blood, thy righteousness, O Lord my God.

Another hymn that can be traced to a particular event is one entitled 'Yet there is Room'. In one of the Moody and Sankey campaigns, Ira Sankey was in trouble. He had planned to sing lines written by the poet Alfred Lord Tennyson, based on the parable of the ten virgins, which he had set to music:

> Late, late, so late, and dark the night and chill,
> late, late, so late, but we can enter still.
> Too late, too late! Ye cannot enter now!

But when Tennyson's publishers withdrew permission for the lines to be used or printed, Sankey turned to Bonar. Could he help him by composing lines in the same metre to fit his tune? And so the Scottish poet produced:

> Yet there is room! The Lamb's bright hall of song,
> with its fair glory beckons you along.
> Room, room, still room; O enter, enter now!

It is recorded that one young woman had been invited to hear Moody preach at one of the missions, but attended only under duress and was not in the least touched by the message. However, when Sankey sang Bonar's hymn with its warning in the final line of the last verse, 'No room, no room! O woeful cry, No room!' she was convicted of her need and converted.

Hymns and poems were by no means the only literary productions of Bonar's Kelso years. No fewer than sixteen other publications flowed from his ready pen. One who knew him well commented that he seemed to be always writing, always working. Late into the night a lamp would be burning in his study. Titles such as *Night of Weeping*,[2] *Words Old and New*,[3] *Fifty-Two Short Sermons for Family Reading* and others were products of these years.

Yet more significant were the Kelso Tracts. These evangelistic pamphlets written by Horatius numbered thirty-six in all and proved highly popular. Published by his brother Andrew, they included such titles as *Believe and Live, God's Way of Peace* and *God's Way of Holiness*. With a heart full of compassion for the lost, Bonar used every means that he could to persuade the unbeliever to turn in faith to Christ. Some were critical of the tracts suggesting that his appeal to sinners went beyond Scripture — but not Dr Thomas Chalmers, who declared, 'I hold by that theology. It is the theology of the open door of salvation. Dr Bonar is a master in a presentation of a free gospel to the chief of sinners.' Even Queen Victoria knew and loved to read *Believe and Live*. This one title had a worldwide circulation with more than a million copies distributed. *God's Way of Peace* achieved a circulation of 280,000 copies.

Despite all this intense activity, Horatius Bonar was essentially a family man. He loved little children, and as he walked around Kelso he might well find a small hand placed in his, as some local child looked up confidently at him and began to tell him all his day's activities. Eleven children were born into the Kelso manse, but sadly Jane and Horatius lost five of their family in death during infancy or childhood. It is likely that his early book, *Night of Weeping,* published in 1845, and offering an interpretation of suffering in the lives of believers, sprang from thoughts relating to the death of their first child. In a book that has brought consolation to many troubled Christians over the years, Bonar describes suffering as the family badge and privilege of all true believers as they follow Christ, the Man of Sorrows.

Always a private man, Bonar did not allow many to share in his personal griefs but instead would commit his thoughts to the pages of his notebook in the form of poetry. He stipulated in his will that no biography should ever be written of him. However, by comparing entries in his brother Andrew's published diary with dates given for some of the poems, we may glean an idea of the sorrows that Jane and Horatius Bonar experienced as their family circle was depleted by death.

In June 1850, while Horatius was away from home, he received a message telling of the sudden illness and death of a baby daughter. Referring to this painful circumstance, his brother Andrew commented, 'May the Lord speak to my brother's heart and to Jane's for he has withered their gourd.' This loss was followed eight years later by the death of Lucy. Describing the helpless anguish of parents who can only watch as some dearly-loved child slips away, Bonar wrote:

All night we watched the ebbing life,
    as if its flight to stay;
till as the dawn was coming up
    our last hope passed away.

'Farewell,' with weeping hearts we said,
    'child of our love and care!'
And then we ceased to kiss those lips,
    for Lucy was not there.

But years are moving quickly past,
    and time will soon be o'er.
Death shall be swallowed up of life
    on the immortal shore.

1869 was a hard year for Jane and Horatius Bonar as two more of their children died; in March, an infant son, Henry. In a poem entitled 'Taken from the evil to come', Bonar writes:

> He died to live; for Jesus died:
>   he lives to die no more.
> Why weep for one whose tears are dried,
>   for whom all death is o'er?
>
> In the first opening stage of life
>   the little traveller failed;
> too rough the road, too full of strife —
>   the gentle spirit quailed.
>
> In the first storm the little bark
>   went down beneath the foam;
> in its first flight the little lark
>   soared to its kindred home.

But when Kitty died only four months later, grief appears to have silenced the poet. No words mark her passing. A hymn that has brought blessing to many others may well have come from this trial:

> Thy way, not mine, O Lord,
>   however dark it be!
> Lead me by thine own hand;
>   choose out the path for me.
>
> Take thou my cup, and it
>   with joy or sorrow fill,
> as best to thee may seem:
>   choose thou my good and ill.

Such experiences turned Bonar's mind frequently to the eternal city where pain and death are gone for ever. Thoughts of the imminent return of Christ and his own 'homesickness' for that better country are reflected in many of his hymns and poems. Once very popular, but not so well known today, were the lines he entitled 'A Pilgrim's Song', beginning 'A few more years shall roll':

> A few more struggles here,
> a few more partings o'er,
> a few more toils, a few more tears,
> and we shall weep no more.
> Then, O my Lord, prepare
> my soul for that blest day;
> O wash me in thy precious blood,
> and take my sins away.

A further bereavement in the family many years later had a direct bearing on the lives of Horatius and Jane Bonar. The death of their son-in-law left their daughter and her five young children in a desperate situation. With a heart of compassion, the couple, now elderly themselves, invited the family to come and share their home. Surrounded once more by the chatter of young children, Bonar saw in these circumstances a compensation from God for the five he and Jane had lost. Writing to a friend, he said, 'God took five [of my] children from [this] life some years ago; and he has given me [an]other five to bring up for him in my old age.'

After a ministry spanning twenty-three years in Kelso, Horatius Bonar received a call to undertake the ministry as first pastor of the newly-formed Chalmers Memorial Church in Edinburgh. Glad of the privilege and honour of being associated in this way with Thomas Chalmers, whom he considered the greatest man he had known, he accepted the invitation, holding the position with dignity and with considerable blessing on his preaching, until well after his seventy-fifth birthday. In 1883 he was appointed as Moderator by the Free Church General Assembly — the highest honour his denomination could bestow on one of its own.

For Horatius Bonar the last years of life were hard. The death of his wife Jane in 1884 left him bereft. Like many in old age he often reminisced over past years:

> I miss the well-remembered faces,
>> the voices, forms, of fresher days:
> time ploughs not up these deep-drawn traces,
>> these lines no ages can erase.

Now, however, his thought focused yet more on a brighter world to come:

> My hopes are passing upward, onward,
>> and with my hopes my heart has gone;
> my eye is turning skyward, sunward,
>> where glory brightens round yon throne.

But in 1887, three years after Jane's death, he himself was taken ill with a terminal condition that was accompanied by increasing pain. With few drugs to alleviate his sufferings, the seventy-nine-year-old poet found writing impossible and concentrated thought difficult. Dark days of depression and pain at times overwhelmed his sensitive spirit. 'Useless, useless, useless,' he would cry, particularly after a sleepless night. Perhaps he then recalled words he had written for a friend a few years earlier:

> Sleep cometh not when most I seem to need
>> its kindly balm. O Father, be to me
> better than sleep; and let those sleepless hours
>> be hours of blessed fellowship with thee.
> 'In me you shall have peace.'

But on better days he would say, 'O what a mercy to be free from pain! Let us say the 103rd Psalm!' Only the knowledge of the changeless love of God sustained him in the long-fought battle with debilitating pain. Maybe he thought back on words written many years before:

> The clouds may come and go,
>   the storms may sweep my sky —
> this blood-sealed friendship changes not:
>   the cross is ever nigh.

> I change, he changes not
>   the Christ can never die;
> his love, not mine, the resting place
>   his truth, not mine, the tie.

And when the end finally came on 31 July 1889, Horatius Bonar, like many other Christian men and women before him, found no consolation in anything he had been, done or written, but only in the atoning sacrifice of Christ for sinners. In his dying he could truly say:

> Not what I am, O Lord, but what thou art!
>   That, that alone can be my soul's true rest;
> thy love, not mine, bids fear and doubt depart,
>   and stills the tempest of this tossing breast.

Notes

1. In Bonar's ms. version of this hymn the first line reads, 'Here Lord, I meet thee, love thee, and embrace...'
2. Republished 1997 under the title *When God's Children Suffer*, Grand Rapids: Kregel Press Inc.
3. Republished Edinburgh, Banner of Truth Trust, 2000.

Frances Ridley Havergal
(1836-1879)

'In full and glad surrender'

Take my life and let it be
consecrated, Lord, to thee;
take my moments and my days,
let them flow in ceaseless praise.

Take my voice and let me sing
always, only for my King;
take my lips and let them be
filled with messages from thee.

Frances Ridley Havergal

Frances Ridley Havergal
(1836-1879)

'In full and glad surrender'

Resting her elbows on the window ledge of her attic bedroom, Frances Ridley Havergal, then a child of eight, gazed out at the small patch of sky and trees that she could see between the red brick of warehouses and the grey walls of St Nicholas Parish Church in Worcester. Beyond lay the hills and fields of the Worcestershire countryside, but the girl could not see them. Frances was a lonely child. Born at the close of 1836, only months before Queen Victoria came to the throne, she was the sixth and youngest in William and Jane Havergal's family. Her three older sisters, Miriam, Maria and Ellen, and her brother Henry were by this time all young adults. Only Frank, now fifteen, had been a companion of her childhood years. But Fanny, as she was called, was lonely for other reasons. Her father, recently appointed rector of St Nicholas, followed the norms of Victorian upper-middle-class standards, feeling it inappropriate that his children should mix with the local children. Fanny had therefore been home-educated and had few companions.

For the first five years of life Fanny had lived in Astley, also in Worcestershire, and then for three years in Hallow, north of Worcester. In both homes the child had been privileged to roam freely in unspoilt countryside, developing an early love for the beauties in nature which would remain a strong characteristic throughout life. Now, following the move to Worcester in 1846, when nine years old, she was deprived of such freedom. Her father would describe his bright-eyed youngest child as 'a caged lark'. Musical, vivacious and affectionate, Frances was a natural favourite in the home; but there was a more hidden side to her nature as well. Deep anxieties regarding her spiritual state burdened her young mind, but she built around herself an impenetrable wall of reserve, refusing to confide in any of her well-meaning sisters or even in her parents. Only in the natural world around her and in her love of both music and poetry did she find consolation.

The greatest sorrow of her childhood years came with the death of her mother in 1748, when Frances was eleven. Watching the departure of the funeral cortege from her bedroom window was an experience that haunted her for long years to come:

> My intense sorrow, childish though it was, seems now, after a lapse of eleven years, a thing of which I do not like to speak... I did not at all expect her departure and shut my ears in a very hardened way to those who tried to prepare me for it. I did not, *would* not see God's hand in it and the stroke left me worse than it found me.

Frances Havergal's first real contact both with her peers and with any outside her family circle came at the age of thirteen when it was decided that she should attend a boarding school. Situated near Camden Hill in Kensington, London, Great Campden House school catered for sixty to eighty boarders drawn from the aristocracy and upper echelons of society. The girls were required to speak French at all times, with Italian also given priority on the curriculum. Music and art were high on the agenda to prepare the girls for society life. The school had won renown for its instruction in dance, but when the headmistress, a Mrs Teed, experienced a true spiritual conversion, the subject was dropped from the timetable. Instead it was replaced by a strong emphasis on Scripture teaching. Pupils were expected to learn most of their lessons by rote, particularly Scripture passages, and Frances, with her quick and accurate memory, was soon able to recite long portions of the Bible, including the Psalms, Isaiah, the four Gospels and many other books of the New Testament.

The brief time that Fanny spent at Great Campden House — for the school itself was soon to close — was one of the happiest in her life. But still her inner longings for spiritual certainty remained unresolved. Soon, however, a former member of staff, Catherine Cooke, was to have a profound influence on her life. As a long-standing friend of her sister Miriam, Catherine Cooke would visit Miriam at her home in Oakhampton, in the Astley parish where Frances was born and had spent her early years. When Fanny, now fifteen years of age, was also there on one occasion, she felt able to confide her spiritual unrest to her sister's friend. The conversation that followed led Frances to turn unreservedly to Christ in faith. Later she could write: 'There and then I committed my soul to the Saviour … and earth and heaven seemed bright from that moment — *I did trust the Lord Jesus.*'

One thing that Frances did not realize, however, was that a friendship was developing between her sister's friend and her own father. Only months later Catherine Cooke was married to William Havergal — he was fifty-eight with poor health and failing eyesight; she, thirty-eight and full of energy. Fanny had always enjoyed a special place in her father's affections. His own abilities both as a hymn-writer and as a musician — gifts which she had inherited to a marked degree — created a close bond between them, and Fanny's position as the youngest in his family endeared her to him. Now, with his remarriage, the teenager had a stepmother and one with whom it would seem she could relate. But it would not always be so. Jealousy of the strength of affection that existed between William Havergal and his youngest child soon led to a worsening relationship between Fanny and her stepmother, and would subsequently become one of the severest problems of Frances Havergal's life.

Shortly after the marriage, William Havergal's deteriorating eyesight led to an extended stay in Germany where he received treatment from a well-reputed Prussian eye specialist. Frances accompanied him and for some months attended a girls' school in Düsseldorf; all her lessons were now in German. After this she spent a year with a German pastor and his family, studying under his tuition. But the life of a young Victorian woman born into a middle-class home could be singularly uneventful. As Frances grew to adulthood her days were largely spent helping her father in the parish.

These parish activities were punctuated by visits to Switzerland, Austria and Germany, where the breathtaking beauty of the Alps never failed to move and inspire her to write both verse and longer descriptive pieces of prose. During a return visit to the German pastor and his family she noticed a picture of Christ on the cross in his home. It moved her deeply. Underneath were the words, 'I gave my life for thee. What hast thou done for me?' As she thought about the significance of Christ's sacrifice for her, she wrote:

> I gave my life for thee,
>   my precious blood I shed,
> that thou might'st ransomed be,
>   and quickened from the dead.
> I gave my life for thee;
> what hast thou given for me?

Three other verses followed, but as Frances reread her work she was so displeased with it that she crumpled up the paper and threw it into the fire. Her aim was not very accurate and though the sheet was singed it fell out again on to the hearth. Uncrumpling the page she put it to one side, but then eventually decided to show it to her father. He encouraged her to keep it and wrote a tune to accompany the words. The second verse confessed her deep sense of indebtedness to the Saviour:

> I spent long years for thee
> > in weariness and woe,
> that an eternity
> > of joy thou mightest know:
> I spent long years for thee,
> hast thou spent one for me?

This would become one of Frances Havergal's best-loved hymns. In order to make it more suitable for public worship, she agreed to transpose the words so that the 'speaker' in each case might be the worshipper, rather than Christ. The last verse, as it appears in hymn books today, expresses a sentiment which could be called the theme tune of Frances Havergal's life:

> O let my life be given,
> > my years for thee be spent;
> world-fetters all be riven,
> > and joy with suffering blent:
> thou gav'st thyself for me;
> I give myself to thee.

In her personal manuscript copy of these words Frances matched each line with a verse of Scripture.[1] However, she never considered herself a natural poet or hymn-writer and was often dissatisfied with her work. Nor, she maintained, could she write to order, but felt that each verse, each line, each word had to be divinely 'given'. Although we may understand what she meant, the way she expressed this fact can easily suggest

that she claimed a degree of God-given inspiration for her lines
— a claim rightly reserved only for Scripture itself:

> Writing is praying to me, for I never seem to write even a
> verse by myself, and feel like a little child writing... I ask
> that every line he would give me, not merely thoughts
> and power, but also every word, even the very rhymes.

Frances Havergal's growing popularity as a singer and
speaker often brought her before the public eye; as a result she
had several offers of marriage during her twenties and early
thirties. Although she often felt the pain of her singleness and
the lack of any home of her own, none of her suitors seems
to have appealed to her. Another factor in her singleness was
her high view of consecration to 'her King and Master', as she
frequently described God. Life as a wife and mother would
necessarily mean less time for the Christian service that had
previously engaged her time and strength, and so she firmly
rejected the option of marriage. In her own family circle,
however, the number of nieces and nephews was steadily
multiplying and 'Aunt Fanny' cared about these children with
all their spiritual and emotional needs as if they had been her
own. As her relationship with her stepmother deteriorated,
Frances appreciated the opportunities she was given to visit
her sisters' homes; but it was her eldest sister Miriam's growing
family in Oakhampton which was to be the major focus of her
care and attention. For seven years, between 1860 and 1867,
she became their governess.

Shortly after these events Frances, now thirty-one years of
age, made the acquaintance of a Charles Snepp, vicar of a parish in Lichfield, north of Birmingham. And through this contact
many of those long-felt desires to use her gifts to the full in the
service of God came to fruition. Snepp was at that time compiling a hymn book to be called *Songs of Grace and Glory*. In

1870 he wrote to Frances in Leamington Spa, where she now lived following her father's retirement in 1867, initially to ask for permission to use her father's musical compositions in his book. William Havergal had died in April of that year. Shaken by the loss, Frances was glad to help Snepp in this way and as her confidence in him grew she gradually began to submit her own compositions to him for his approval and possible inclusion in his collection. By this means many of the young hymnwriter's verses appeared in print and first gained popularity.

Although Frances had professed faith as a teenager and her energies were oriented towards pleasing and obeying the one she undoubtedly loved, there had always seemed to be a missing ingredient in her spiritual life, resulting in a recurring lack of assurance. But in December 1873, at almost thirty-seven years of age, Frances had a spiritual experience that left a profound impression on her. No dramatic fanfare or crowded emotional meeting could explain the event and what surprised her most was the unexpected and sovereign nature of the divine blessing. Writing to her sister Maria, Frances describes the occasion:

> You know how singularly I have been withheld from attending all conventions and conferences; man's teaching has, in consequence, had little to do with it. First I was shown that 'the blood of Jesus Christ, his Son, cleanseth us from all sin', and then it was made plain to me that he who had thus cleansed me had power to keep me clean; so I utterly yielded myself to him, and utterly trusted him to keep me.

These things were to have a transforming effect, not only on her spiritual understanding but also on the hymns that she wrote. It is noteworthy that almost all the hymns for which her name is still loved today were written after December

1873 when this experience occurred. One of the first of these expresses her new commitment to Christ:

> In full and glad surrender
>   I give myself to thee,
> thine utterly and only
>   and evermore to be.
>
> Reign over me, Lord Jesus;
>   O make my heart thy throne!
> It shall be thine, dear Saviour,
>   it shall be thine alone.

Teachings on holiness and living 'the victory life' had been in circulation in Christian circles throughout the early 1870s, and in 1875 the Keswick Convention was inaugurated. Christians then began to flock to Keswick in the Lake District each year for a week of special meetings aimed at promoting holiness of life. Many were influenced by what has subsequently become known as the 'Keswick message' and were taught to pray earnestly for certain blessings, later to be called the 'Keswick blessing'. This took the form of a new experience of the grace and power of God that would deliver the one who received it from the daily struggle against indwelling sin. All that was required was to relinquish striving after holiness and to 'Let go and let God' accomplish it in the believer's life. Although some of her writings suggest that Frances confused her own liberating experience with this teaching, in the view of B. B. Warfield,[2] she remained convinced that sanctification was not a gift to be appropriated by an act of faith — as taught by the 'Keswick message'.

Continuing tireless in her efforts to win others for the kingdom of God, Frances Ridley Havergal packed into the short remaining years of her life more than most would accomplish in a long lifetime. Her constant prayer was:

> Take my life and let it be
> consecrated, Lord, to thee;
> take my moments and my days,
> let them flow in ceaseless praise.

The couplets of this, her best-known hymn — one that has been translated into many different languages including those of African and Asian countries — were written in 1874 when she was visiting friends in Stourport. Ten others were staying in the house at the time, and Frances had a strong desire that each person should receive a blessing from the Spirit of God. 'Lord, give me all in this house,' had been her prayer. It was a prayer God heard. After speaking with two of the girls in the family who had seemed unconcerned but had at last expressed spiritual interest, Frances went to her bedroom too happy to sleep. As she renewed her own personal consecration to God, the words of this hymn flowed into her mind, concluding with the pledge:

> Take myself, and I will be
> ever, only, all for thee.

Many opportunities for service were open for one as ardent as Frances Havergal to influence others for the kingdom of God. With her musical and speaking gifts there were invitations to join evangelistic endeavours, and to address smaller and larger gatherings both in song and through her messages. It was even as she had prayed:

> Take my voice, and let me sing
> Always, only, for my king;
> take my lips, and let them be
> filled with messages from thee.

Perhaps as she wrote those words she recollected that only the previous year she had been invited to sing the part of the wicked queen of Israel, Jezebel, in a production of Mendelssohn's *Elijah* for the Kidderminster Philharmonic Society. Flattered by the honour, she would have accepted, until rebuked by her friend Charles Snepp, who suggested that as a Christian woman it would surely be inappropriate that she should impersonate so idolatrous a character.

Another of Frances Havergal's well-known hymns also expresses her same single-minded desire for the blessing of God on her undertakings:

> Lord, speak to me, that I may speak
> > in living echoes of thy tone;
> as thou hast sought, so let me seek
> > thine erring children, lost and lone.
>
> O use me, Lord, use even me
> > just as thou wilt, and when, and where,
> until thy blessed face I see,
> > thy rest, thy joy, thy glory share.

Her burning concern for the salvation of others, together with a call for total dedication to the service of Christ, form the core theme for many of her hymns. Her metres are generally simple, and the frequent use of a refrain as in 'Who is on the Lord's side?' makes her hymns memorable and easy to sing. Constricted by her Victorian sentiments, her staunch Anglican loyalties and the limited and privileged circle in which her days were spent, her hymns and poems do not have the same appeal today as they once had, but their earnest spirit and devotion to Christ still shines through and has ensured for them continued popularity.

Frances Havergal's writings proved increasingly popular in her own day and her readers were constantly clamouring for more from this gifted and godly woman. At least twenty-five separate publications from her pen were in circulation before her death, some subsequently translated into other European languages, including Russian and also into Arabic. Her booklet, *Kept for the Master's Use,* would sell in its thousands throughout the English-speaking world, to a public eager for her work. Nor was her poetry confined to hymns. Her poetic gift was recognized when *The Oxford Book of Mystical Verse* carried extracts from 'Under his Shadow', one of her longer poems. But it is for her hymns that Frances Havergal is remembered today.

Frances Havergal never lost sight of the primary aim in all her writing. Royalties and success played little part in her thinking, even though her publishers constantly urged her to write further books, doubtless for their own profit as well as for the benefit of their readers. The Bible was the sourcebook for all her material, and in a preface to a collection of her hymns she could claim, 'almost every line has been directly drawn from Holy Scripture, or may be proved thereby'.

With a temperament so lively and intense it is not surprising that Frances Havergal also suffered periods of exhaustion with its accompanying depression of spirits, and, in addition, several prolonged bouts of illness. In 1874 she contracted typhoid fever and at one point her life seemed in the balance. The pain was intense and sometimes she thought she could endure it no longer. Then she would feel she had failed her God: 'I felt I had not glorified him in the fires because I had lost all my strength and could not bear the pain without moaning and crying out.' But in pity the Lord consoled her with such words as 'He knows our frame; he remembers that we are dust'. It was during this time of distress that she wrote the well-known words:

Like a river, glorious
    is God's perfect peace,
over all victorious
    in its bright increase…

Stayed upon Jehovah,
    hearts are fully blest,
finding, as he promised,
    perfect peace and rest.

Two years later she was again taken seriously ill while on a visit to Switzerland. Struggling to bear acute pain with patient submission, she could see that even such physical distress was a mark of divine love and wrote:

I take this pain, Lord Jesus,
    from thine own hand,
the strength to bear it bravely
    thou wilt command.

'Tis thy dear hand, O Saviour,
    that presses sore,
the hand that bears the nail-prints
    for evermore.

When Frances Havergal's stepmother died in 1778, Frances and her sister Maria had the difficult task of clearing up the family home. As she did so, Frances discovered many items of jewellery which she scarcely needed. 'Take my silver and my gold,/not a mite would I withhold' she had written in her hymn of consecration. Now she collected all her necklaces, rings and brooches together, keeping only one or two of particular significance. Fifty-three articles were packed in a box and sent to the Church Missionary Society for sale. Together they realized £50 — a considerable sum in days when that would be the yearly wage of many working men and women. Frances at last felt free to make her own decisions in life, and with her sister Maria set up home near Swansea. At forty-two years of age, Frances still felt the problem of her singleness. Affectionate and warm by nature, she had often sensed the need of someone with whom to share her life. And her resolve to remain unmarried may well have been severely tested when she received yet another proposal in 1878. Four years earlier she had prayed:

> Take my love; my Lord I pour
> at thy feet its treasure-store.

Once again she turned her suitor down, but not without pain. Her sister records: 'She bravely and unreservedly severed a correspondence and friendship which [had] scathed her heart.' Perhaps a poem written at this time is referring to this experience:

> Take what thou wilt, beloved Lord,
>   for I have all in thee!
> My own exceeding great reward,
>   thou, thou thyself shalt be.

Did Frances Havergal sense that she had not long to live? Certainly she had already experienced times of life-threatening illness. Only a few months later she was taken seriously ill once more and her doctor soon diagnosed peritonitis. Since that December day in 1873 Frances had been able to rest all the concerns for her eternal welfare on the power of Christ to cleanse her from all sin and to keep her through life: so now in her dying, she had no fear. Among her own hymns, Frances had one particular favourite:

I am trusting thee, Lord Jesus,
      trusting only thee,
   trusting thee for full salvation,
      great and free.

I am trusting thee for cleansing
      in the crimson flood;
   trusting thee to make me holy
      by thy blood.

This was the hymn her friends and family sang for her as they gathered around her bed, and this was the hymn that was found tucked in the back of her Bible after her death. In spite of the severe pain she was suffering, her faith did not waver. 'There has not failed one word of all his good promise,'[3] she quoted as the end drew near. 'Splendid to be so near the gates of heaven,' she was heard to repeat over and over again. And as if she could hardly wait for that moment when she would pass through those gates, she prayed, 'Come, Lord Jesus, come and fetch me, Oh! run! run!' 'That child will die singing,' someone had once said of Fanny when she was very young. And so she did. Singing in a low but clear voice the entire first verse of a favourite hymn written by a friend of hers, and a tune she herself had written, Frances Ridley Havergal joined those celestial choirs that praise the Lamb of God day and night:

Jesus, I will trust thee,
      trust thee with my soul,
   guilty, lost and helpless,
      thou canst make me whole.

She was buried in Astley, Worcestershire, near the graves of her parents. The words inscribed on her gravestone were those of 1 John 1:7, the beacon that had guided her through her last six years of life, 'The blood of Jesus Christ His Son cleanseth us from all sin.'

Notes

1. See Sharon James, *In Trouble and in Joy*, Evangelical Press, 2003, p.217.
2. B. B. Warfield, *Perfectionism*, Presbyterian and Reformed Publishing Co., 1958, p.266.
3. 1 Kings 8:56.

Fanny J. Crosby
(1820-1915)

Compulsive hymn-writer

Blessed assurance, Jesus is mine:
O what a foretaste of glory divine!
Heir of salvation, purchase of God,
born of his Spirit, washed in his blood.

This is my story, this is my song,
praising my Saviour all the day long.

Fanny Crosby

Fanny J. Crosby
(1820-1915)

Compulsive hymn-writer

A young mother drew her five-year-old daughter close to her and began to read her a poem: a strange poem to read to a child of five. It was John Milton's well-known sonnet 'On his Blindness'. With deep expression she read the poignant words:

> When I consider how my light is spent,
> ere half my days, in this dark world and wide,
> and that one talent which is death to hide
> lodged with me useless, though my soul more bent
> to serve therewith my Maker, and present
> my true account, lest he returning chide,
> doth God exact day-labour, light denied,
> I fondly ask...

Little Frances Jane Crosby was blind. She was not blind from birth, but at six weeks old had developed an eye infection. Well-meaning friends had suggested a poultice should be applied to the infant's eyes. The result was disastrous and had robbed the child of her sight altogether.

Born in 1820 in Putnam County, not far from New York, Fanny, as she was always known, was the child of parents who could trace their stock back to the days of the Pilgrim Fathers.

A forebear on her father's side was among the founders of the University of Harvard and her mother's family, with strong Puritan traditions, came from New England. An only child, Fanny had lost her father before her first birthday, and the strongest influence in her young life was that of her grandmother who took especial delight in introducing her blind granddaughter to the beauties of nature. She taught her to identify the flowers by touch and scent, and described in vivid language the glories of rivers, lakes, bird-life, sunrise, sunset and the wide canopy of the skies at night. Fanny could recognize the different trees by the feel of the leaves. But more than this, her grandmother taught her to love the Scriptures and soon Fanny was committing long passages to memory.

The family still entertained the hope that something could be done for Fanny and when the child was five her mother took her to New York, a long and tiring journey, where she was to see an eminent oculist. The situation was hopeless, the specialist had told Fanny's mother after he had examined the girl's eyes: apart from being able to distinguish light from darkness, she would be blind for the rest of her life. It was at this sad juncture that Fanny's mother read Milton's poem to her child, little realizing its double relevance for the future of her poet-daughter.

Despite her disability Fanny Crosby was a cheerful child. Early in life she began to express her thoughts in verse and at eight years of age she wrote:

> Oh, what a happy soul am I!
>   Although I cannot see,
> I am resolved that in this world
>   contented I will be.
>
> How many blessings I enjoy,
>   that other people don't!
> To weep and sigh because I'm blind
>   I cannot and I won't.

A move from Putnam County to Ridgefield, Connecticut, at this time proved an important one for Fanny and her mother. At the Methodist Episcopal Church in Ridgefield Fanny came under clear biblical teaching. In addition, the landlady from whom Mrs Crosby rented rooms was a woman whose influence on her daughter was wholly good. Like Fanny's own grandmother, who now lived at a distance, she taught the child the Scriptures. Soon Fanny, whose powers of rote learning were probably heightened due to her blindness, could recite most of the New Testament, the Psalms, and long passages from the Pentateuch as well.

But the child missed her grandmother, and remembering how she had taught her to recognize the trees by their leaves, the eleven-year-old wrote:

> 'Tis only a leaf, a withered leaf,
>> but its story is fraught with pain;
> 'Twas the gift of one who is far away,
>> and will never come back again.

A highly intelligent girl, Fanny Crosby felt an overwhelming desire for education, but with no local facilities for teaching blind children, it seemed that her wishes could not be met. One of her earliest personal spiritual experiences was her prayer to God one night alone in her room. She asked that somehow he would provide a way for her to receive an education. Four years later her mother learned of the recently opened New York Institution for the Blind, a charitable organization on a Christian foundation. Shortly before her fifteenth birthday Fanny found herself on the way to New York to be enrolled as a pupil — an answer to her prayer.

The system of braille, originated by Louis Braille in 1827 when Fanny was nine years of age, was coming into widespread use, and Fanny Crosby benefited from it in her studies. But it was poetry and the great poets of the past and present that secured her first love. And Fanny continued to write her own excellent verse too. Possibly her blindness drew extra attention to her gift, but as a young teenager she had the honour of being called upon to recite her verse before both Houses of Congress as well as on many other public occasions. She was presented to the president of the day and to other literary figures. Such attention may well have fanned the flames of ambition and pride in the girl, and produced an inflated sense of the extent of her own abilities. Realizing the pitfalls this would present, her tutor discouraged her from writing verse and then unwisely forbade it altogether. As a blind girl, he insisted, she should concentrate on acquiring a skill that would provide a future means of support.

At this juncture a phrenologist visited the institution. Whether he had heard of Fanny's reputation we do not know, but on examining the various contours of Fanny's head, he exclaimed: 'This young lady is a born poetess. She should be encouraged … teach her to appreciate the best poetry, and I doubt not you will some day hear more of her.' Now Fanny was free to study the subject nearest her heart and at twenty-four years of age published her own first volume of verse entitled *A Blind Girl, and Other Poems*.

Even though Fanny Crosby could recite long passages of Scripture, she had as yet no personal knowledge of the Saviour. In her mid-twenties she had a strange dream. In it a close friend who was apparently dying asked her whether or not they would meet again in heaven. On waking she could not forget the question. For some years she carried with her a nagging fear that if she should die she would be disqualified to enter that eternal city where only the redeemed of Christ are welcomed. Not until 1850, when Fanny was thirty years of age and on the teaching staff of the institution, did the head knowledge of many years become true heart experience of the grace of God. A movement of God that was touching a number

of American cities had reached New York and Fanny joined her
friends in attending meetings that were being held each night
at a Methodist church near the institution. Always sensitive to
poetry, it was through the words of a hymn by Isaac Watts that
Fanny Crosby was converted. As the congregation sang 'Alas!
and did my Saviour bleed', Fanny was deeply moved:

> Was it for crimes that I had done
>   he groaned upon the tree?
> Amazing pity! grace unknown!
>   and love beyond degree!

But when it came to the last verse she was melted down in
thankfulness and love:

> But drops of grief can ne'er repay
>   the debt of love I owe;
> here, Lord, I give myself away;
>   'tis all that I can do.

Now her motivation in life was no longer to bring glory to herself
as a renowned poet, but in devotion to Christ to consecrate her
gifts to the Giver.

Soon after this Fanny Crosby published her further anthology
of verse entitled *A Wreath of Columbia's Flowers*, and with it
attained national recognition for her work. As yet the thought of
writing hymns had not crossed her mind. Coupled with her ear
for rhythm, Fanny also had a deep appreciation of music — a
factor that undoubtedly played a part in her growing friendship
with Alexander van Alstyne. 'Van', as she called him, was also
blind and had become a student at the institution a few years
after Fanny. A gifted musician, he shared Fanny's love of verse.
Her poems moved and charmed him, though possibly this was
not unconnected with his growing affection for Fanny herself.

She delighted in his music and it can have been no surprise to others at the institution when Fanny and Van announced their forthcoming marriage in 1858. A year later, at thirty-nine years of age, Fanny became a mother, but the brief life of their only child was an intense grief for Van and Fanny.

Fanny van Alstyne was in her mid-forties before she wrote her first hymn. William Bradbury, a capable musician whose tunes are still to be found in many collections of hymns,[1] approached her with a suggestion: had she thought of using her gift for writing verse in the composition of hymns? Apparently she had not, and the idea appealed to her. Fanny began at once. These were the days of the Civil War in America with all its tragic loss of life — a backdrop to much of Fanny's thought at this time. The words of her first hymn, written in 1864, were on the beauties of heaven:

> We are going, we are going
>   to a home beyond the skies,
> where the fields are robed in beauty
>   and the sunlight never dies;
> where the fount of joy is flowing
>   in the valley green and fair;
> we shall dwell in love together,
>   there shall be no parting there.

And it was as a hymn-writer that Fanny Crosby — for she continued to write and publish under her maiden name — now saw her role in life.[2]

A further remarkable providence in Fanny's life was her association with Robert Lowry, Professor of Rhetoric at Brooklyn University, New York, and later pastor of a Baptist church. Lowry, himself the writer of a number of hymns,[3] was highly gifted musically. He encouraged Fanny to continue writing hymns and set some of her best-known compositions to music.[4] So it was that a blind woman who all her life had to rely on the help of others in dangerous or difficult circumstances could write:

> All the way my Saviour leads me,
>   cheers each winding path I tread,
> gives me grace for every trial,
>   feeds me with the living bread.
> Though my weary steps may falter
>   and my soul athirst may be,
> gushing from the rock before me,
>   lo! a spring of joy I see.

Another early hymn still in use today was born out of days of revival and begins: 'Pass me not, O gentle Saviour'.

> Let me at a throne of mercy
>   find a sweet relief;
> kneeling there in deep contrition,
>   help my unbelief.
>
> *Saviour! Saviour!*
> *Hear my humble cry;*
> *and while others thou art calling*
> *do not pass me by.*

This hymn, translated into languages worldwide including Chinese and Japanese, was extensively used in the Moody and Sankey campaigns in England during 1873-1875. Many were the stories reported to the blind hymn-writer of men and women who found their hearts arrested by her moving words and were then converted to Christ. One young man, fast drifting into a life of drink and degradation, told her that he had heard the words sung at a Moody and Sankey meeting and found in his heart a wistful longing that he too might find a place in the mercy of God. Returning night after night to hear the message of redeeming grace, he was converted. Eventually he became a successful businessman in America and for forty years he carried about with him a copy of 'Pass me not, O gentle Saviour', the hymn that had led to his conversion.

A hymn, considered by many to rank among Fanny Crosby's best, though seldom sung today, begins 'Safe in the arms of Jesus'. The seed thought had come to Fanny when she heard of an incident in New York of a crowd stampede in which many lives were put in jeopardy. A mother lifted her frightened child above the crush and said, 'You are safe now in my arms.' Soon afterwards a musician friend called at her home, telling Fanny that he only had forty-five minutes to spare, but asking her to listen to a tune he had composed and provide him with some words. With a blind person's acute concentration, Fanny listened to the tune and then said, 'Why, that sounds like "Safe in the arms of Jesus".' Hurrying upstairs she began to scribble down words and thirty minutes later reappeared with the final draft — a hymn that has been sung at many a believer's funeral and brought consolation:

> Jesus, my heart's dear refuge,
> Jesus has died for me;
> firm on the Rock of Ages
> ever my trust shall be:
>
> *Safe in the arms of Jesus,*
> *safe on his gentle breast,*
> *there by his love o'ershaded,*
> *sweetly my soul shall rest.*

Many were the stories of men and women snatched from a downward spiral of a life of misery and sin by Fanny Crosby's arresting hymn:

> Rescue the perishing, care for the dying,
>> snatch them in pity from sin and the grave.
> Weep o'er the erring ones, lift up the fallen,
>> tell them of Jesus, the mighty to save.

Another writer, with a style far different from Fanny van Alstyne's, found herself drawn out in affection for the blind hymn-writer; Frances Ridley Havergal composed a long poem in honour of her American counterpart:

> Dear blind sister over the sea,
>> an English heart goes forth to thee.
> We are linked by a cable of faith and song,
>> flashing bright sympathy swift along;
> one in the East and one in West,
>> singing for him whom our souls love best.

Fanny van Alstyne became a compulsive hymn-writer. Her output of hymns was prodigious. It is computed that she probably wrote 7,000-8,000 pieces, sometimes producing as many as seven or eight in a single day. Clearly their quality was uneven and less than a hundred survived much beyond her own lifetime. Her publishers, fearful that their public would not credit the authenticity of such abundant productivity, invented no less than 216 pseudonyms under which her hymns were marketed. These included such creations as Jenny Glenn; Grace J. Frances; Kate Grinley; Viola V.A.; Ella Dale, together with a host of variant initials such as F.A.N. or J.C.F.

Fanny van Alstyne was as bubbly and vivacious a personality as her hymns might suggest. At eighty-five years of age she would still hurry down the stairs singing a little tune to herself, or sit in her familiar rocking chair, her knitting needles clicking as she produced endless wash-rags [face-flannels] for the needy. Alternatively she would be anxious to visit some friend or acquaintance who was ill or in trouble. A constant stream of visitors flocked to her home wishing to meet her. Longevity was in the family and she wished to live to a hundred and three if she could. 'I made up my mind, years ago, that I would never become a disagreeable old woman,' said Fanny when she was ninety. 'It is my purpose in old age to grow ripe and rich and heavenly.' She frequently gave the royalties accruing from her vast number of publications to the less fortunate. 'During these ninety years I have never served for pay,' she declared. 'Gold is good in its place, but when it becomes our master it places a crown of thorns upon the brow that crushes the strongest to earth.'

In his *Dictionary of Hymnology* published in 1892, John Julian is less than charitable to Fanny van Alstyne. Although recognizing that sales of her work could be numbered in millions, he says, 'With few exceptions [they are] very weak and poor, their simplicity and earnestness being their redeeming features.' Certainly her hymns lack profundity and some appear superficial. Placed side by side with a piece from the pen of a Watts or a Wesley her lines are clearly inferior. Yet they have their merits. They take up themes that lie at the heart of Christian experience and echo the desires of many believers. We may cite:

> Jesus, keep me near the cross:
>   there a precious fountain,
> free to all, a healing stream,
>   flows from Calvary's mountain.
>
> Near the cross! O Lamb of God,
>   bring its scenes before me;
> help me walk from day to day
>   with its shadow o'er me.

Or:

> Here from the world we turn,
>   Jesus to seek;
> here may his loving voice
>   tenderly speak.
> Jesus, our dearest friend,
> while at thy feet we bend,
> O let thy smile descend!
>   'tis thee we seek.

In almost all her hymns Fanny Crosby aims to lift our eyes to the eternal city and the glory awaiting the children of God. It was uncertainty over her own eternal destiny that led the poet herself to seek assurance of forgiveness of sin. As we have seen, the joys of heaven formed the subject of her first hymn, and to that theme she returns again and again in much of her subsequent work. Concluding her best-known hymn, 'To God be the glory', she could write:

> Great things he hath taught us, great things he hath done,
> and great our rejoicing through Jesus the Son;
> but purer and higher and greater will be
> our wonder, our transport, when Jesus we see.

The blind hymn-writer's words touch a chord in the singer's heart, even though the words may seem simplistic at times. Such lines as these, coming from one whose condition often meant dependence on others, carry their own pathos:

> Hold thou my hand: my way is dark before me
>   without the sunlight of thy face divine;
> and when by faith I catch its radiant glory,
>   what heights of joy, what rapturous songs are mine.

Deprived of her natural sight, Fanny Crosby's mind often turned to the day when she would at last *see* her Saviour. It is noteworthy that many of her lines have some reference to spiritual sight. Her constant prayer is expressed in words such as these:

> Come to our hearts' delight,
> make every burden light,
> cheer thou our waiting sight;
>   we long for thee.

Despite their lack of depth at times, her hymns have outlasted those of many of her contemporaries. Some still remain high on the list of favourites, especially owing to the prominence given to them in the 1950s during the Billy Graham crusades. Many can remember surprising scenes on the London Underground in 1954 when strains of:

> Blessed assurance, Jesus is mine:
> O! what a foretaste of glory divine!
> heir of salvation, purchase of God,
> born of his Spirit, washed in his blood,

would burst out spontaneously from travellers returning from a Billy Graham meeting in Harringay, regardless of the bemused looks from fellow-travellers. Or sometimes it would be:

> To God be the glory! great things he has done!
> so loved he the world that he gave us his Son;
> who yielded his life an atonement for sin;
> and opened the life-gate that all may go in.

And despite the plethora of new hymns that have become popular in recent years, it is interesting to note that some of

Fanny Crosby's hymns, including these last two, find their way into most modern hymnals, including *Common Praise* (2000), the successor to *Hymns Ancient and Modern*.

Fanny van Alstyne did not achieve her desired a hundred and three years but was taken to the land where faith is turned to sight at the advanced age of ninety-four with scarcely a day's illness. Now she knew in experience the joys she had long awaited:

> Some day the silver cord will break
> and I no more, as now, shall sing:
> but, O the joy when I shall wake
> within the palace of the King!

> *And I shall see him face to face,*
> *and tell the story — saved by grace.*

Notes

1. William B. Bradbury's tunes include 'Even Me', set to 'Pass me not O gentle Saviour' and 'Solid Rock' which is set to 'My hope is built on nothing less'; also several children's hymns including the tune to 'Jesus loves me! this I know'.
2. Surprisingly, biographies of Fanny Crosby contain no further reference to her husband Alexander, although they enjoyed forty-two years of married life.
3. Best known today of Lowry's hymns is 'Low in the grave he lay, Jesus my Saviour'.
4. Lowry's hymn tunes include 'Dim Ond Jesu', set to the theme hymn of the 1904 Welsh Revival: 'Here is love, vast as the ocean', and also to Rev. Vernon Higham's hymn 'Have you heard the voice of Jesus?' Lowry also wrote the tune commonly set to Isaac Watts' hymn, 'Come, we that love the Lord', that includes the refrain, 'We're marching to Zion'.

'Time would fail me to tell of...'

other hymn-writers

We sing the praise of him who died,
of him who died upon the cross;
the sinner's hope let men deride,
for this we count the world but loss.

Thomas Kelly

The village of Broughton, home of Anne Steele

'Time would fail me to tell of...'

other hymn-writers

Even a hasty count of the names of hymn-writers in the index pages of a popular hymnal such as *Christian Hymns*, first published in 1977, reveals at least 350 whose work was considered of sufficient merit to be included in the collection. When the writer of the Epistle to the Hebrews was recording the triumphs of faith in the lives of men and women during the Old Testament era, he exclaimed: 'What more shall I say, for time would fail me to tell of...' In the same way, neither time nor space permits an adequate coverage of the many worthy hymn-writers of past generations. We can now only briefly mention the lives and achievements of a selected few.

Anne Steele

Anne Steele (1717-1778) was one whose modesty prevented her from publishing her work under her own name. Instead she adopted the pseudonym 'Theodosia' when her two leather-bound volumes, *Poems on Subjects Chiefly Devotional,* were first published in 1760. As the earliest woman hymn-writer of any note, Anne Steele was indeed a 'gift of God' to his church, although it is unlikely that she intended to convey that meaning when she chose such a pen-name. Born in the village of Broughton, Hampshire, in 1717, Anne would remain in the same village all her life, dying there in 1778 at the age of sixty-one. She was a member of a Particular Baptist church of which her father, William Steele, was the minister. The Particular Baptists were a group of men and women of clear Calvinistic persuasion who also held that the only proper candidates for baptism were those who had made a personal profession of faith. Their early history has been traced back to the years immediately preceding the Civil War in the 1640s. The Broughton church had its own beginnings in 1653 with a membership of one hundred and eleven. Many of Anne's hymns were written for use by the congregation of her day, and covered a wide range of topics, many with biblical references attached.

Anne Steele faced much suffering in life, a fact reflected in a number of her hymns, making her compositions especially helpful to others passing through such times. She and her brother William lost their mother when Anne was only three. Her father remarried three years later, and Anne's stepmother took over the care of the children, showing warm affection for them. The anecdote telling of the death of Anne's fiancé in a drowning accident on the day before their marriage is questionable, but the fact of an earnest proposal for her hand made by the noted Baptist preacher, Benjamin Beddome, has manuscript evidence to back it. In his proposal he quotes Milton to describe the 'sweetness into my heart unfelt before' that the sight of Anne had brought to him. She, however, chose to remain single despite her various suitors. Some of her light-hearted verse represents this as her preferred option in life.[1]

Constant ill-health undoubtedly coloured many of Anne Steele's hymns. Her stepmother's diary is peppered with references to Anne's illnesses — ailments which eighteenth-century antidotes seemed only to exacerbate. Living close to both a river and marshy ground, as she did, would appear to account for her constant fevers, probably a form of malaria prevalent among the population living in such areas.[2] Weakness in her back after a fall from a horse also had a permanently debilitating effect. References to such trials can be found throughout her hymns:

> If pain and sickness rend this frame,
>   and life almost depart,
> is not thy mercy still the same
>   to cheer my drooping heart.

But one day all pain would be gone for ever, and so she could write:

> When I survey life's varied scene,
>   amid the darkest hours,
> sweet rays of comfort shine between,
>   and thorns are mixed with flowers.
>
> Lord, teach me to adore the hand
>   from whence my comforts flow,
> and let me in this desert land
>   a glimpse of Canaan know.

The emphasis in many of the Particular Baptist churches of Anne's day tended to discourage the practice of inviting the unbeliever to seek Christ for forgiveness of sin, stressing instead the need to detect inner evidences of God's work in the heart before one could hope for salvation. Anne Steele was not inhibited by this discouraging emphasis:

> See, Jesus stands with open arms;
>   he calls, he bids you come:
> guilt holds you back, and fear alarms;
>   but see, there yet is room.

> Room in the Saviour's bleeding heart:
>   there love and pity meet;
> nor will he bid the soul depart
>   that trembles at his feet.

Although she was bold enough to invite sinners to come to Christ without a list of prior qualifications, when it came to her own case, we find a different emphasis. Here, there is a note of diffidence pervading her hymns. Words such as 'O could I know my sins forgiven!' or 'And may I hope that Christ is mine?' can be found scattered throughout. She is always questioning, always hoping, but rarely seems quite certain that she herself is accepted by God:

> Jesus, my soul adoring bends
>   to love so full, so free;
> and may I hope that love extends
>   its sacred power to me?

Anne Steele's role model was undoubtedly Isaac Watts. She had learnt to sing his hymns from early childhood and not surprisingly she followed his style. Much of her work was written in four-line verses and predominantly in common or long metres, for these were most easily adapted to tunes familiar to congregations that had only sung metrical psalms before Watts published his work in 1707. Always conscious of his superior gift, she could exclaim:

> O for the animating fire
> that tuned harmonious Watts's lyre
> to sweet seraphic strains!

Yet Anne had her own distinctive contribution and for this reason gentle 'Theodosia's' work still finds a place in collections of hymns published in the twenty-first century. Her hymn on the Scriptures is rarely missing from modern books:

> Father of mercies, in thy word
> what endless glory shines!
> For ever be thy name adored
> for these celestial lines.

As John Newton would later do in *Olney Hymns*, Anne Steele sometimes employed what has been called the 'argument of faith': reasoning from a truth that she knew to be certain to establish her confidence in something of which she was less certain:

> If my immortal Saviour lives,
> then my immortal life is sure;
> his word a firm foundation gives:
> here let me build and rest secure.
>
> Here, O my soul, thy trust repose;
> if Jesus is for ever mine,
> not death itself, that last of foes,
> shall break a union so divine.

One of our most gifted women hymn-writers, Anne Steele's use of adjectives prevents the singer from assuming the expected in her lines: 'dreadful glories', 'healing radiance', 'heaven-born grace'; sin is a 'dire contagion'; earth has 'alluring joys'. These form just a few examples picked at random. Her hymns cover a wide spectrum of subjects that a congregation might meet: communion services, funeral services, days of national repentance, even a hymn of thankfulness for the delivery of the land from the Gunpowder Plot of 1605. Her style is individual, characterized by numerous exclamation marks and thoughts added in parentheses:

> God's only Son (stupendous grace!)
>   forsook his throne above;
> and swift to save our wretched race,
>   he flew on wings of love.

Her use of rhetorical questions emphasizes the wonder of the atonement:

> And did the Holy and the Just,
>   the Sovereign of the skies,
> stoop down to wretchedness and dust,
>   that guilty worms might rise?

and she answers her own question with a resounding:

> Yes; the Redeemer left his throne,
> his radiant throne on high —
> surprising mercy! love unknown! —
> to suffer, bleed and die.

Anne lived only to the age of sixty-one: during the final hard years of life she became little more than an invalid, dying at her brother William's home in 1778. Despite her personal spiritual uncertainty, she was confident in death: her last words were, 'I know that my Redeemer lives.'

John Cennick

Born in 1718, only a year after Anne Steele, was another whose hymns are still sung today: John Cennick. The story of his protracted search for forgiveness of sins and acceptance with God — a search that extended over three and a half years — forms the backdrop against which we view his hymns. All but a handful were written in the immediate aftermath of that day when he could at last exclaim, 'I was overwhelmed with joy and believed there was mercy. My heart danced for joy and my dying soul revived. I heard the voice of Jesus saying, "I am thy salvation".' Popular, witty and worldly, John Cennick, still only eighteen years of age, was now a changed man. His collection of more than one hundred and fifty hymns, published

John Cennick

four years later in 1741, has a freshness and exuberance about it. Of his conversion he writes:

> Lo! glad I come; and thou, blest Lamb,
> shalt take me to thee as I am!
> Nothing but sin have I to give;
> nothing but love shall I receive.
>
> Now will I tell to sinners round,
> what a dear Saviour I have found!
> I'll point to thy redeeming blood,
> and say, 'Behold, the way to God!'

And that is exactly what he did for the remainder of his short life. Before his death at the age of thirty-six he had witnessed a powerful work of the Spirit of God in Dublin, and had established ten chapels and over forty Societies in Ballymena and the surrounding area. John Cennick had worked in harmony with Wesley in Bristol for a period following his conversion, but in 1741 when doctrinal differences arose between the two men, Wesley dismissed his young assistant. Cennick continued to work with George Whitefield, but gradually found himself increasingly attracted to the Moravians, whom he joined in 1746.

Cennick's hymns, published five years before this date, were not characterized by the Moravian emphasis on the physical sufferings of Christ. Nor do they carry the imprint of Charles Wesley's influence on them, for Charles had published little of his verse at the time when Cennick was writing. Like Anne Steele, he follows more naturally in the steps of Isaac Watts, but unlike Watts writes almost exclusively in rhyming couplets. 'Children of the heavenly king', with its strong emphasis on the Christian life as a pilgrimage and heaven its ultimate goal, is typical of Cennick's verse:

> We are travelling home to God,
>   in the way the fathers trod;
> they are happy now, and we
>   soon their happiness shall see.
>
> Lift your eyes, you sons of light!
>   Zion's city is in sight:
> there our endless home shall be,
>   there our Lord we soon shall see.

Cennick experienced in full measure the mindless persecutions meted out on these early Methodist preachers: placed in the stocks, stoned, nearly murdered on several occasions — circumstances that contributed to his early death. In his hymns he would pray for strength to sustain him in such trials:

Shall I my blessed Lord deny?
Or leave the fold of Christ and fly?
Forbid it, Jesu! Let man rage,
they cannot spoil thy heritage.
May I, O Saviour, thankful be
for this great blessing granted me.
Ere I thy sacred truth deny,
permit me strength, and let me die.

Two of Cennick's hymns are surprisingly different from the rest: their 8.33.6.D metre, unusual at the time, and their internal rhyming pattern mark them out and carry the hymn along. Greeting a new day, Cennick prays:

Rise, my soul, adore thy Maker:
angels praise;
join their lays,
with them be partaker.
Thou this night wast my protector,
with me stay
all the day,
ever my director.

And as he comes to the end of a day he is thankful for all the blessings he has received:

Ere I sleep, for every favour
this day showed
by my God,
I will bless my Saviour.
Thou my rock, my guard, my tower,
safely keep,
while I sleep,
me, with all thy power.

A deeply sensitive man, Cennick had found the trials of his life hard to bear, and when he learnt that he was dying in 1755, even though he must leave his wife Jane and two young daughters, he was content. 'Saviour, give me patience' was his last prayer, for he was ready to exchange earth for heaven. Many years earlier he had written:

> Fear not, brethren, joyful stand
> on the borders of your land;
> Jesus Christ, your Father's Son,
> bids you undismayed go on.

Samuel Medley

Samuel Medley was another eighteenth-century preacher whose hymns attained considerable popularity, though few are sung today. Born in 1738, that remarkable year which saw the beginnings of the evangelical revival, Samuel Medley soon turned his back on the religion he had learned from his parents and grandparents. As a young naval officer Medley suffered a serious leg injury; when gangrene set in, it appeared that amputation was the only way to save his life. In desperation the young man turned to his father's God in prayer. When the surgeon came to operate the following day he could only marvel at the improvement in Medley's condition — and the leg was spared. Some months later, while convalescing at his grandfather's home,

Samuel Medley was obliged to listen to a sermon by Isaac Watts, read to him by his grandfather. As he listened, however, God showed him his waywardness and unbelief and when his grandfather had left the room Medley urgently prayed for mercy and forgiveness:

> Hear, gracious God, a sinner's cry,
> for I have nowhere else to fly.
> My hope, my only hope's in thee:
> O God be merciful to me!
>
> To thee I come, a sinner weak,
> and scarce know how to pray or speak;
> from fear and weakness set me free:
> O God be merciful to me!

And later he wrote:

> He saw me ruined in the Fall
> yet loved me, notwithstanding all;
> he saved me from my lost estate:
> his loving-kindness, O how great!

Samuel Medley would eventually become a preacher in a Particular Baptist church in Liverpool. When he began his ministry in 1772 he discovered only sixteen dispirited members, who were grieving over their former pastor's open fall into immorality for which he had expressed no repentance. Gradually, under Medley's preaching, the church built up, and numbers increased to such an extent that a new and enlarged building was required. Like Doddridge, Medley wrote most of his hymns to supplement and re-enforce the truths he had just been preaching. To make those truths yet more memorable he would frequently use the last line of each verse as a type of refrain, repeating the theme in varying forms. Writing at a time when congregations were singing without copies of the words, Medley often used rhyming couplets for ease of memory. However, as printing became an easier undertaking, he was among the first to break with the custom of 'lining' out the hymns, producing word sheets for distribution to the congregation. The hymn for which he is best known sold many hundreds of copies on the Liverpool streets:

> Awake, my soul, in joyful lays
> and sing thy great Redeemer's praise;
> he justly claims a song from thee:
> his loving-kindness, O how free!
>
> Often I feel my sinful heart
> prone from my Saviour to depart;
> but though I have him oft forgot,
> his loving-kindness changes not!

Many of a poet's finest compositions spring from days of sorrow, and this is true of Medley. When the pram in which his baby was sleeping accidentally began to roll down a steep street, the child was thrown out and instantly killed. The grieving father expressed his bewilderment and consolation in these words:

> God shall alone the refuge be,
>   and comfort of my mind;
> too wise to be mistaken, he,
>   too good to be unkind.
>
> Though I may not his goings see,
>   nor all his footsteps find;
> too wise to be mistaken, he,
>   too good to be unkind.

When he was dying in 1799 Samuel Medley was heard to declare, 'I never saw so much of the excellency, glory and the suitableness of Christ as an all-sufficient Saviour.' In those words he was fulfilling his own wish written many years earlier:

> O may my last expiring breath
> his loving-kindness sing in death!

Thomas Kelly

The work of both Thomas Kelly and Josiah Conder, whose compositions still find a place in modern hymnals, reveal a marked transition from the hymns of the eighteenth-century revival. Although Conder was born in 1789, twenty years after Kelly, both were writing at the same time and both died in 1855. In their hymns they seemed to turn from the intensity of the personal dealings of God with the soul, so characteristic of the eighteenth century, aiming instead to supply songs of worship for the gathered church. Lines expressing desires for new depths of spiritual experience, such as we find throughout Charles Wesley's hymns, have little place in Kelly's work. This is undoubtedly a loss: it is not easy to find instances of the use of the pronouns 'me', 'my', 'I' or 'mine' in any of the better-known hymns from the pen of Thomas Kelly. Only inclusive pronouns such as 'we', 'us' and 'ours' are used as Kelly seeks to turn the worshipper away from himself to the glories of Christ and to the progress of his kingdom.

The son of an Irish judge, Thomas Kelly graduated from Trinity College, Dublin, and planned to follow his father to the Bar. While studying in London he came across some of the works of William Romaine, the renowned preacher of St Ann's, Blackfriars. His reading brought the young law student into a deep awareness of his inability to please God by his own works, and instead he looked to Christ for salvation. With little heart now for a legal career, Kelly was ordained in 1792 at the age of twenty-two, and returned to Dublin, fearlessly preaching justification by faith alone wherever he had opportunity. Soon he found himself banned from that city's pulpits by the Archbishop of Dublin. Undeterred, Kelly turned instead to meeting houses used by Dissenters, and before long cut his ties with the Church of Ireland and joined the ranks of Dissent. Favoured with ample financial means, Kelly was responsible for erecting a number of churches in and around Dublin. His generosity to the poor became a by-word and in the great potato famine of the mid-1840s his liberality saved many destitute families from disaster and death. His heart went out in a particular way to suffering Christians:

> Poor and afflicted, yet they sing,
> for Jesus is their glorious King;
> through sufferings perfect now he reigns,
> and shares in all their griefs and pains.
>
> Poor and afflicted, but ere long
> they'll join the bright celestial throng;
> their sufferings then will reach a close,
> and heaven afford them sweet repose.

Kelly's hymns were composed over a period of fifty-three years. The first book to contain only his hymns was published in 1804, entitled *Hymns on various Passages of Scripture*. It included ninety-six hymns; the last edition of that same collection was published forty-nine years later in 1853 and included all 753 that he had written. The work of Christ in his death and in his exaltation is at the heart of all Kelly's compositions:

> Glory, glory everlasting
>   be to him who bore the cross!
> who redeemed our souls, by tasting
>   death, the death deserved by us:
>   spread his glory,
>   who redeemed his people thus.

There is a robust exuberance about these hymns, achieved in part by the close-knit rhyming schemes Kelly employs. The popular hymn commemorating the ascension of Christ, 'Look, ye saints, the sight is glorious', is a good example:

> Hark, those bursts of acclamation!
>   Hark those loud triumphant chords!
> Jesus takes the highest station:
>   O what joy the sight affords!
>   Crown him! Crown him!
>   King of kings and Lord of lords!

The tone of triumph in much of Kelly's work, echoing Christ's victory over sin, Satan and hell, is also achieved by the bright fast-moving metres he chooses. One that Kelly employs to good effect is the 87.87.47 metre. William Williams had used it in 'Guide me, O thou great Jehovah', and also in 'O'er the gloomy hills of darkness'. John Cennick had occasionally used it, as had Joseph Hart in 'Come, ye sinners, poor and wretched', but it was Thomas Kelly who popularized the metre in numerous compositions. We find an example above, but also in these lines:

> In thy name, O Lord, assembling,
>   we thy people now draw near;
> teach us to rejoice with trembling;
>   speak, and let thy servants hear;

> hear with meekness,
> hear thy word with godly fear.

Kelly's lines are memorable; John Julian suggests that some of them rank with the first hymns in the English language, citing several as examples:

> The head that once was crowned with thorns
>   is crowned with glory now;
> a royal diadem adorns
>   the mighty victor's brow.

> The highest place that heaven affords
>   is his, is his by right;
> 'THE KING OF KINGS AND LORD OF LORDS',
>   and heaven's eternal light.

For sixty-three long years Thomas Kelly preached faithfully. Looking back as he approached the end of his ministry, he was able to declare that the same truths that had sustained him at the first were still those on which he was building the foundation of his life and ministry — a fact borne out in all his hymns.

With the dawn of the nineteenth century came a plethora of hymn books. Julian lists as many as forty-two separate publications — mainly collections of psalms and hymns — between 1801 and 1820, produced for use in individual parish churches where hymns had not yet received official approval. Each denomination had also begun to compile or increase its own collection, with the Methodists adding supplement after supplement to Wesley's 1780 edition of 525 hymns. The first General Baptist books were appearing by the 1790s, replacing the popular 1785 *Barton Hymns,* largely composed and published by Samuel Deacon of Barton-in-the-Beans.

Josiah Conder

As we have seen, the Congregationalists had led the way in hymnology with the hymns of Isaac Watts in 1707. In the following century Josiah Conder was at work compiling and editing *The Congregational Hymn Book* finally published in 1836. Like Montgomery, Conder was one of the few Christian laymen to write quality hymns that survive today. Born in 1789, he showed exceptional ability, becoming an avid reader by the age of four. But while still a small child Josiah suffered a setback which seemed to cast a shadow of uncertainty over his young life: as the result of an immunization against smallpox he lost sight in his right eye. Unable to join in the normal activities of childhood, Josiah gave himself to study and to cultivating literary skills. He was writing articles for publication at the age of ten; as a teenager some of his poetry was considered good enough for publication. When he was thirteen Conder followed his father into the map-making and book-selling business. Surrounded by books from his earliest days, it is not surprising that his contribution to his own generation would be in articles and other literary work, but his wider and more enduring legacy to the church of Christ has been in the hymns which he composed.

With broad sympathies and a desire for fellowship with all true believers regardless of their denominational label, Conder was the right man to be chosen as editor of the new Congregational hymn book. Although he was assisted by a small committee, all final decisions were his own, and he was one of the first beyond the bounds of Methodism to recognize the outstanding worth of the hymns of Charles Wesley. Conder shared the reaction, if not the prudery, of the nineteenth century to the devotional content of many eighteenth-century hymns. He regarded Wesley's work as 'bold, careless and unequal to an extreme and requires a pruning hand to render his hymns fit for general use'. Like all who tamper with Wesley's hymns, he failed; happily, later editors have largely reverted to Wesley's originals.

The Congregational Hymn Book was a highly successful publication and sold 90,000 copies in the first eight years. Among its 620 hymns were fifty-six of Conder's own compositions, many of which had already gained popularity in the denomination. Their inclusion in the book, by popular demand, secured for Conder a lasting name as a hymn-writer. Among his best known are his lines composed on words in Revelation 19:6: 'Alleluia, for the Lord God omnipotent reigns.' Glorying in the thought of the just, all-powerful and wise reign of the King of glory, Conder begins with the memorable words:

> The Lord is King; lift up thy voice,
> O earth, and all ye heavens, rejoice!

He speaks of the irresistible rule of God over all his creatures:

> The Lord is King! who then shall dare
> resist his will, distrust his care,
> or murmur at his wise decrees,
> or doubt his royal promises?

He then turns his gaze to the Saviour at God's right hand in heaven, describing him in some of the most evocative of all his lines:

> and he is at the Father's side,
> the Man of love, the crucified.

Encouraged by that one representing us to the Father, Conder urges his singers:

> Come, make your wants, your burdens known:
> he will present them at the throne;
> and angel bands are waiting there,
> his messages of love to bear.

The two verses which follow speak of the wide extent of God's kingdom, but these are normally omitted; however, without them Conder's reference to the universal reign of God in the first line of the final verse makes little sense — although few who sing them seem to notice!

> One Lord, one empire all secures:
> he reigns, and life and death are yours;
> through earth and heaven one song shall ring,
> 'The Lord omnipotent is King!'

Throughout life Conder championed the cause of the downtrodden, standing against the social injustices of his day. Like any Christian willing to suffer ignominy for the sake of Christ, he experienced the hostility of the world. One of his most moving hymns has these words:

> Privations, sorrows, bitter scorn,
>   the life of toil, the mean abode,
> the faithless kiss, the crown of thorn —
>   are these the consecrated road?

> Lord, should my path through suffering lie,
>   forbid it I should e'er repine;
> still let me turn to Calvary,
>   nor heed my griefs, remembering thine.

After his death in 1855, Josiah's son published all his father's collected poems, which, he said in a preface, were 'transcripts of personal experience', many springing from the trials and sorrows he had known in his life.

Charlotte Elliott

One of the best-known hymns of any woman writer came from the pen of Charlotte Elliott:

> Just as I am — without one plea,
> but that thy blood was shed for me,
> and that thou bidd'st me come to thee —
>   O Lamb of God, I come!
>
> Just as I am — and waiting not
> to rid my soul of one dark blot,
> to thee, whose blood can cleanse each spot,
>   O Lamb of God, I come.

Charlotte Elliott, born in 1789, the same year as Josiah Conder, was the granddaughter of the well-known eighteenth-century preacher Henry Venn, friend of William Grimshaw and later of Charles Simeon of Holy Trinity Church, Cambridge. During her lifetime Charlotte received over a thousand letters from men and women who had read or sung these words and been deeply moved by them. And could she have known it, the number of those touched by that one hymn would multiply a hundredfold in the future, particularly as a result of its use at the Billy Graham crusade meetings in the mid-1950s, chosen, undoubtedly, because it was instrumental in Graham's own conversion. Charlotte's brother, Henry Elliott Venn, who had conducted a long and fruitful ministry, could say that he felt more good had been done by this one hymn than by all his sermons.

Even though Charlotte was privileged with a home where she was taught the Christian faith from earliest years, it was not until 1822 when she was thirty-two that she was converted. In that year César Malan, distinguished Swiss evangelist, was visiting her Clapham home. Despite all her knowledge, the young woman was perplexed and distressed about the way of salvation; her sins seemed to rise as a mountain of evil before her troubled conscience. Even terms such as 'coming to Christ', so frequently used to present the gospel, baffled her. When Malan challenged her over her spiritual state, she was initially defensive but then spoke to him of her deep need. 'I should like to come to Christ, but I do not know how.' Malan's answer was surprisingly simple: 'Come just as you are.' Malan corresponded regularly with Charlotte after he left her home, urging her to take that 'one look, silent but continuous and faithful at the cross of Jesus'. At last the light of the gospel shone in Charlotte's heart as she did exactly that, and with it came the joy of knowing that Christ had accepted her.

Cheerful and bright by nature, Charlotte also had a natural sympathy with any who were passing through suffering. From early years she had experienced much ill-health and, in common with many Victorian women, would become a lifelong invalid. But although frequently restricted to just a single room in the house, there was one gift that she could and did use to great effect to serve God — her gift as a poet. Soon sheets of verse were coming from that sickroom, directed to those who, like her, knew much pain and weakness. To the bereaved, the weary, in fact to any who 'feel life's path a tough and thorny path' she addressed her volume of poems called *Hours of Sorrow*, first published in 1836 — a book that ran through many editions.

Like many who experience constant illness, depression of spirit was never far away, and particularly was this true on one occasion twelve years after Charlotte Elliott's conversion. All her brother's family with whom she was presently living were busy preparing for a grand sale of work in aid of a school for the daughters of Anglican ministers. Charlotte felt useless and discouraged. She even began to question her own salvation. One night in particular she wrestled with many doubts and fears. When all the family were out at the sale and she was left alone in the house, Charlotte faced up to her troubled condition before God. She recalled the words of her friend César Malan: 'come just as you are', and expressed her

Charlotte Elliott

renewed spiritual confidence in the words of her well-loved hymn:

> Just as I am — though tossed about
> with many a conflict, many a doubt,
> fightings and fears within, without —
>   O Lamb of God, I come!

Each word in this simple hymn is evocative, mirroring the thoughts and anxieties common to all believers. It moves steadily on to a climax, first as the sinner knows himself accepted by a merciful God:

> Just as I am, thou wilt receive,
> wilt welcome, pardon, cleanse, relieve;
> because thy promise I believe —
>   O Lamb of God, I come!

and then on to an assurance of his love:

> Just as I am — thy love unknown
> has broken every barrier down —
> now to be thine, yea, thine alone,
>   O Lamb of God, I come.

The hymn was first published anonymously until, it is said, Charlotte's doctor came across it. Certain that such words would comfort his patient he showed them to Charlotte. We can imagine his surprise when he discovered she had in fact written them herself.

The repeated, shorter fourth line of this hymn adds to the ever-growing commitment of the soul to Christ, the Lamb of God. Charlotte Elliott employed this same poetic technique in a number of her hymns. Another well-known composition begins with the words, 'Christian, seek not yet repose', each verse ending with the refrain 'Watch and pray'. As she develops the concept of the unseen spiritual battle raging around the believer, she creates a growing sense of the urgency of remaining watchful:

> Principalities and powers,
>   mustering their unseen array,
> wait for thy unguarded hours:
>   Watch and pray.
>
> Watch as if on that alone
>   hung the issue of the day;
> pray that help may be sent down:
>   Watch and pray.

A lesser-known hymn in which Charlotte Elliott employs the same structure speaks of the believer's need of the intercession of Christ to keep him to the end:

When weary in the Christian race,
far off appears my resting place,
and fainting I mistrust thy grace,
    then, Saviour, plead for me.

When Satan, by my sins made bold,
strives from the cross to loose my hold,
then with thy pitying arms enfold,
    and plead, O plead for me.

And when my dying hour draws near,
darkened with anguish, grief and fear,
then to my fainting sight appear,
    pleading in heaven for me.

Despite being a lifelong invalid, Charlotte Elliott lived to the age of eighty-two. Her last days were not 'darkened with anguish, grief and fear' but peaceful, as one who knew her informs us. And in 1871 she entered into that experience she had written about almost forty years earlier:

Just as I am, of that free love
the breadth, length, depth and height to prove,
here for a season, then above,
    O Lamb of God, I come.

Cecil Frances Alexander

Three women who became known as the 'Three Fannys' dominated the Victorian scene in their capacity as women hymn-writers. Having looked at two 'Fannys' in some detail, Fanny Crosby and Frances Ridley Havergal, we must now glance at the remaining member of the trio, Cecil Frances Alexander.

Born in Wicklow, Ireland, in 1818, Fanny Humphreys was to marry William Alexander in 1850. Alexander, then serving as a rector in County Tyrone, would eventually become Primate of All Ireland. From a child Fanny had delighted to compose verses, often shyly hiding her scraps of paper under some rug. Two years before her marriage she published her best-known book, *Hymns for Little Children* — a book that would sell 250,000 copies in the next twenty years. In days when women were not readily accepted as hymn-writers in a male-dominated world, the composition of children's hymns was one avenue open to them and Frances Alexander excelled at such verses.

Cecil Frances Alexander

With a supreme gift as a story-teller, the rector's wife wrote in the 'Once upon a time' style so loved by children. Even her best-known and arguably greatest hymn is told almost as an artless tale. 'There is a green hill far away...' it begins, and we may imagine Fanny gazing at the green hills of Ireland. She then narrates the story of the crucifixion with utmost clarity. We can anticipate the unspoken question of her first singers: 'But why did he have to die?' and she answers with superb simplicity:

> He died that we might be forgiven,
> he died to make us good,
> that we might go at last to heaven,
> saved by his precious blood.

> There was no other good enough
> >to pay the price of sin,
> he only could unlock the gate
> >of heaven, and let us in.

And the believing response to such love can be nothing else except:

> O dearly, dearly has he loved,
> >and we must love him too,
> and trust in his redeeming blood,
> >and try his works to do.

The plan which Frances Alexander adopted as she wrote her *Hymns for Little Children* was to take the important teachings of the Apostles' Creed and put them into simple verse. So for the incarnation she wrote the popular Christmas hymn, 'Once in royal David's city'. Again, the narrative style predominates, and we can imagine the appeal to children as she develops her strange sad story of the child who had only 'a manger for his bed'. Like them, he too was 'little, weak and helpless', sharing all their joys and sorrows. Throughout his 'wondrous childhood', he would 'honour and obey' his parents. Frances Alexander then adds an exhortation to her first young singers:

> Christian children all must be
> mild, obedient, good as he.

The reference in these lines to 'Christian' children points to one of the defects in Alexander's verse: she assumes that all children baptized into the church must be 'Christian', and should therefore be exhorted to Christlike behaviour. Other verses in this volume of forty-one hymns are of the same character:

We were only little babies,
    knowing neither good nor harm,
when the priest of God most holy
    took us gently on his arm.

And he sprinkled our young faces
    with the water clean and bright,
and he signed our Saviour's token
    on our little foreheads white.

Such thoughts are followed up with earnest, but impossible, admonitions to holy living:

Do no sinful action,
    speak no angry word,
you belong to Jesus,
    children of the Lord.
Christ is kind and gentle;
    Christ is pure and true,
and his little children
    must be holy too.

Frances Alexander lived through the harrowing days of the potato famine in Ireland. All around she saw poverty-stricken families suffering, and children dying. Such scenes would have deeply distressed her sensitive nature. Perhaps to rationalize in her own mind that degree of destitution, Fanny Alexander adopted an almost fatalistic interpretation of society: it was God's purpose so to order a community that the privileged and the impoverished should remain in their respective situations. Words in one verse of her popular hymn, 'All things bright and beautiful', now omitted from all hymn books, demonstrate this:

> The rich man in his castle,
>> the poor man at his gate,
> God made them, high or lowly,
>> and ordered their estate.

The same thought is expressed in lines addressed to children from poor homes:

> God made thy cottage home so dear,
>> gave store enough for frugal fare;
> if richer homes have better cheer,
>> 'twas God who sent it there.

Without disputing the sovereignty of God in the circumstances surrounding an individual or even a nation, the idea of any possibility of improvement in a man's social condition by personal effort seems to be foreign to Fanny Alexander's thought in such lines.

Despite the enormous popularity that the Irish poetess enjoyed in her lifetime, most of her work has now been forgotten, and very few of today's children would be happy to sing such words as 'We are but little children weak'. However, for her succinct statements of the atonement in her best-known hymn, 'There is a green hill far away', we honour the memory of Cecil Frances Alexander, who died in 1895.

Henry Baker

The second half of the nineteenth century was dominated by the work of Anglican writers. The Church of England had been slow to acknowledge or accept the changes introduced into services of worship by the singing of any words other than the Psalms or Scripture paraphrases. But in 1820, as we have seen in the study of the work of James Montgomery, the Established Church at last formally allowed such compositions to be sung within its walls. By the 1850s, with the multiplicity of private collections and supplements prepared for use within individual churches, it became imperative that the Church of England should follow the other denominations and produce its own hymn book. First published in 1861, *Hymns Ancient and Modern* was a success story of astounding proportions, due in part to its timing and in part to the hugely competent, though ruthless editorial policy followed by Sir Henry Baker. Accepting hymns from all strands of opinion within the Church itself, whether High Church or Low Church, together with the best of Watts, Wesley, Doddridge, Montgomery and many other writers, the small, rather unattractive-looking book held 273 hymns and had sold four and a half million copies within seven years.

Henry Baker held Anglo-Catholic views and was a prominent member of the Oxford Movement. He served as a vicar for twenty-six years in the quiet English village of Monkland in Herefordshire. As an editor he was highly skilled, capable of judging his market, picking the right men to help him with his project and, with a callous streak in his character, enabling him to dismiss those who did not comply with his suggestions. He altered and edited other people's hymns with a free hand — so much so, that the title *Hymns Ancient and Modern* came, in jest, to stand for '**h**ymns **a**sked for and **m**utilated'. But often this was not a bad thing, for it was Henry Baker who reshaped William Whiting's hymn, 'O thou who bidd'st the ocean deep', turning it into 'Eternal Father strong to save' — a hymn that proved one of the most popular in a day when much travel was by sea.[3]

Despite his Anglo-Catholic views, Henry Baker, who was born in 1821, wrote some of the most lasting and beautiful of our hymns. One often sung at evangelistic services begins:

> God made me for himself to serve him here
> With love's pure service and in filial fear...

Certainly, lines of this hymn are Arminian in character, and therefore some may well be unhappy with it, but taken from the perspective of the awakened sinner, turning from his sins and seeking at last to find forgiveness through Christ, the lines are evocative and moving:

> All needful grace was mine through his dear Son,
> whose life and death my full salvation won...
>
> And I, poor sinner, cast it all away;
> lived for the toil or pleasure of each day;
> as if no Christ had shed his precious blood,
> as if I owed no homage to my God.
>
> O Holy Spirit, with thy fire divine,
> Melt into tears this thankless heart of mine;
> Teach me to love what once I seemed to hate,
> And live to God before it is too late.

Among other lines that came from the pen of the vicar of Monkland is a hymn on the enduring value of the Word of God:

> Lord, thy Word abideth,
> and our footsteps guideth;
> who its truth believeth,
> light and joy receiveth.

All Baker's work is closely rhymed, his words well chosen and memorable. Perhaps his best-known piece, and the one that will endure the longest, is his version of Psalm 23:

> The King of love my Shepherd is,
>> whose goodness faileth never;
> I nothing lack if I am his,
>> and he is mine for ever.

A verse sometimes omitted from this hymn betrays Baker's Anglo-Catholic views, for here he interprets David's 'cup that runs over' as the chalice used in the sacrament of the Holy Eucharist:

> Thou spread'st a Table in my sight,
>> thine Unction grace bestoweth,
> and O, what transport of delight,
>> from thy pure Chalice floweth!

Like Watts, Baker sought to 'Christianize' David's Shepherd Psalm, adding New Testament references. We catch an echo of Luke 15 where the Good Shepherd seeks his lost sheep in these poignant words — words which proved a comfort to Baker himself as he lay dying in 1877 at the age of fifty-eight:

> Perverse and foolish oft I strayed,
>> but yet in love he sought me,
> and on his shoulder gently laid,
>> and home, rejoicing, brought me.

John Monsell

A number of Anglican clergymen, taking courage from the popularity of *Hymns Ancient and Modern,* began to produce their own collections of hymns. John Monsell, an Irishman born near Londonderry in 1811, spent most of his life in England exercising his ministry as vicar of Guildford in Surrey.

He published a number of separate books, and many of his three hundred compositions suggest the hushed atmosphere of an ornate parish church. Perhaps best known is:

> O worship the Lord in the beauty of holiness;
>   bow down before him, his glory proclaim;
> with gold of obedience and incense of lowliness,
>   kneel and adore him, the Lord is his name.

A hymn sung mainly at Communion services catches the longings of believers:

> I hunger and I thirst;
>   Jesus my manna be;
> ye living waters, burst
>   out of the rock for me.

> Thou bruised and broken bread,
>   my lifelong wants supply;
> as living souls are fed,
>   O feed me, or I die.

Monsell died in 1875 as the result of an accident. According to John Julian, he fell from the roof of his Guildford church while inspecting some rebuilding work in progress.

William Walsham How

William Walsham How, born in 1823 and who became the suffragan bishop in East London, is one whose hymns are still sung today. Most notable is his hymn on the Word of God, with its highly memorable lines:

O truth, unchanged, unchanging
O light of our dark sky!

Some of his hymns are written in an unadorned and direct style
as if for small children; yet they express profound truths:

O my Saviour, lifted
from the earth for me;
draw me in thy mercy,
nearer unto thee.

Lift my earth-bound longings,
fix them Lord, above;
draw me with the magnet
of thy mighty love.

Edward Bickersteth

Nor was William How the only bishop to discover that he had
a gift for composing hymns. Bishop Edward Bickersteth, born
in 1825, lived on into the twentieth century, dying in 1906. An
earnest evangelical man, he was responsible for editorial work
on several hymn books. Best known is his hymn 'Peace, perfect
peace', set very unusually in rhyming couplets: the first line
expressing a problem common to all, the second providing the
antidote for the Christian:

Peace, perfect peace, in this dark world of sin?
The blood of Jesus whispers peace within.

Peace, perfect peace, by thronging duties pressed?
To do the will of Jesus, this is rest.

> Peace, perfect peace, death shadowing us and ours?
> Jesus has vanquished death and all its powers.

Sabine Baring-Gould

But it was Sabine Baring-Gould, travel writer, novelist and composer of light-hearted verse, who took the Christian Church marching into the twentieth century, with the hymn, 'Onward Christian soldiers'. A favourite with Winston Churchill, it is set to the steady beat of tramping feet, echoing the onward march of British colonialism:

> Onward Christian soldiers,
>   marching as to war;
> with the cross of Jesus[4]
>   going on before.
> Christ, the royal master,
>   leads against the foe;
> forward into battle,
>   see his banners go!

Notes

1. See Sharon James, *In Trouble and in Joy*, Evangelical Press, 2003, for a fuller account.
2. See Antonia Fraser, *Cromwell: Our Chief of Men* (London: Weidenfeld and Nicolson, 1973), pp.670-1.
3. When President Roosevelt and Sir Winston Churchill met secretly aboard the HMS *Prince of Wales* in North Atlantic waters, this was the hymn Churchill asked should be sung by the men serving in those perilous conditions.
4. Evangelical editors, unhappy with the concept of marching after the cross, have normally replaced these words with 'Looking unto Jesus, who is gone before.'

Hymns today

Psalm 96

O sing a new song,
O sing to the Lord;
O sing all the earth:
his name be adored!
Tell forth his salvation
as day follows day;
among all the peoples
his wonders display.

David G. Preston

Bishop Timothy
Dudley-Smith

Stuart Townend

Hymns today

By the time Sabine Baring-Gould died in 1924, the church of God in Britain was not moving forward 'like a mighty army'. Instead it was in sad decline. As liberal theology prevailed in the pulpit, the vital spiritual life of the churches ebbed away, the pews emptied, its hymnology became muted. During the first sixty years of the twentieth century, relatively few writers of any significance added to the wealth of song that had been steadily accumulating for the past three hundred years.

A few exceptions stand like points of light in the gloom. When *The Methodist Hymn Book* of 1933 first included the Swiss pastor Edmond Budry's hymn, 'Thine be the glory, risen conquering Son', translated from the French by Richard Hoyle, it was immediately popular. The words rang with the triumph of the resurrection of Christ as the shadow of war once more hung over Europe:

> No more we doubt thee, glorious Prince of life;
> life is nought without thee: aid us in our strife;
> make us more than conquerors, through thy deathless love;
> bring us safe through Jordan to thy home above.

Frank Houghton

Two hymns written by the veteran missionary Frank Houghton who died in 1972 are still popular today. He had braved much personal danger during his service in China with the China Inland Mission and in 1931, when political unrest had brought severe disruption to missionary work there, the needs of that vast land lay as a heavy burden on the young missionary's heart. In 1929 the General Director of the mission had issued an impassioned plea for two hundred new workers to volunteer for service in inland China within the next two years. By 1931 two hundred and three had responded.[1] And yet still more were needed. In May of that year Frank Houghton wrote the moving words of this hymn:

> Facing a task unfinished,
>   that drives us to our knees,
> a need that, undiminished,
>   rebukes our slothful ease,
> we, who rejoice to know thee,
>   renew before thy throne
> the solemn pledge we owe thee
>   to go and make thee known.

In 1951 it fell to Frank Houghton, among others, to preside over that last sad withdrawal from China when the Communist government expelled all Christian missionaries. Grieved to think of the many who might now never hear the gospel, and to leave an infant church to face certain persecution, he would surely have recalled words he had written in the second verse of that same hymn:

> Where other lords beside thee
>   hold their unhindered sway,

> where forces that defied thee
>   defy thee still today,
> with none to heed their crying
>   for life and love and light,
> unnumbered souls are dying,
>   and pass into the night.

On a far different theme, Houghton's hymn on the incarnation added to our repertoire of Christmas hymns one of real worth:

> Thou who wast rich beyond all splendour,
>   all for love's sake becamest poor;
> thrones for a manger didst surrender,
>   sapphire-paved courts for stable floor.[2]

Vast cultural changes had begun to take place in post-war Britain, and accelerated during the 'swinging sixties', as the decade became known. With them came a fundamental change in the style and character of written English. For more than three hundred and fifty years the Authorized Version of the Bible had been in regular use and had shaped the English language. Demand now grew for modern translations of the Scriptures and in 1957 the *Revised Standard Version,* published some years earlier in the United States, was brought across the Atlantic to meet this need in the British Isles. This was followed by the New Testament of the *New English Bible* in 1961. Following these new translations of Scripture a new hymnology began to emerge.

Timothy Dudley-Smith

As he read a review copy of the New Testament in the *New English Bible,* the thirty-four-year-old Assistant Secretary of the

Pastoral-Aid Society was struck by the rendering of the opening words of Mary's song in Luke 1. From early childhood Timothy Dudley-Smith, born in 1926, had learnt to love poetry, inspired by the example of his father. Now these words affected him strongly: 'Tell out, my soul, the greatness of the Lord', and soon a new and popular hymn was born:

> Tell out, my soul, the greatness of the Lord!
>   unnumbered blessings, give my spirit voice;
> tender to me the promise of his word;
>   in God my Saviour shall my heart rejoice.

But he had accomplished something more. With the publication of this hymn in the *Anglican Hymn Book* in 1965, Timothy Dudley-Smith, who would become suffragan bishop of Thetford in 1981, had pointed the way for a new generation of Anglican writers to combine a modern style of expression with the structures of traditional hymnody. Many more of his hymns were to follow and words such as these have gained widespread popularity:

> Lord, for the years your love has kept and guided,
>   urged and inspired us, cheered us on our way,
> sought us and saved us, pardoned and provided:
>   Lord of the years, we bring our thanks today.
>
> Lord, for our land, in this our generation,
>   spirits oppressed by pleasure, wealth and care;
> for young and old, for commonwealth and nation,
>   Lord of our land, be pleased to hear our prayer.

Timothy Dudley-Smith was also an important contributor to *Psalm Praise,* a collection of a number of psalms rendered into a modern metrical form — together with twenty-one hymns — first published in 1973. His version of Psalm 91 is among his best:

> Safe in the shadow of the Lord,
> beneath his hand and power,
> I trust in him,
> I trust in him,
> my fortress and my tower.

By the 1980s Dudley-Smith's hymns had found their way into almost eighty current hymnals from many different parts of the world: America, Canada, Australia, New Zealand and even Africa and India. In 1984 Bishop Dudley-Smith, known affectionately as T. D-S, published a volume of his hymns and early poems entitled *Lift Every Heart*. In a separate section at the end of this book, he tells us the circumstances that lay behind many of his compositions. For example, the hymn, 'Lord, for the years your love has kept and guided,' was not conceived in any quiet or cloistered study, but in a railway carriage as the writer travelled from Nottingham to London in 1967, and was specifically written for the centenary celebrations of the Scripture Union. Many of the three hundred or more other hymns from the bishop's pen were composed for special occasions in the church calendar with a number particularly adapted for singing at Christmas and Easter. Throughout his writing we detect a pastoral attempt to address the sense of emptiness so common in our day:

> Above the voices of the world around me,
> my hopes and dreams, my cares and loves and fears,
> the long-awaited call of Christ has found me,
> the voice of Jesus echoes in my ears:

> 'I gave my life to break the cords that bind you,
> I rose from death to set your spirit free;
> turn from your sins and put the past behind you,
> take up your cross and come and follow me.'

We are glad that Bishop Dudley-Smith has not yet laid his pen aside, but has continued to add to his repertoire of hymns that have enriched today's church. His pieces find a place in ceremonies of national importance, and on the occasion of Queen Elizabeth II's Golden Jubilee celebrations in 2002, words he had composed formed a fitting expression of our thoughts:

> O Christ the same, through all our story's pages,
>   our loves and hopes, our failures and our fears;
> eternal Lord, the King of all the ages,
>   unchanging still, amid the passing years:
> O living Word, the source of all creation,
>   who spread the skies and set the stars ablaze,
> O Christ the same, who wrought our whole salvation,
>   we bring our thanks for all our yesterdays.[3]

Michael Saward

It would be invidious to attempt a critical evaluation of the contributions of today's authors to the hymns of the church. Apart from a few comments on the best features of the work of some writers, it would be wiser to allow time itself to be the arbiter of the value and durability of their labours. One whose hymns have proved popular in recent years is Rev. Michael Saward. His composition 'Lord of the cross of shame', first published in *Psalm Praise,* has gained widespread acceptance:

> Lord of the cross of shame,
> set my cold heart aflame
> with love for you, my Saviour and my Master;
> who on that lonely day
> bore all my sins away,
> and saved me from the judgement and disaster.[4]

James Seddon (1915-83) is another whose words are frequently sung today, with a hymn such as 'Go, forth and tell, O Church of God, awake!' found in many modern hymnals. Less known in Britain is the Canadian hymn-writer, Margaret Clarkson, also born in 1915, whose work, published over a forty-year period, addresses the needs of our generation with sensitivity and compassion.

Vernon Higham

Another name we must include is that of Rev. W. Vernon Higham — well loved by all who have sung from the first edition of *Christian Hymns* published in 1977. Mr Higham was born the same year as Bishop Dudley-Smith and served a long and honoured pastorate of forty years at Heath Church, Cardiff. Throughout the years he has transcribed his deep personal experiences into verse, and some of these lines have formed hymns which are sung and loved, not only in his native Wales, but throughout Britain and further afield. After a time of serious illness Vernon Higham wrote the words of one of his most moving hymns:

> I saw a new vision of Jesus,
>   a view I'd not seen here before,
> beholding in glory so wondrous
>   with beauty I had to adore.
> I stood on the shores of my weakness,
>   and gazed at the brink of such fear;
> 'twas then that I saw him in newness,
>   regarding him fair and so dear.

A hymn that has gained popular acclaim is Mr Higham's rendering of verses in 1 Timothy 3. Accompanied by the prize-winning Eisteddfod tune, *Pantyfedwen*, this hymn has become a regular choice at church anniversaries and other occasions:

> Great is the gospel of our glorious God,
>   where mercy met the anger of God's rod;
> a penalty was paid and pardon bought,
>   and sinners lost, at last to him were brought.
>
> *O let the praises of my heart be thine,*
> *for Christ has died that I might call him mine,*
> *that I might sing with those who dwell above,*
> *adoring, praising Jesus, King of love.*

Graham Kendrick

As the Charismatic Movement gained increasing prominence during the last half of the twentieth century, a new type of worship song began to emerge. The name of Graham Kendrick has become synonymous with these songs. Born in 1950, the son of a Baptist pastor, Dr Kendrick is not only a capable poet but also a musician. For the most part his hymns carry irregular metres but he has composed music to match the words — melodies that support and interpret the mood of his lines. Like the work of most other writers, his hymns vary both in quality and in content, but the best are already showing signs of lasting, and are sung worldwide.

Dr Kendrick's hymns touch on the central themes of the Christian gospel: the incarnation, the substitutionary atonement of Christ, the resurrection, and the justification of the sinner by faith:

> My Lord, what love is this
> that pays so dearly,
> that I, the guilty one,
> may go free!

Amazing love! O what sacrifice,
the Son of God given for me!
My debt he pays,
and my death he dies,
that I might live,
that I might live.

On the same theme we may cite words such as:

We worship at your feet
where wrath and mercy meet,
and a guilty world is washed by love's pure stream.
For us he was made sin —
O help me take it in.
Deep wounds of love cry out, 'Father, forgive!'
I worship, I worship
the Lamb who was slain.

In many of his hymns the core doctrines of the gospel are portrayed in a remarkable manner, compelling the worshipper to marvel afresh at the grace of God. Kendrick's use of striking contrasts or oxymora in some of his hymns is one that would have pleased Charles Wesley himself. This is particularly notable in one beginning:

What kind of greatness can this be
that chose to be made small?

Kendrick continues:

The One in whom we live and move
in swaddling clothes lies bound.
The voice that cried, 'Let there be light,'
asleep without a sound.

> The One who strode among the stars
>   and called each one by name,
> lies helpless in his mother's arms,
>   and must learn to walk again.[5]

Stuart Townend

Another writer whose work has come to prominence is Stuart Townend. With a return to more regular metres, Townend has composed hymns expressing profound truths in a fresh idiom. Such words as these reach to the heart of the Christian faith:

> How deep the Father's love for us,
>   how vast beyond all measure,
> that he should give his only Son
>   to make a wretch his treasure.
> How great the pain of searing loss —
>   the Father turns his face away,
> as wounds which mar the chosen One
>   bring many sons to glory.[6]

Equally moving is another hymn by the same writer:

> In Christ alone my hope is found,
>   he is my light, my strength, my song;
> this cornerstone, this solid ground,
>   firm through the fiercest drought and storm.
> What heights of love, what depths of peace,
>   when fears are stilled, when strivings cease!
> My Comforter, my all in all,
>   here in the love of Christ I stand.

No Christian can fail to feel the vibrant confidence expressed in the final verse:

> No guilt in life, no fear in death,
>> this is the power of Christ in me;
> from life's first cry to final breath,
>> Jesus commands my destiny.
> No power of hell, no scheme of man,
>> can ever pluck me from his hand;
> till he returns or calls me home,
>> here in the power of Christ I'll stand![7]

Nor can he fail to identify with the anticipation and desire expressed in words such as:

> Then one day I'll see him as he sees me,
> face to face, the Lover and the loved:
> no more words — the longing will be over,
>> there with my precious Jesus.[8]

It is only possible to include a few sample names from the numerous composers of new hymns and songs, but words such as those quoted above suggest a hopeful future for the English hymn.

The apostle Paul urged his Ephesian readers to encourage one another with 'psalms, hymns and spiritual songs' — an apt description of modern Christian hymnody. As we review the whole sweep of hymn-writing down the centuries, we can raise our hearts in thankfulness to God for these men and women whose work we have considered. They have provided us with words for our songs, enabling the church to fulfil the Apostle's further injunction to 'sing and make melody in your hearts to the Lord'. Heaven is a place of song. There the triumphant hosts of redeemed men and women join the swell of that great paean of victory, praising the Son of God. One day all his people will unite in a song that will exceed anything they have known on earth: 'Worthy is the Lamb who was slain to receive power and riches and wisdom, and strength and honour and glory and blessing!' Until then, perhaps old Richard Baxter should have the last word:

My soul, bear thou thy part,
triumph in God above,
and with a well-tuned heart
sing thou the songs of love.
Let all my days
till life shall end,
whate'er he send,
be filled with praise.

Notes

1. My own father was among that number.
2. © OMF International.
3. All above texts © Timothy Dudley-Smith in Europe (including UK and Ireland) and in all territories not controlled by Hope Publishing Company.
4. © Michael Saward/Jubilate Hymns.
5. Hymns by Graham Kendrick © Make Way Music, PO Box 263, Croydon, CR9 5AP, UK.
6. © Stuart Townend, 1995, Thankyou Music, tym@kingsway.co.uk. Used by permission.
7. © Stuart Townend and Keith Getty, 2001, Thankyou Music, tym@kingsway.co.uk. Used by permission.
8. © Stuart Townend, 1999, Thankyou Music, tym@kingsway.co.uk. Used by permission.

Select bibliography and suggestions for further reading

Horatius Bonar

Horatius Bonar – A Memorial, 1889.
Memories of Horatius Bonar, 1909.

William Cowper

John Piper, *Tested by Fire,* IVP, 2001.
Gilbert Thomas, *William Cowper and the Eighteenth Century,* 1935.
Thomas Wright, *Life of William Cowper,* 1892.

Fanny Crosby

J. R. Casswell, *The Blind Poetess.*
S. Travena Jackson, *Fanny Crosby: The Story of Ninety-Four Years.*

Philip Doddridge

Alan C. Clifford, *The Good Doctor,* 2002.
Various, ed. Geoffrey Nuttall, *Philip Doddridge, his Contribution to English Religion,* 1942.
Charles Stanford, *Philip Doddridge,* 1880.

Joseph Hart

Thomas Wright, *The Life of Joseph Hart*, 1910.

Frances Ridley Havergal

T. H. Darlow, *Frances Ridley Havergal*, Nisbet & Co., 1927.
Janet Grierson, *Worcestershire Hymnwriter*, 1979.
Sharon James, *In Trouble and in Joy*, Evangelical Press, 2003.
Maria Havergal, *Memorials of Frances Ridley Havergal*, Nisbet & Co., 1909.

Henry Lyte

H. J. Garland, *Henry Francis Lyte and the story of Abide with Me*, 1909.

James Montgomery

James Montgomery, *The Christian Psalmist*, William Collins, 1846.
A. Thomson, *Memoir and Poetical Works of James Montgomery*, 1866.

John Newton

Josiah Bull, *But now I see, Life of John Newton*, reprinted, Banner of Truth Trust, 2000.
Brian Edwards, *Through Many Dangers*, Evangelical Press, 2001.
D. Bruce Hindmarsh, *John Newton and the English Evangelical Tradition*, W. B. Eerdmanns Publishing Co., 1996.
An Authentic Narrative, Newton's letters on his life written by himself, first published 1764.

Augustus M. Toplady

Paul E. G. Cook, 'The Saintly Sinner', Evangelical Library Annual
    Lecture, 1978.
George Lawton, *Within the Rock of Ages,* James Clarke, 1983.
Thomas Wright, *The Life of Augustus M. Toplady,* London, 1911.

Isaac Watts

David Fountain, *Isaac Watts Remembered,* Henry Walter, 1974.
Paxton Hood, *Isaac Watts, his Life and Hymns,* Ambassador, 2001.
Bernard Lord Manning, *The Hymns of Wesley and Watts*, Lutterworth
    Press, 1954.
Thomas Wright, *The Life of Isaac Watts,* 1914.

Charles Wesley

Frank Baker, *Charles Wesley's Verse,* Epworth Press, 1988.
Arnold Dallimore, *A Heart Set Free,* Evangelical Press, 1988.
Frederick Gill, *Charles Wesley,* Lutterworth Press, 1964.
Bernard Lord Manning, *The Hymns of Wesley and Watts,* Lutterworth
    Press, 1954.
Charles Wesley, Poet and Theologian, Ed. St Kimbrough, Kingswood
    Books, Tennessee, 1992.

William Williams

Edward Morgan, *Brief account of the Great Progress of religion under
    the ministry of Rev. W. Williams,* 1847.
William Williams of Wern, *Welsh Calvinistic Methodism,* first published
    1872 (contains considerable material on William Williams,
    Pantycelyn), republished Bryntirion Press, 1998.

General books on hymnody

Benson, Louis F., *The Hymnody of the Christian Church*, Philadelphia, 1927.

Benson, Louis F., *The English Hymn,* London, 1915.

Brownlie, John, *Hymns and Hymn-Writers of the Church Hymnary,* 1911.

Gadsby, John, *Memoirs of the Principal Hymn writers and compilers*, London, 1861.

Gillman, F. J., *The Evolution of the English Hymn,* Allen & Unwin, 1927.

Great Hymn Stories, Ambassador Publications, 1994.

Houghton, Elsie, *Christian Hymn-writers,* Evangelical Press of Wales, 1982.

Julian, John, *Dictionary of Hymnology*, 1909.

Montgomery, James, *The Christian Psalmist*, William Collins, 1846.

Routley, Erik, *Hymns and Human Life,* Murray, 1952.

Routley, Erik, *I'll Praise my Maker,* Independent Press, 1951.

Strathan, Jack, *Hymns and their Writers*, Gospel Tract Publications, 1989.

Watson, J. R., *An Annotated Anthology of Hymns*, OUP, 2002.

Watson, J. R., *The English Hymn, A Critical and Historical Study,* OUP, 1997.

Whittle, Tyler, *Solid Joys and Lasting Treasure,* Ross Anderson Publications, 1985.

Index